MW01092213

CHEMICAL-BIOLOGICAL
DEFENSE

CHEMICAL-BIOLOGICAL DEFENSE

U.S. Military Policies and Decisions in the Gulf War

ALBERT J. MAURONI

Foreword by
Lieutenant General Daniel R. Schroeder, USA (Ret.)

Best Regards
Albert J Mauroni
3-02

PRAEGER

Westport, Connecticut
London

Library of Congress Cataloging-in-Publication Data

Mauroni, Albert J., 1962–
    Chemical-biological defense : U.S. Military policies and decisions
in the Gulf War / Albert J. Mauroni ; foreword by Daniel R.
Schroeder.
        p.   cm.
    Includes bibliographical references and index.
    ISBN 0–275–96243–1 (alk. paper)—ISBN 0–275–96765–4 (pbk.)
    1. United States—Defenses.   2. United States—Armed Forces—
Operational readiness.   3. Chemical weapons—Iraq.   4. Biological
weapons—Iraq.   5. Persian Gulf War, 1991.   6. United States. Army.
Chemical Corps.   I. Title.
    UA23.M323   1998
    358'.3'0973—dc21   97–46531

British Library Cataloguing in Publication Data is available.

Library of Congress Catalog Card Number: 97–46531
ISBN: 0–275–96765–4 (pbk.)

First published in 1998

Praeger Publishers, 88 Post Road West, Westport, CT 06881
An imprint of Greenwood Publishing Group, Inc.
www.praeger.com

Printed in the United States of America

The paper used in this book complies with the
Permanent Paper Standard issued by the National
Information Standards Organization (Z39.48–1984).

10 9 8 7 6 5 4 3 2 1

Copyright Acknowledgments

The author and publisher gratefully acknowledge use of the following material:

Excerpts from *Personal Perspectives on the Gulf War* by the Association of the United States Army,
Arlington, VA: Institute of Land Warfare, 1993. Reprinted by permission of the Institute of Land
Warfare.

Dedicated to the memory of a Chemical Corps leader:

Major General John G. Appel, Commanding Officer, Pine Bluff Arsenal (1962–1964); Commanding General, Deseret Test Center (1966–1969); Director, Chemical and Nuclear Operations Directorate, Office of the Assistant Chief of Staff for Force Development (1970–1973), died August 24, 1995.

My greatest regret and disappointment was the fact that the Army chose to consider disestablishment of the Corps in the 1970s without consulting me even though I was the principal advisor to the Chief of Staff for NBC at the time. That decision, done in "secret," was a mistake from which the Corps will never fully recover. The latest decision regarding Fort McClellan, done in a similar way, brought back sad memories of the 70s. Some people NEVER learn. No doubt they are not students of history.

—Major General (Ret.) John G. Appel, March 1990

Contents

Tables and Figures   ix

Foreword by LTG Daniel R. Schroeder   xi

Preface   xv

Acknowledgments   xvii

Abbreviations   xix

1.   Incidents in the Gulf   1

2.   Deployment to the Desert   19

3.   Building Up the Defense   43

4.   Move to the Offense   61

5.   Tensions Rise in the Gulf   75

6.   Operation Desert Storm Begins   91

7.   ". . . And Then We Are Going to Kill It"   109

8.   After-Action Report   129

9.   Agent Orange Revisited?   151

10. Conclusion   169

Appendix A   Chemical Defense Units Serving in Southwest Asia   187
                (Shield and Storm Task Organizations)

Appendix B   XVIII ABN Corps G-3-NBC Significant Events: 191
                24 January–18 March 1991

Appendix C   Glossary   201

Notes   209

Selected Bibliography   227

Index   231

Tables and Figures

TABLES

1.1	Changes to Chemical Corps Doctrine	2
1.2	Active Duty Chemical Units (Re)Activated, 1979–1990	3
7.1	Status of Iraqi Chemical Munitions as of August 1991	125
8.1	Chemical Agent Detection Equipment Limits	147

FIGURES

1.1	Growth of the Army Chemical Corps versus the Total Army, 1968–1990	4
2.1	Scheduled Cumulative Purchases of Protective Suits versus Actual Cumulative Deliveries	37
4.1	Suspected Iraqi NBC Warfare Targets	69
6.1	Locations of Biological Detection Teams	106
7.1	Declared Iraqi CBW Agent Stockpiles	126
9.1	Locations of Major Commands Relative to Khamisiyah	160

Foreword

It must be said to our shame that we sent our army into that most modern war with weapons and equipment which were quite inadequate, and we had only ourselves to blame for the disasters which early overtook us in the field when fighting began in 1940.

—Montgomery of Alamein

The professional world of my generation was defined in a bipolar context, with intense competition between two superpowers—Russia and the United States. That nonambiguous threat provided a rational approach to the study of the operational art, focused our training and shaped the supra-national alliance, NATO. With the fall of the Berlin Wall, the national security environment became more confusing: threats were ambiguous, NATO was reestablishing a new relevance and the operations tempo of the US armed forces was increasing. While some looked to claim a "peace dividend," Saddam Hussein claimed sovereignty over Kuwait and proceeded to invade. The US-led coalition's response was remarkable. Desert Shield and Desert Storm were unprecedented operations: they brought a focus in the United States that had not been seen since the early 1940s. America's military doctrine, equipment and personnel were demonstrating impressive capabilities, which were reported upon worldwide. The fact that Iraq had used chemical weapons as recently as 1988 was not lost on military planners and commanders.

This lucid and thorough study covers heretofore unexamined territory in the contemporary analysis of chemical-biological defense. What follows is a superb history of the people and events that shaped the coalition's response to the very real threat of weapons of mass destruction being used on the battlefield. It chronicles the efforts of individuals and organizations to mitigate what was viewed by many as the near certainty that Saddam would use chemical weapons. While it was generally agreed that battlefield effectiveness of coalition forces would be diminished by the use of chemical weapons, there was no lack of conviction that the force would be successful. After having contemplated the exceptional efforts described in this analysis, the real question is, where do we go from there?

The strategic environment today sees a continued evolution of disparate threats. While there is no peer competitor of the United States, there are more and increasingly ambiguous threats to US interests. Rogue states, trans-national antagonists, proliferation of weapons of mass destruction and divergent regional interests make the world a dangerous place.

While this study provides tremendous insights into the Gulf War, its greater value may be in extrapolation. The issue is broader than chemical specialists/units in ground operations providing chemical-biological defense. It is truly a joint and interagency issue in an environment that sees the distinction among strategic, operational and tactical levels of warfare becoming less clear. Specifically, the asymmetrical use of chemical-biological weapons could produce a disproportionate outcome.

Joint Vision 2010 describes four principles as key to force projection for a more CONUS-based armed force:

- forward deployed
- forward presence
- pre-positioned equipment, ashore and afloat
- rapid projection of joint forces from CONUS.

The literature is replete with Desert Shield/Desert Storm lessons to be learned by potentially hostile players:

- do not allow the US to build a coalition
- do not allow the US (and allies) to build up massive forces
- do not try to fight the US military strength to strength
- neutralize US strengths by asymmetrical means.

Chemical-biological weapons will continue to be with us and may well become the weapons of choice of some insidious regimes or groups. The asymmetry may well be their smaller-scale use within a joint battlespace that includes ports of embarkation for any power projection. The "full spectrum dominance" spoken to in various journals and studies has to address weapons of mass destruction when they are not used for mass destruction, when their use is not limited to the classical battlefield and when there is no apparent "smoking gun."

The conclusions of this report should not cause one to think this is a parochial appeal. Rather, reflect on the broader implications of this often-overlooked dimension of what Ralph Peters describes as "multiple conflicts in mutating forms around the globe." Presidential Decision Directive (PDD) 56, "Management of Complex Contingencies," should now address the jurisdictional issues and establish a rigorous command and control architecture. In that context, organization and responsibilities of chemical-biological incident first responders, on the battlefield and in more benign environments, should be resolved now and their tactics, techniques and procedures developed and exercised.

Saddam may well have been dissuaded from using his chemical weapons because of fear of retaliation or having seen the capabilities of the coalition. This provocative study should cause us to think more deeply about how to address this possible mutation of conflict in the future.

Daniel R. Schroeder
Lieutenant General, US Army (Ret.)

During his active service, Lieutenant General Schroeder served as: Deputy Commander-in-Chief, US Army Europe, Commanding General, Joint Task Force Support Hope (Africa); Assistant Deputy Chief of Staff for Operations and Plans, Department of the Army; Commandant, US Army Engineer Center; Chief of Staff, XVIII Airborne Corps, Commanding General, Joint Task Force Golden Pheasant (Honduras); Chief of Staff, 24th Infantry Division (Mechanized); Chief of Contingency Plans, US Readiness Command.

Preface

A former colleague of mine, Captain Bill Gregg, came back from the Persian Gulf War after augmenting the headquarters of the Tiger Brigade, 2d Armored Division, as a brigade chemical officer. He told war stories of the chemical defense support, the difficulties of procuring chemical defense equipment, and the military leadership's concerns about the threat of chemical-biological warfare. He told me that the story of the Chemical Corps during the war would make a great book. I casually agreed and promptly let the subject go. It wasn't until three years later that I noticed a disturbing trend in the many books written about Operation Desert Shield/Storm. All stressed that the political and military leadership were concerned about the chemical-biological weapons threat from Iraq. All of these books detailed the heavy, hot protective clothing, the protective masks ever present around the waists of soldiers, and the Fox reconnaissance vehicles present to warn of the threat. Most scholars agreed that the massive conventional attacks against the nuclear, biological and chemical (NBC) weapons production and storage sites, combined with not-so-veiled diplomatic threats of retaliation, had been a factor in stopping Saddam's use of weapons of mass destruction, as they were termed. Many books also quoted General Schwarzkopf's statement about Iraq's potential for chemical-biological warfare attacks: "We just thank goodness that they didn't!"

No one was bothering to ask *why* the US military, having the skills and resources of the Army Chemical Corps so readily available, was unprepared for an opponent using World War I and II chemical-biological agents in 1990. The reason had to be more than the military distaste and public revulsion for these unconventional weapons. The second point that irritated me was that I, as an Army chemical officer, didn't know what my colleagues had done in the Persian Gulf. Obviously, there was a failure somewhere to communicate exactly what had transpired among the professionals within the NBC defense community. After a limited open-source literature search, I realized that the best sources of information were the many chemical officers and non-commissioned officers that had served in the combat units and chemical defense units, in the Pentagon offices, at the Chemical Research, Development and Engineering Center at Edgewood, and of course, at the Chemical School at Fort McClellan. I began calling these chemical officers and discovered a wealth of information, lessons learned, and unit histories. I talked to general officers and senior chemical officers who had been responsible for rebuilding the Chemical Corps as it emerged from its decade of banishment (1969 to 1979). Without the efforts of these soldiers from 1979 to 1990 recasting the Chemical Corps in a brand new vision, there would have been no chemical defense preparations to speak of. Without these chemical defense preparations, the story of Operation Desert Shield/Storm would have been much, much different.

As I interviewed the senior chemical officers who contributed to this book, I was struck by how many insisted they had had no great measure of success in developing the Corps that had defended our forces in the Gulf War. These generals and colonels pointed to the young chemical captains, lieutenants, sergeants and specialists working as chemical staffers in the many combat arms and combat service brigades, battalions and companies. These were the men and women who, with very little senior supervision, ordered chemical defense equipment where they found shortages, conducted NBC defense training in the desert, advised commanders during the war, and did what needed to be done for a force that was not initially prepared for NBC warfare. These individuals, in part due to their excellent training at Fort McClellan's Chemical School and Chemical Defense Training Facility, had the confidence, experience and strength that really formed the bulkhead of Central Command's (CENTCOM's) NBC defense.

The *raison d'etre* of this book is to ask the eternal question, where does the military go now, knowing what we do? With a steadily shrinking military force, the political and military leadership are called upon to make tough decisions, based on defense priorities and congressional interests. It is altogether too easy to state, since there were no chemical-biological weapons used against the US military in the Persian Gulf War, that the US military must be doing everything right, that there is no need to increase spending or change program directions. In a world where B-2 bombers, F-22 fighters, Comanche helicopters, and Seawolf submarines fight for funds, it is easy to forget the drab, unexciting military programs (like heavy truck transport, strategic airlift capability, sealift capability, communications and NBC defense). I suggest that this view is inappropriate, even criminally neglectful. The military combat arms should review the lessons learned here and game the future possibilities through their Battle Labs and other wargaming applications. If they do not continue the necessary reforms of integrating NBC defense equipment and doctrine into their operations, both by understanding the threat and its effects on the soldier, and through integration of chemical defense units at brigade, division and corps level, we'll soon see the US military faced again by an opponent with NBC weapons. The next time, the US military won't have six months to prepare.

Acknowledgments

I could not have completed this book without the assistance of many individuals and organizations, to whom I will be forever in their debt. Within the military ranks, I would like to thank General (Ret.) Barry McCaffery, Lieutenant General Ronald Blanck, Lieutenant General (Ret.) Dan Schroeder, Major General (Ret.) Bob Orton, Major General (Ret.) Jan Van Prooyen, Major General (Ret.) John Stoner, Major General (Ret.) Gerald Watson, Brigadier General (Ret.) Walt Busbee, Brigadier General (Ret.) Pete Hidalgo, Colonel Mike Ahern, Colonel (Ret.) Eric Azuma, Colonel (Ret.) Ray Barbeau, Colonel (Ret.) Gary Eifferd, Colonel (Ret.) Gene Fuzy, Colonel Darryl Kilgore, Colonel (Ret.) Nate Licata, Colonel Harold Mashburn, Colonel Ted Newing, Colonel Walt Polley, Colonel Rick Read, Colonel (Ret.) Bob Thorton, Lieutentant Colonel (Ret.) Jeff Adams, Lieutenant Colonel Mike Brown, Lieutenant Colonel (Ret.) Mike D'Andries, Lieutenant Colonel (Ret.) Fred Evans, Lieutenant Colonel George Fahlsing, Lieutenant Colonel Stephen Franke, Lieutenant Colonel (Ret.) W.A. Funderberg, Lieutenant Colonel (Ret.) Jim Hansen, Lieutenant Colonel Randall Kennedy, Lieutenant Colonel (Ret.) Vicki Merryman, Lieutenant Colonel Mark Wagner, Major Dave Alegre, Major (Ret.) Howard Beardsley, Major Shirley DeGroot, Major Eric Henderson, Captain Darryl Briggs, Captain Dennis Cantwell, Captain Mark Lee, Captain Ed Marshall, Captain Andrew Murray, Captain Paul Neese, Captain Tom Shea, Captain Nick Swayne, Captain Mike Standish, Command Sergeant Major (Ret.) George Murray, and Specialist Frank Clark. I would like to offer a special thanks to Mrs. Jane Appel, widow of the late Major General (Ret.) John Appel, for her husband's personal papers.

Among the irreplaceable civilians, I would like to thank Dr. Billy Richardson, former Technical Director at Edgewood and former Deputy Assistant to the Secretary of Defense (Atomic Energy) (Chemical-Biological Matters), Mr. Jeff Smart, CBDCOM historian; Dr. Burton Wright, US Army Chemical School historian; Mr. Steve Cook, Chemical Defense Training Facility; Mr. Bill Dee, a former CBDCOM arms control expert. I wish also to thank the Public Affairs Officers: Ms. Suzanne Fournier at CBDCOM, Mr. Mike Abrams and Sergeant Todd at Fort McClellan, Ms. Carol Fruik at Dugway Proving Ground, Mr. William Thomas at Rocky Mountain Arsenal, Mr. Mickey Morales at PM Chemical Demilitarization, and the PAOs at Pine Bluff Arsenal, Fort Detrick and CENTCOM Headquarters. Last, thanks to the Freedom of Information Act offices at CBDCOM (Ms. Cheryl Fields) and the US Army Medical Research Institute of Chemical Defense (Mr. Lloyd Roberts). I'm sure I have forgotten others; please excuse my unintentional omissions. If there are any shortcomings or errors, they are completely my responsibility. The analysis and interpretation are my own, for better or for worse.

Special thanks to Eric Azuma, Mike D'Andries, Chuck Kelly, Vicki Merryman, Walt Polley, Nate Licata, Rick Read and Dr. Billy Richardson for their insightful comments on my drafts. Thanks to my colleagues at Booz·Allen & Hamilton, Inc., for their support and encouragement. Not least, thanks to my editor Heather Ruland, production editor Norine Mudrick, and Praeger Publishing for taking a chance on a first-time author.

Finally, and above all, I want to acknowledge the consistent and unswerving support from my wife Roseann, who put up with my wild muttering over arcane subjects, my constant failures to perform household chores, my choosing to peck at a keyboard instead of keeping her company in the evenings and over the weekends, and perhaps most of all, for enduring the difficult and thankless role of a military officer's wife.

Abbreviations

ABN	Airborne
ACCB	Air Cavalry Combat Brigade
ACDA	Arms Control and Disarmament Agency
ACR	Armored Cavalry Regiment
AFB	Air Force Base
AFMIC	Armed Forces Medical Intelligence Center
AMC	Army Materiel Command
AMCCOM	Armaments, Munitions and Chemical Command
ANBACIS	Automated Nuclear, Biological and Chemical Information System
APC	Armored Personnel Carrier
AR	Armor
ARCENT	Army Component, Central Command (3rd Army HQ)
ASARDA	Assistant to the Army for Research, Development and Acquisition
ASTD(AE)	Assistant to the Secretary of Defense for Atomic Energy
BDA	Battle damage assessment
BDO	Battledress Overgarment (protective clothing)
BDE	Brigade
BRAC	Base Realignment Committee
BW	Biological warfare
BWC	Biological Weapons Convention
CAM	Chemical Agent Monitor, M1
CANA	Convulsant Antidote for Nerve Agents
CANE	Combined Arms in a Nuclear/Chemical Environment study
CARC	Chemical Agent Resistant Coating
CAV	Cavalry
CB	Chemical-biological

CBDCOM	Chemical and Biological Defense Command
CBR	Chemical, biological and radiological
CBW	Chemical-biological warfare
CDC	Centers for Disease Control
CDE	Chemical defense equipment
CDTF	Chemical Decontamination Training Facility
CENTAF	Central Command, Air Force Component (9th Air Force HQ)
CENTCOM	Central Command
CG	Commanding General
CINC	Commander-in-Chief
CINCCENT	Commander-in-Chief, Central Command
CINCEUR	Commander-in-Chief, European Command
CO (Co)	Company
CONUS	Continental United States
COSCOM	Corps Support Command
CPE	Collective Protection Equipment
CPOG	Chemical Protective Overgarment
CPS	Collective Protection System
CRDEC	Chemical Research, Development & Engineering Command
CSL	Chemical Systems Laboratory
CTC	Combat Training Center
CW	Chemical warfare
DA	Department of the Army
Decon	Decontamination
DIA	Defense Intelligence Agency
DIV	Division
DLA	Defense Logistics Agency
DNA	Defense Nuclear Agency
DoD	Department of Defense
DPSC	Defense Personnel Support Center
ENG	Engineer
EOD	Explosives Ordnance Disposal
EPW	Enemy prisoner of war
FMIB	Foreign Materiel Intelligence Battalion
FORSCOM	Forces Command
FROG	Free Rocket Over Ground
GA	Tabun nerve agent (non-persistent)
GB	Sarin nerve agent (semi-persistent)
GD	Soman nerve agent (persistent)
GDLS	General Dynamics Land Systems
GDSC	General Dynamics Services Company
GF	Cyclosarin nerve agent
GVO	Green Vinyl Overboot
GWS	Gulf War Syndrome

HD	Mustard agent (persistent non-lethal)
HHC	Headquarters and Headquarters Company
HMMWV	(also "humvee") High Mobility Multi-Purpose Wheeled Vehicle
HQ	Headquarters
HQ DA	Headquarters, Department of the Army
HTH	High Test Calcium Hypochlorite
ICAD	Individual Chemical Agent Detector
IND	Investigational New Drug
JACADS	Johnston Atoll Chemical Agent Disposal System
JCMEC	Joint Captured Materiel Exploitation Center
JCS	Joint Chiefs of Staff
JPO-Bio	Joint Program Office for Biological Defense
JSCC-CDE	Joint Service Coordinating Committee for Chemical Defense Equipment
JSTARS	Joint Surveillance Target Attack Radar System
KFIA	King Fahd International Airport
KKMC	King Khalid Military City
KTO	Kuwait Theater of Operations
LANL	Los Alamos National Laboratory
LDS	Lightweight Decontamination System, M17
MARCENT	Marine Corps Component, Central Command (I Marine Expeditionary Force Headquarters)
MCRDAC	Marine Corps Research, Development and Acquisition Command
mg-min/m^3	milligram-minutes per cubic meter (gaseous measure)
MILPERCEN	Military Personnel Center
MLRS	Multiple Launch Rocket System
MODA	Ministry of Defense and Aviation (Saudi)
MOPP	Mission Oriented Protective Posture (levels 1-4)
MPS	Maritime Prepositioning Squadron
MRDC	Medical Research and Development Command
MRICD	Medical Research Institute of Chemical Defense
MRIID	Medical Research Institute of Infectious Diseases
MSG	Master Sergeant
MTT	Mobile Training Team
NAAK	Nerve Agent Antidote Kit, Mark 1
NAPP	Nerve Agent Pyridostigmine Pretreatment
NATO	North Atlantic Treaty Organization
NAVAIR	Naval Air Systems Command
NAVCENT	Naval Component, Central Command
NAVSEA	Naval Sea Systems Command
NBC	Nuclear, Biological and Chemical
NBCC	NBC Center
NBCRS	Nuclear, Biological and Chemical Reconnaissance System (FOX)
NBCWRS	NBC Warning and Reporting System

NCO	Noncommissioned Officer
NRDEC	Natick Research, Development and Engineering Center
ODCSLOG	Office of the Deputy Chief of Staff for Logistics
ODCSPER	Office of the Deputy Chief of Staff for Personnel
ODCSOPS	Office of the Deputy Chief of Staff for Operations and Plans
OPCON	Operational control
ORF	Operational readiness float
OSD	Office of the Secretary of Defense
OASD(HA)	Office of the Assistant to the Secretary of Defense for Health Affairs
OTSG	Office of the Surgcon General
PAO	Public Affairs Officer
PARC	Principal Assistant Responsible for Contracting
PB	Pyridostigmine bromide
PFC	Private First Class
Plt	Platoon
PM	Program/project/product Manager
R&D	Research and development
RCA	Riot Control Agents
RDA	Research, development and acquisition
Recon	Reconnaissance
REFORGER	Return of Forces to Germany
RSCAAL	Remote Sensing Chemical Agent Alarm, XM21
SCALP	Suit, Contamination Avoidance, Liquid Protection
SGT	Sergeant
SOCCENT	Special Operations Command, Central Command
TEU	Technical Escort Unit
TRADOC	Training and Doctrine Command
ug/liter	micrograms per liter (liquid measure)
UNSCOM	United Nations Special Commission
USANCA	US Army Nuclear and Chemical Agency
USAREUR	US Army Europe
USACMLS	US Army Chemical School and Center
VA	Veterans Administration
VX	Persistent nerve agent

CHEMICAL-BIOLOGICAL DEFENSE

CHAPTER 1

Incidents in the Gulf

War is less costly than servitude. The choice is always between Verdun and Dachau.
— Jean Dutourd, preface of Alistair Horne's *Price of Glory*

Since its renaming in 1946, the US Army's Chemical Corps has had the responsibility of preparing the US armed forces to survive and sustain military operations in a nuclear, biological and chemical (NBC)–contaminated environment. From 1946 to 1969, the Chemical Corps's mission, organization and goals remained fairly consistent as those of a technical support branch of the Army. Most Chemical Corps officers had master's degrees and doctorates in chemistry, chemical engineering, and biology—and rightly so, given their positions at chemical depots, laboratories, and division and corps headquarters. These were the only positions for active duty chemical officers, as brigade and lower combat units still relied on officers who were not Chemical Corps branched to execute NBC defense programs as an additional duty. Virtually all combat positions were gone, since chemical mortar units, chemical defense companies and battalions had been inactivated and formed as reserve units after 1955. A successful career Chemical Corps officer relied on laboratory and depot positions at Edgewood Arsenal, Fort Detrick, Dugway Proving Ground, Rocky Mountain Arsenal, and similar noncombat positions to help him rise to the position of Chief Chemical Officer. This created a "white lab coat" image of the "Chemistry Corps," which persisted from prior to the Korean War into the late 1970s.[1]

This technical bent may have been what eventually doomed the Chemical Corps. In October 1972, General Creighton Abrams, Army Chief of Staff, ordered the formation of a special study group, to determine how to disestablish the Chemical Corps, as part of the Army's restructuring plan after Vietnam. This group recommended putting a smaller Chemical Corps under the Ordnance Corps, as a special weapons branch. While Congress did not grant this disestablishment, General Abrams froze recruitment and career progression in the Chemical Corps.

The Chemical School shut down at Fort McClellan, Alabama, and moved to Aberdeen Proving Ground, Maryland, as a technical subelement to the Ordnance Corps for special weapons (chemical munitions).

Chemical defense training and leadership in the Army vanished for nearly a decade, for all practical purposes. Then the emergence of chemical warfare threats in the Arab-Israeli War brought it back from the edge of extinction, as the US military examined the Soviet's growing offensive chemical warfare capability. The Secretary of the Army reinstated the Chemical Corps in 1979, and the NBC defense program was running smoothly again by 1982. The Chemical Corps restructured its doctrine, force structure and equipment modernization program in a crash effort to regain an NBC defense capability for the armed forces. The new doctrine stressed a three-tiered approach, of contamination avoidance, protection and decontamination.[2] This doctrine emphasized that combat forces should continue the mission even if contaminated, highlighting the need to accept NBC warfare as an environment or condition, not as a separate mission in itself. This was a major change from the past, when combat units had expected to be completely decontaminated before continuing operations (see Table 1.1).

Table 1.1
Changes to Chemical Corps Doctrine

	Pre-1980	Post-1980
Doctrine and Training	Chemical Corps concern	Army-wide concern
Operational Emphasis	Minimize chemical casualties	Minimize mission degradation
Degree of Risk	Zero risk	Take intelligent risks
Control of Chemical Defense Operations	Centralized under division NBC element	Decentralized, flexible down to brigade level
Decontamination Operations	Complete decontamination of troops and equipment	Partial decon—enough to continue the mission

Chemical staff specialists slowly joined every level of command from company through corps, developing an in-house expertise on NBC defense doctrine, intelligence, training and logistics in every unit. It would not be until the mid-1980s until all divisions could claim they had chemical-biological (CB) defense experts from company through division headquarters, but the shift from being seen as technicians toward becoming true combat supporters had been made. The Army activated twenty-eight active duty chemical defense companies between 1979 and 1989, revitalizing the Army's divisions with dedicated chemical defense specialists (see Table 1.2 and Figure 1.1).

Table 1.2
Active Duty Chemical Units (Re)Activated, 1979–1990

Division	Chemical Unit	Date
1st Cavalry Division	68th Chemical Company (Hvy Div)	7/1/79
82d Airborne Division	21st Chemical Company (Smoke/Decon)	9/16/79
3rd Armored Division	22d Chemical Company (Hvy Div)	9/21/79
8th Infantry Division	25th Chemical Company (Hvy Div)	9/21/79
1st Armored Division	69th Chemical Company (Hvy Div)	9/21/79
3rd Infantry Division	92nd Chemical Company (Hvy Div)	9/21/79
101st Airborne Division	63rd Chemical Company (Smoke/Decon)	3/1/80
1st Infantry Division	12th Chemical Company (Hvy Div)	3/1/80
2d Armored Division	44th Chemical Company (Hvy Div)	3/1/80
III Corps	181st Chemical Company (Corps/TA)	9/1/80
V Corps	10th Chemical Company (Corps)	9/16/80
VII Corps	11th Chemical Company (Corps/TA)	9/16/80
V Corps	95th Chemical Company (Corps/TA)	9/16/80
III Corps	172d Chemical Company (Smoke) (Mech)	3/1/81
9th Infantry Division	9th Chemical Company (Motorized)	9/1/81
4th Infantry Division	31st Chemical Company (Hvy Div)	9/1/81
III Corps	46th Chemical Company (Smoke) (Mech)	9/1/81
III Corps	84th Chemical Company (Smoke) (Mech)	9/1/81
24th Infantry Division	91st Chemical Company (Hvy Div)	9/1/81
I Corps	164th Chemical Company (Smoke)(Mech)	9/1/81
XVIII Airborne Corps	101st Chemical Company (Decon)	8/16/83
5th Infantry Division	45th Chemical Company (Hvy Div)	9/1/83
I Corps	813th Chemical Company (Corps/TA)	10/1/84
10th Mountain Division	59th Chemical Company (Smoke/Decon)	3/16/85
25th Infantry Division	71st Chemical Company (Smoke/Decon)	10/16/86
V Corps	13th Chemical Company (Decon)	9/16/87
7th Infantry Division	761st Chemical Company (Smoke/Decon)	10/1/87
8th Army	23rd Chemical Battalion (HHD)	9/20/88

Source: "Lineage and Honors," *Army Chemical Journal*, Spring 1986, p. 15.[3]

Figure 1.1
Growth of the Army Chemical Corps versus the Total Army, 1968–1990

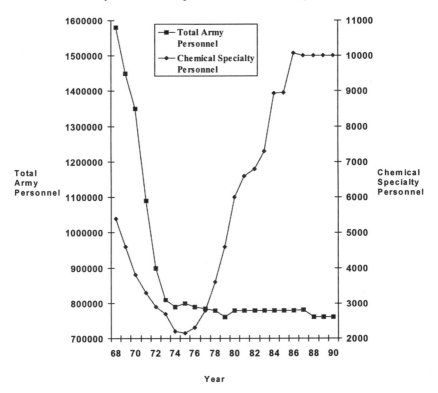

Year

   While this gave the US Army an immediate credible defensive capability, its leaders had risen in an Army without chemical defense units (between the Korean Conflict and 1980); learning how to properly employ them would come slowly. Decon companies served as "car washes" more often than they were realistically exercised. Likewise, many smoke generator platoons received missions as artillery smoke markers rather than large area smoke obscuration. Change would come slowly to some divisions, more quickly to others.

   A series of studies called Combined Arms in a Nuclear/Chemical Environment, or CANE, conducted in the mid to late-1980s, emphasized the psychological isolation and physical degradation felt by soldiers as they attempted to perform individual and group combat operations wearing protective clothing and masks. These studies also quantified the increases in time to mount an offensive, the overall decrease in combat strength and the increased difficulties leaders faced trying to command their forces in a chemical environment. While these findings were generally understood, this was the first time anyone had attempted to quantify and assess these effects. The Chemical Defense Training Facility (CDTF) opened on March 3, 1987. There, potent nerve agents were introduced into various training rooms; students garbed in full protective clothing and masks practiced using agent detectors and decontaminating equipment in a toxic agent environment. As of the summer of 1997, over 40,000 students had passed through the facility without one accident. This facility continues to be invaluable as a confidence builder for chemical defense personnel, teaching them the effectiveness of their equipment and training.

The equipment modernization plan shot forward, fielding M8 and M9 chemical detector paper and M256A1 chemical detector kits, giving all soldiers, not only the specialists, the ability to identify chemical agents. The M8A1 automatic chemical agent alarm provided more reliable point warnings than its predecessor, while the new M1 Chemical Agent Monitor (CAM) allowed personnel to pinpoint chemical contamination on troops and equipment. There was an improved protective ensemble, called the Battledress Overgarment (BDO), offering twenty-four hours protection against liquid agents. New decontamination systems such as the M13 Decon Apparatus, Portable (DAP), and the M17 Lightweight Decon System (LDS) offered battalions the ability to clean themselves during combat rather than moving off the line to a chemical decon company's site. Collective protection systems in vehicles and tanks meant less physical and psychological degradation to the crews, who would not have to wear masks and clothing while in the vehicles.

Other developmental systems in the 1980s were not so quickly fielded. A new protective mask (M40-series), replacing the M17-series masks, still waited in the wings, leading to the Army's decision to modernize its Vietnam-era M17 masks to the M17A1/A2 masks in 1983–85. The NBC reconnaissance vehicle (the XM93 NBC Reconnaissance System or "Fox" NBCRS) and a long range chemical agent detector (the XM21 Remote Chemical Stand-Off Agent Alarm [RSCAAL]) had slipped their delivery dates to the early 1990s. Biological agent detectors, miniature chemical agent detectors and decontamination systems that did not use massive amounts of water fell into the "too hard" column. Still, there were tremendous strides in one decade, which the Army had yet to absorb. With less than five years to train with these new items, suddenly the call to battle sounded.

READY FOR DESERT SHIELD?

In the mid-to-late 1980s, there was a certain quiet pride in being a member of the armed forces. It seemed that the malaise of the Vietnam years and the resulting hollow military of the 1970s had finally faded away, with the unprecedented peacetime buildup that occurred in the Department of Defense (DoD) during the Reagan-Bush administrations. With the actions in Grenada and Panama under their belts, modern combat equipment, and a new joint philosophy termed "Air-Land Battle," the call of an Army career attracted the top talent from the pool of American citizens. When the call went out to mobilize for deployment to Southwest Asia, there was a mixture of dread and eagerness: dread because no logical military individual seeks out the battlefield to test his or her skills on other human beings, and the fear of death always dampens excitement. Yet this is what the men and women of the armed services trained to do—to work as a team to carry out the Commander-in-Chief's orders and to act in the interests of national security. The question of whether they could do the job for which they had been trained sat in the back of their minds, even as they deployed into the combat theater. Confidence in themselves and their equipment, excellent training and leadership would tell over time.

These thoughts and fears existed in the minds of every chemical soldier in the Army as well. On the one hand, no one knew more than chemical personnel that the potential danger of an NBC agent environment was real. These individuals had donned protective gear and trained in the CDTF at Fort McClellan. Although some in the military might not think so, even chemical soldiers dislike having to train in full protective posture with chemical protective clothing, mask, boots and gloves. Yet they understood and respected the threat, knew how to survive in an NBC environment, and most important, understood that they *could* operate in a toxic environment. Many chemical soldiers looked forward to using their unique knowledge to help their comrades survive and sustain combat operations.

Because the US military had not suffered the effects of NBC warfare since World War I, many combat arms units (infantry, armor, artillery and aviation) had relegated their chemical soldiers to secondary positions within their commands (such as administrative clerks, supply assistants, training officers). Many had ignored the need to integrate NBC training and equipment in the years since the Chemical Corps had returned from the dead. Now as the call to deploy went through the ranks, concerned voices spoke out. Where are those chemical agent detectors? How exactly do we build these collective protection shelters? What do you mean, we don't have enough mask filters and agent detector batteries for thirty days? When was the last time I checked the fit of my protective mask?

The flurry of individual and unit NBC defense training that began at US bases in August and carried over in Saudi Arabia was evident to CNN cameras and other media. What wasn't as public was the feverish twenty-four-hour work being conducted at Aberdeen Proving Ground–Edgewood Area, Maryland, site of the Army's Chemical Research, Development and Engineering Center (CRDEC); at Natick, Massachusetts, home of the Army's Natick RD&E Center (NRDEC); at Rock Island Arsenal, Illinois, home of the Armament, Munitions and Chemical Command (AMCCOM); at Fort McClellan, Alabama, within the US Army Chemical School (USACMLS); at Dugway Proving Ground, Utah, home of the Joint Test Center; at Pine Bluff Arsenal, Arkansas, the long-standing depot for chemical-biological defense equipment (and in the past, both biological and chemical agent weapons); at Fort Detrick, home of the US Army Medical Research and Development Command (MRDC) and, of course, at the various staff sections working for the services and Joint Chiefs of Staff (JCS) in the Pentagon. This is their story, and the story of the Army's chemical soldiers—a story of sacrifice, hardship, unending optimism and faith that their skills would find a use in a military that had stopped believing in NBC warfare.

TALES FROM THE SOLDIERS—OPERATION DESERT SHIELD

I was at Fort Leavenworth, Kansas, attending the Combined Arms and Services Staff School course along with about thirteen hundred other company-grade officers on August 2, 1990, when we heard the news about the Iraqi invasion into Kuwait. Officers soon began disappearing from the two-month course to mobilize with their units. When the 82nd Airborne Division began airlifting its troops to Saudi Arabia a few days later, my first thoughts were, "Those guys are in trouble. If they get hit by chemical agents, the entire division will lock up in protective postures and freeze in place like a deer in the headlights." I had visited the 82d Airborne Division in 1987, where a brigade chemical officer had explained that the 82d ABN DIV's soldiers trained with masks only for riot control situations. "The 82d believes that none of their missions will call for deployment into an area where we will see the actual employment of CB agent weapons. We'll bring protective masks into areas where military or police forces use riot control agents. We're into low intensity conflict scenarios," he explained. This attitude was typical of most "light infantry" fighters in the 1980s, and the Army's generals knew that this was the case in August 1990 as well. I remember thinking that this was the reason why there was so much public footage of soldiers training in the desert with protective equipment, and why President George Bush, Secretary of Defense Richard Cheney, and other political figures were so quick to warn Saddam against the use of chemical agents. Other soldiers told me of their brushes with CB defense preparations during the mobilization and deployment to the Persian Gulf.

Colonel Mike Ahern, Division Chemical Officer, 2d Armored Division

"I had arrived at the Division (Fort Hood) only about three weeks prior to Saddam's invasion of Kuwait. 2AD [2d Armored Division] had already been earmarked for inactivation. Its remaining ground brigade, the 'Tiger Brigade,' was then attached to the 1st Cav [Cavalry] Division for deployment to the Gulf. Other units from the division base were also included, such as the Division's 44th Chemical Company. The only role that I and the 2AD division chemical section played was the important (but not very glamorous) work that everyone was doing—refresher training for the troops deploying, and a huge effort to get serviceable masks, protective clothing, and NBC supplies on hand and issued to the troops. Our unreadiness in the area of supplies, which were supposed to be on hand but weren't, and the masks, which were supposedly serviceable until needed for a real war, was my real heartburn. We also conducted some NBC staff exercises for the deploying troops, and then after they'd gone, kept busy by continuing to keep our own battle staff expertise up by participating in numerous Corps-level CPXs [command post exercises].

"It wasn't a real fun time when so many of our Dragon soldiers [Chemical Corps soldiers] were going off to war and we in 2AD were not. I think every single one of us was looking for a way to go over, but the Division Commander (Major

General Phil Mallory) was striving to keep the division staff intact as a trained and ready battle staff that could be deployed as a replacement or augmentation to a Corps or Division HQ if needed. I think we all realized the sensibility of this as the Division continued to downsize, but it sure didn't make us any happier."[4]

Lieutenant Colonel Mike D'Andries, Product Manager for NBCRS, Office of the Project Manager for NBC Defense Systems

"I had left the M43 Apache Protective Mask team to join the PM NBC office in mid-July 1990, where I was to take over the Fox project. Because of my past experience both on the mask team and as an aviator, I agreed to be available for all major meetings concerning the M43 mask up to August.

"An example of these meetings included briefing the status of the M43 Apache Protective Mask to a quarterly general officer steering committee for fielding the Apache helicopter at Fort Lee, Virginia. HQ DA [Headquarters, Department of the Army] had stated that the Apache helicopter could not be fielded without a compatible protective mask for its pilots, which brought much attention to this particular mask program. When the Scott Aviation M43 production contract was canceled, we were left without a production source until Mine Safety Applications picked up the contract. Earlier in the year, I had explained that this contract transition would delay the mask until the summer of 1990. I also explained a skin irritant problem for some pilots as a technological challenge—the labs couldn't use silicone rubber for the M43 as they were planning for the M40/42. The mask production needed to use a blend of butyl and natural rubber to avoid chemical agents absorbing and off-gassing through the thin rubber facepiece. The general officers tasked our mask team to explain this in depth at their next quarterly meeting.

"As mentioned earlier, I left to move into the Fox NBCRS office. I planned on attending an In-Progress Review meeting at General Dynamics Land Systems in Detroit on August 6, and then flying to Fort Hood, Texas, to brief the Apache general officer steering committee on August 7. To assist in technical expertise, CRDEC had added a civilian member—Rick Decker—who would meet me in Austin. During the drive from the Austin airport to Fort Hood (a two-hour drive), we recognized that we were walking into an unfriendly meeting. The commander of the 6th Air Cavalry Combat Brigade (stationed at Fort Hood) was planning to brief the panel on the deficiencies of M43 mask—pilots thought the mask's motor blower was too heavy and they didn't like the skin irritant problem. The Program Manager for Apache knew that the aviators hated the mask, and the mask was two years late (delaying vital Apache program milestones). The Army's Commander of the Safety Center also planned to tell the panel that the irritant was a hazard to flight safety. Our briefing on the skin irritant issue was not positive—we had planned to tell the aviators that there was no alternative but to use the butyl-natural rubber blend.

"When we arrived to meeting at Fort Hood's officers club, we saw lots of stars (Major General Arwood, ODCSLOG; Major General Greenburg, AMCCOM; Jim Morgan, PARC from Rock Island Arsenal), FORSCOM's aviation officer, and the brigade commander of the 6th ACCB) laying in wait for the CRDEC mask team. This was not a friendly audience. We told each other (in the manner of individuals resigned to a sure fate), 'If you see them measuring us and carrying hammers and nails, RUN!' and 'We should tell the CRDEC office that if they can't find us tomorrow, to look for our bodies in the Texas desert!' The meeting opened with administrative comments and the meeting agenda, which showed the mask briefing in the morning. As the meeting opened, one officer rose to suggest that the group take a break to review President Bush's address about the crisis in the Gulf. We had missed much of the news about the Iraqi invasion. The group moved into a bar where there was a television. President Bush announced his act of drawing a 'line in the sand' and the deployment of US troops to Saudi Arabia. CNN followed up the President's address with a report on the 82nd Airborne Division's deployment, Air Force and Navy deployments. CNN also reported that the Iraqi military was loading 'gas bombs' on their aircraft. The mood at the briefing immediately turned somber. Rick Decker ran to the phone to call Mine Safety Applications [MSA, the industry partner] and the CRDEC lab to establish how many M43 masks he could build immediately. As the brief resumed, the general officers had forgotten about the skin irritant problem. They had forgotten about the heavy motor-blower problem and the two-year program lapse. All they wanted to know was how many masks could be built and how soon. Rick replied that they could engineer 243 masks in four weeks using test articles and spare parts at Edgewood, but he couldn't promise that these masks would last for their expected full seven-year life.

"Since we were the only chemical defense specialists at the meeting, the Army aviators asked us where they could find additional M8A1 alarms for aviator units (not that we knew). We received permission from Jim Morgan to incentivize MSA by giving them a bonus for delivering masks sooner than contracted. Major General Greenburg pulled me aside, saying 'You tell me who you need me to kick in the butt, and I'll use my size 9 shoes. And I'll make my personal plane available to ship any M43 spare parts or masks.' The general officers loved us. We left the meeting after lunch, but not before the 6th ACCB commander stated darkly, 'You guys got lucky.' Not only did we survive the pogrom, we came back as heros."[5]

Colonel Rick Read, Chemical Section, Office of the Deputy Chief of Staff for Operations and Plans

"The first week after the invasion, I got into the office about 0630 or 0645 one morning, and the phone rang—it was the Army PAO. He said, 'I need you to get down here right away. You need to go over to CNN studios here in Washington. They need somebody to brief them up on NBC.' I said, 'What? Who's cleared this?' 'It's already cleared, DCSOPS said you can go.'

"We had a mannequin that we kept inside the door dressed in MOPP [Mission Oriented Protective Posture] gear. So we grabbed this mannequin, and we were going to take him with us along with the mask and a detector kit and a few other odds and ends we had there. As we picked him up, the mannequin disassembled in the middle. We had these big old grocery carts that people used to get supplies from self-help. They loaded this thing in so that the top of the torso was sticking out at one angle and the legs out the other. We're pushing this thing down, charging down the halls and quarters of the Pentagon, took the elevator downstairs to the second floor, ran into PAO. We raced out the door, piled into a waiting CNN van, and roared across town.

"At the CNN building, I entered the elevator, standing there in Class A's [service-dress uniform] with that damn mannequin. People were staring at me like I was crazy. When I got upstairs, they ushered me back into the Green Room, where [Colonel (Ret.)] Harry Summers and the president of STI, Inc., were waiting. 'OK, Colonel, here's what we're going to do. Colonel Summers is going to go on as an NBC expert. You need to make him an expert before he goes on camera. And then the second speaker will talk about his company's atropine injectors.'

"After Summers came back from makeup, we chatted a little bit. He said, 'OK, take me through this. I can't remember much of this stuff, it's been years.' We talked about the nomenclature of the mask, the purpose of the suit, and the M9 paper and the way it changed color. When the time came, he charged out on the floor. I watched my 'student' perform on the monitor, and he did a fairly credible job. He did the pitch, everybody liked it, and I took it all back to the Pentagon. No sooner did I get back (about noon), the PAO called again. 'That worked well this morning. We need to you bring it all back downstairs this afternoon.' 'What? What's going on?' 'We've got Sam Donaldson coming over. He wants to do a stand-up piece.' So we trotted back downstairs to a room that was set up, and put the mannequin up. It was interesting times. That was the kind of stuff that was going on."[6]

Master Sergeant Gregory Drake, S-1 [Personnel] NCO, 210 Field Artillery Brigade, 2d Armored Cavalry Regiment

"I rarely heard a soldier complain about the requirements to have his helmet and protective vest on at all times, and just as seldom would I find a soldier without his load-bearing equipment, M-17 protective mask, weapon and ammunition. Spare chemical suit, water, and rations were part of every vehicle's load plan. Due to the increased threat of chemical weapons deployment by the Iraqi forces, soldiers took chemical protective measures very seriously. Everyone knew what each level of MOPP was, and how to use the individual detection kits. Pyridostigmine Bromide tablets were taken without fail (with NCOs checking as part of their nightly ritual), and M8 chemical detection alarms were deployed and checked almost hourly. Some vehicles had more than one M-11 decontamination device, and no one was without a healthy supply of DS-2 [decontaminant]."[7]

Specialist Frank Clark, 220th MP Company, Colorado National Guard, at the 402d Enemy Prisoner of War Military Police Camp

"We were activated 2 January 1991 and spent our prep and training time at Fort Carson. There we had daily training and reinforcement in NBC training along with mission-specific training. We worked with the individual detection kits, M8 chemical detection units. Spent lots of time talking about MOPP, about nerve agent antidotes, etc. Another interesting fact was that we couldn't be deployed until every protective mask passed a 100 percent function check and visual check. Some masks had to be turned in because of potential problems.

"Late in January we were finally deployed to Southwest Asia. At Fire Base Mike, chemical preparedness was taken seriously, as at the airports. But within the time of about a week, this went downhill fast. After the first few Scud attacks, we were no longer forced to MOPP up and actually slept through half of them. I usually put my mask on just to be on the safe side; usually the all-clear was given only minutes after a Scud attack. As far as I know, there were no chemical alarms set up in the area of Fire Base Mike. The lack of detection equipment worsened as we moved forward. Our company had very little chemical detection equipment, and its use was even more inconsistent. Chemical monitoring might have been done diligently by the front line and infantry, but we were right behind them (within twenty miles of the border) before the ground war, and were even Scud'ed at the 402d [location], but no chemical precautions were taken or encouraged. This posture and attitude was prevalent throughout the desert during my time there."[8]

Lieutenant Colonel Stephen Franke, Assistant Army Attaché, American Embassy, Saudi Arabia

"I was assigned as to DAO's Defense Attaché System as an Assistant Army Attaché. I became intimately familiar with Saudi Arabian Ministry of the Interior and Municipality of Riyadh. They were the main Saudi Arabian government bodies responsible for civil defense and countermeasures/recovery against (dreaded) chemical warfare attack by Scud SSM [surface-to-surface missiles] (Hussein and al-Abas variants). While assisting them, I accompanied the Saudi police and civil defense guys to Scud impact sites, helped carry bodies, assessed damages, showed that the US shared concern and the danger, and interviewed witnesses and survivors.

"On a side and somewhat still-humorous note, I remember the panic and indignation by the resident expatriate British community because their embassy wouldn't get gas masks for their horses! Those valiant horsemen swore up and down that since the British had gas masks for their military horses in WWI, then Her Majesty's Government certainly must have a stock back in the United Kingdom, or they could get some made and delivered posthaste to Saudi Arabia. Her Majesty's ambassador was most firm, clear, and not delicate in his negative reply."[9]

TALES FROM THE SOLDIERS—OPERATION DESERT STORM

First Lieutenant Russell Baggerly, Pier Operations Officer, 24th Transportation Battalion, 7th Transport Group, 22d Support Command

"It was January 16th, the deadline had passed and the air war finally started. Almost at the very moment we saw that Peter Arnett was foolishly not keeping his head down, came the wail of Damman's air raid sirens. 'Scud warning!' said the radio and we scrambled to get into mission-oriented protective posture (MOPP). I gathered with the rest of the off-shift soldiers in a nearby warehouse, and then realized that due to the heat, and my almost constant sweating over the last few months, I had lost enough weight that my mask didn't fit anymore. Air bubbled through the sweat pooled in the chin cup of my mask. Trying in the best traditions of the Officer Corps to stay calm, because, "panic is contagious," I tried to set the example while I desperately held the chin of my mask firmly against my face and sat with the soldiers. I also tried to remember first aid for NBC casualties. 'OK, it's atropine for blood agent, no, wait, first the little one, then the big one, no . . . shit.' I remember thinking, 'This isn't how I thought I'd get it.' That Scud supposedly whistled overhead for a not-even-near miss in the gulf, and the sirens sounded the all clear.

"Later, after our 'fifty-seventh' Scud warning we got a bit nonchalant about the whole thing. When the siren went off, we would run to the railing of the barge to watch the fireworks. Some of the ships reacted to the Scud warnings by hitting every fire hose on the ship and 'showering' themselves to 'wash off' the chemical agents they feared. To us it was funny, the sirens blew, and the ships disappeared behind a curtain of water. Not that we weren't afraid, but what do you do?"[10]

Captain Andrew Entwistle, commander, 45th Ordnance Company, XVII Airborne Corps

"When it [the Scud attacks of January 17] finally came, the message that awakened me was all that I'd expected. 'It's started. Have your guys take their pills, get into MOPP and be ready to go to the bunkers.' Turning on the portable radio we listened with the rest of the world as Bernard Shaw of CNN witnessed what we could not. I paused in dressing, thinking aloud to LT [Lieutenant] McPeak: 'This is history, happening right now. You just tore open a brand-new protective suit because you really might need it. We're taking these PB tablets for the first time ever in the field. None of this stuff has ever happened before and we don't know tonight how it will end, or even if either of us will ever see it end.' Our eyes met, and we finished dressing in silence. The Scuds did not come, and at dawn we held stand-to, marvelling at the streams of aircraft filling the sky.

"[On the third day he was awakened.] 'Scud launchers are up, some pointed this way. Take the pills and head for the holes.' Each soldier carried a chemical suit tightly rewrapped since its first exposure. We'd been told that this could preserve it [after being worn once], but we'd never heard that before and few of us believed it, especially later, as the number of 'reusable' days was increased almost daily. Inside the commo shack, panic broke out with the whooping of an M8 alarm set on the perimeter. I could hear it as they screamed to me over the commercial walkie-talkie, and I thought about those letters I dreaded. It never occurred to any of us at that moment that we hadn't seen any type of delivery system, or that no one else's alarm was sounding. We were not going to die! Screaming at the top of my lungs, I raced around the perimeter. The company exploded into action, heading for MOPP level 4 in record times that will never be broken. A soldier without his gear bolted for his tent barely touching the ground. Someone yelled that I had not yet masked, that they'd carry the word around. Precious seconds burned as I desperately tried to force a bootie on backwards, but I got it on somehow. Masked and ready, we waited.

"And waited. Around the perimeter, soldiers reviewed their lessons: 'One sign of being gassed is sweating . . . I'm sweating!' Through sheer willpower [suggestion] mouths dried out, heads pounded, and the twitching began. The pills made many nauseous, but they couldn't be sick in the mask, and if they couldn't take the mask off . . . A soldier fainted and panic nearly overtook us. There's no telling what our self-inflicted body count would have been had not the sun finally topped the horizon, revealing the tents of the chemical platoon, 50 yards away. Wandering to the four-holers in their t-shirts and flip-flops, they couldn't imagine what the idiot commanding the 45th Ord was doing practicing NBC in the dark. I stared at them, waiting for the first to writhe and fall. None did. Suddenly, things were very clear to me. I had read about, and scoffed at, the self-perpetuating panic of Orson Welles's *War of the Worlds*. Now I scoffed no longer, and was deeply ashamed that I had been so easily stampeded. I decided to prolong the charade just a bit longer, for not to practice the M256 detector kits now would have been to admit utter defeat. We had 220 volunteers for the unmasking procedure, and a few minutes later retaped our chemical suits for what would be the last time of the war."[11]

Captain Shirley DeGroot, Group Chemical Officer, 171st Corps Support Group

"It was the last week in January 1991. I was assigned to the Headquarters Company, 171st Corps Support Group. We were the forward support group with a mission of supporting the Division Support Command, 24th Infantry Division, and all the XVIII Airborne Corps-level troops within the 24th ID area of operation. Our Group had about 2,000 soldiers in it, and I was the only chemical officer, so I was quite busy during Desert Shield coordinating the NBC training and contingency planning for these soldiers. In the midst of all this, I was asked by the Group Commander and the HHC Commander to give a few NBC common task refresher classes to the troops of the HHC before we deployed forward to locate near the 24th ID.

"One of the classes I naturally selected for a unit about to get a scenic, motor-coach tour of southern Iraq was 'Treat Self Using the Nerve Agent Antidote Kit,' as there was at least a minor threat that the Iraqis might utilize a semi-persistent or non-persistent nerve agent on our advancing forces. One of the training aids required to give this class is a 'Dummy' Nerve Agent Antidote Kit (NAAK) that soldiers can use to simulate injecting themselves with the antidote. Since the HHC deployed to Saudi Arabia during September 1990 in a bit of a hurry, there weren't any of the bright blue training aids available (training items being something that didn't get packed in the rush to deploy). As the Chemical Officer, I had custody of the 'live' antidote kits until they were issued to the individual soldiers. As is usually the case in the Army, some of the 'live' kits had been roughly handled during shipment to Saudi, and a few of them had accidentally fired their antidotal contents into the protective packing around the auto-injector. Because there weren't any 'dummy' kits, my Assistant Instructor, Sergeant Bob Brasco and I decided to make use of the used 'live' kits, which are colored olive-drab, just like everything that's an operational item in the Army. We carefully cut the exposed needles off with wire cutters, and marked the injector syringes 'FOR TRAINING USE ONLY.' Now we were ready to give the class.

"On the appointed day, Sergeant Brasco and I gathered the personnel from Headquarters Company into the Mess Tent for NAAK class. As an aside, it never failed to amaze me how popular NBC training was in Saudi Arabia. Having been commissioned into the Chemical Corps in 1985, I was used to having soldiers do anything, up to and including volunteering for KP, to get out of having to practice NBC skills. But NBC training was always a number-one attraction during the Gulf War—amazing what a marvelous training motivator a bit of poison gas can be. To return to the saga, the Mess Tent was full to overflowing and I recall thinking to myself 'Gee, I sure wish I'd arranged for another two or three Assistant Instructors to handle the practical side of this.' However, when I gave the introduction to the task at hand, the soldiers quieted down; soon I had their complete attention as I explained and Sergeant Brasco demonstrated how the NAAK was to be used in case of nerve agent poisoning. The demonstration completed, I split the HHC into small groups, each with a homemade training auto-injector, to practice the skill. Sergeant Brasco and I floated, supervising the practice and testing those soldiers who had mastered the task.

"We were about halfway through the practice period, when I was approached by a lieutenant colonel who had arrived late. He was in a harried state anyway about the upcoming operation and was quite concerned about missing the class; he asked me to catch him up to speed on what to do. The officer had secured an antidote kit, so I told him we'd go over the main points of the task immediately. First, I would explain the symptoms and the procedure, then I would demonstrate it, then he would practice the task on his own, and when he felt confident, I would test him. Agreed. I talked the officer through what would happen if he was exposed to the agent. Then, I grasped the antidote kit and held it in the proper position in my left hand, extended out from my body at 90 degrees. With my right hand, I demonstrated how you 'clear the area,' which means you pat your posterior to ensure you're not preparing to inject the antidote into your wallet or other obstruction. Then, I explained, you grasp the auto-injector in your right hand and swing it down onto the hip that you've cleared, like so . . . 'SHEEEEEITTTT!'

"I ripped the auto-injector from where it had fired into my buttocks. My tardy colonel had somehow taken his 'live' auto-injector out from his protective mask carrier to use as his training aid. Of course, in being Captain Helpful and volunteering to demonstrate the task, I got the full dose of atropine in my behind. The runny nose I had been suffering from for several days cleared (or should I say dried) up immediately. Knowing that I was in for a very pleasant 'trip' in a short while, I ordered Sergeant Brasco to take charge of the class. I reported to my supervisor, the Group Operations Officer, and said that I'd explain more fully in the morning, but that I was going to go lie down on a cot for a while. What followed was the best night's sleep I had during the entire six months of my stay in Southwest Asia. I awoke the next morning with the war's greatest hangover —not even the morning after an epic New Year's Eve party complete with home-distilled, white-lightning brand hooch could compare to how bad I felt following my NAAK class.

"I had a meeting with the 1st Corps Support Command's Chemical Officer that next day. Major Fred Evans was mildly amused at my predicament, and especially at the enormous quantities of water I kept tossing down my dry throat. His only comment was, 'Well, you're not a real chemical officer until you've fired up with an auto-injector.' My only regret is that I didn't have the presence of mind to ask Major Evans exactly what the circumstances were when he'd become duty-qualified."[12]

Colonel Bob Thornton, VII Corps Chemical Officer

"On the night prior to the ground war's initiation, the television show *48 Hours* had sent a video tape to Lieutenant General Franks on a story they had done on the VII Corps's preparation for combat. The only VCR in the Corps Main Command Post was in the Chemical Section, so the general's aide told us the general was going to come down to view the tape. A few minutes later General Franks arrived, and after watching the ten-minute segment, with all of us crowded around him, he sat back and quietly reflected a few moments. Finally, still looking at the darkened screen, he solemnly remarked as if to himself, 'You know, if we've done our job right, we won't lose a lot of people tomorrow.' With that, he rose, spoke a few brief words of encouragement to the chemical staff, and departed for the forward deployed Tactical Command Post, about to begin the attack."[13]

Captain Nick Swanye, Commander, Headquarters and Headquarters Battery, 212th Field Artillery

"I was a commander of an artillery unit in Saudi. We were attached to the 24th ID and did the left hook into Iraq, stopping just west of Basra. We returned via the same route. During the four-plus months we were waiting (near Nayiria on the pipeline road) for the war to start, we had our brand new M8A1 alarms on 24/7 [twenty-four hours a day, seven days a week]. They never went off.

"A brigade HHB doesn't have any organic decon equipment. We were having problems with our CUCV [Commercial Utility Cargo Vehicle] RATT [Radio TeleTypewriter] rigs getting stuck every 100 meters, so I took three 2 ½ ton trucks and mounted RATT rigs on them. There was room left, so we added a three-hundred-gallon fiberglass tank up front. We filled it with water and bleach. I bought gas-powered pumps, high-pressure hose, and made nozzles for them. They worked great for putting out tent fires (using straight water), and with the bleach mix we figured they were better than nothing for decontamination.

"On the first day of the war, I was the lead vehicle. We crossed into Iraq near the west end of the neutral zone. I had wired an M8 [chemical alarm] onto the roof of my 'humvee' to monitor for agents (this is not a recommended solution because the new alarms are so susceptible to dust). Within four hours of crossing the border, the alarm was going off so frequently that we shut it off. Our chemical officer said it was due to the dust (which was so thick, visibility was down to twenty–fifty feet). Our entire brigade, and the 24th ID, stayed in MOPP-1 from day one of the air war until the day we crossed back into Saudi Arabia (10 March). My unit never entered Kuwait, and departed, for the most part, by 10 April."[14]

PURPOSE OF THIS BOOK

The primary goal of this book is to identify the chemical-biological warfare (CBW) challenges learned from the Persian Gulf War. During the months of Operation Desert Shield, the media, the political leadership and the military leadership examined the threat of CBW against US and allied forces in minutia. Many articles and stories examined the chemical attacks during the Iran-Iraq War in the 1980s, the US military's defensive equipment and training (or lack thereof), and the real threat of chemical or biological agent attacks against US forces. Coalition nations' politicians and military leaders warned Saddam both publicly and diplomatically about the consequences of such actions, while praying for enough time to bring their soldiers up to speed on survival skills. When the air campaign began in January 1991, NBC munition production and storage facilities were the number-two target on the priority list, right after Iraqi command and control sites. As Scuds landed on Saudi Arabia and Israel, chemical detection teams raced out to the impact areas to determine whether CBW had been initiated.

When the ground offensive kicked off, commanders donned their chemical protective suits and, as they crossed into Iraq, prayed silently that no CBW munitions would be used. As most accounts of the Persian Gulf War will state, the political and military leadership claims that the combination of their defensive preparations against NBC agents, a massive conventional offensive against Iraqi NBC munition production and storage sites, and highly mobile divisions moving quickly against Iraqi forces kept Saddam from employing NBC munitions against the coalition.

In the aftermath of Operation Desert Shield/Storm, the US military is dangerously close to ignoring the fact that lightning has struck the same spot several times. As it did in World War I and World War II, the US Army went into Southwest Asia initially unprepared to survive and sustain its forces in an NBC-contaminated environment. In all three instances, the military developed a capability that enabled it to fight on a potentially NBC-contaminated battlefield, although not necessarily in the timeframes one would optimally choose. The following chapters will reveal that it took six months of production and six months of training to prepare for NBC warfare, none of which would have been possible had the Army's Chemical Corps not worked hard for ten years prior to 1990. Because of the efforts of chemical soldiers throughout Southwest Asia and the continental US, the coalition would have survived any NBC munitions attacks—in February 1991. Had Saddam ordered the attack to continue into Saudi Arabia before November 1 and used NBC munitions as he had in the Iran-Iraq War, the coalition would have suffered massive casualties General Norman Schwarzkopf has since stated that this was one of his worst fears.

Why then, in all the books and articles written after the war, does no one acknowledge that the Chemical Corps might have been doing something to prepare the armed forces for this effort? This book attempts to show that effort did take place, and was successful in preparing the US Central Command (CENTCOM) for the real threat of NBC warfare. All the concerns about the US military's vulnerability were reported accurately by the media, by political and military leaders before Congress, and were accepted as true statements. But that doesn't explain two things—why did DoD, and more importantly, the military leadership, allow this vulnerability to develop over the years? And what did the Army Chemical Corps do to ensure American soldiers, airmen, sailors and Marines were prepared to overcome these deficiencies prior to the ground offensive?

The general officers in Desert Shield/Storm, who had to face these questions, are retiring and leaving DoD. Chemical warfare specialists who understood offensive chemical munitions employment have long since left, and only a few remain from the US biological warfare program. We are quickly losing the resident expertise that understands how future adversaries might employ chemical and biological warfare munitions. On top of this, the Army is being downsized, chemical defense companies are being moved out of the divisions, Dugway Proving Ground and Fort McClellan are on the Base Realignment Committee list, and the chemical defense community grows smaller every year. Until we get a grasp on this issue and make reasoned decisions based on costs and benefits, the US military remains in grave peril from the NBC warfare threat.

This declaration is not intended to overstate the issue. Only if CB weapons were used on civilians and population centers, would they truly be "weapons of mass destruction." On the military battlefield, these weapons, shorn of the ridiculous air of menace given to them by politicians and the media, are merely another tactical-operational factor like enemy air attacks or unforeseen terrorist attacks; military forces can and do take steps to minimize the effects of chemical-biological contamination. If a military force invests a small amount of time and funds in planning, defensive equipment and training, the immediate threat of mass casualties is avoided, and chemical-biological weapons become merely "weapons of mass *disruption*" instead of destruction. We have the specialists and the right doctrine (both then and now). It's really that simple—if the military invests in equipment and training, they maintain a viable combat force. If they do not, their troops become as vulnerable as unprepared civilians.

The saying is that every military force prepares to fight the last war. In that case, in the early hours of the next conflict the US Army will prepare for CB warfare just as it has in the past, by checking its CB defense "insurance policy" and determining whether or not it has done enough in CB defense equipment and training to protect its investment—the men and women of the US armed forces. When military and political leaders see that the same challenges still exist, they will wave their arms around, push bushels of money at the Army, and improvise a solution as the US military has always done when faced with the threat of CB warfare. But I do not think that next time we will have a six-month grace period to build up the necessary stocks and training expertise.

CHAPTER 2

Deployment to the Desert

> In addition to being outnumbered, there was this overriding concern, overwhelming concern about chemical warfare. This just occupied most of my waking moments.
> —General Walt Boomer, USMC, *Frontline,* 1995

On August 2, 1990, as Iraqi tanks crossed the border into Kuwait, US armed forces were not fully prepared to deploy and fight on a CB-contaminated battlefield in the Middle East. Over the last few decades, the Army had focused upon designing equipment for European conflicts. All the latest CB defense equipment had been meant for fighting the Soviets on a European battlefield, and military units in Europe had priority in receiving it. Realistic CB defensive training was the rule (within bounds).[1] Soldiers used chemical protective overgarments (CPOGs) during field exercises. All the tanks had the latest agent filtration systems, and airfields and command posts had collective protection systems ready. The Army and Air Force stockpiled chemical and tactical nuclear weapons in Europe as a theater retaliatory capability (at least until the summer of 1990, when US Army Europe [USAREUR] implemented plans to remove these systems).

Back in the United States, combat divisions training to deploy and fight outside of Europe ignored these preparations, because they did not expect to encounter CB warfare in their theaters of conflict. Because of production delays, many divisions lacked CB defense equipment issued to their higher-priority European counterparts. Unit commanders chose not to purchase chemical protective clothing that probably would not be used, but spent the funds on other training and maintenance priorities. Reserve and Guard units had even less time for training on topics outside of immediate mission areas. This situation made for an unequal level of individual training, unit training and logistics preparations throughout the Army (and other services). Most important, it meant that CENTCOM's forces were not initially prepared for an adversary who used CB agent munitions.

DEPLOYMENT TO SAUDI ARABIA

General Norman Schwarzkopf first arrived at CENTCOM headquarters in Florida in November 1988, reporting as CINCCENT (Commander-in-Chief, Central Command). One of his challenges was to justify the continuation of a command that had no assigned combat units; any forces that were to deploy to the Middle East would be borrowed from CONUS or Europe. Part of this assessment was accomplished through an annual wargame called "Internal Look," which tested contingency plans for CENTCOM's responses to threats against American interests in the Middle East. Plan 1002, last gamed in 1989, had a scenario assuming that Iran was the main adversary. The Iraq-Iran War had decimated Iran's forces but left intact most of Iraq's modern, mechanized units. Syria, the only other major Arab power that might be hostile to the US, focused its military force against Israel, which was not part of CENTCOM's responsibility. General Schwarzkopf decided that 1990 "Internal Look" would star the Iraqi forces as the adversary.[2]

Plan 1002-90 would focus on the defense of the Arabian Peninsula from an Iraqi invasion into Saudi Arabia through Kuwait. It assumed a twenty-two-division opposing force against the XVIII Airborne Corps in an established defense-in-depth in eastern Saudi Arabia. This plan also assumed that CENTCOM had twenty-one days of warning to mobilize and deploy to Saudi Arabia. Friendly forces included the 82d Airborne Division (ABN DIV), 24th Infantry Division (IN DIV), 101st ABN DIV, a Marine amphibious force, a Navy carrier group, and Air Force tactical fighter wings. The game showed Iraqi armored units, though fiercely attacked by tactical aircraft and helicopters, still able to push nearly 200 kilometers into Saudi Arabia before being stopped around al-Jubayl; XVIII Airborne Corps did hold Dhahran, ad-Dammam and the Abquaiq oil refineries, at the cost of 50 percent of its fighting force. The exercise stressed the need for tank-killers, such as the tactical aircraft and helicopters, a fast sea-lift capability, and for quickly developing a strong combat power advantage.[3]

The "Internal Look" war game probably did not portray Iraq as using CB agent munitions. Integrating realistic CB agent-cloud behavior, as affected by weather and terrain, into tactical wargaming was too difficult in the 1970s and 1980s. Agencies responsible for developing computer models for CB agent effects did not have the ability to verify or validate their models, given the cessation of open-air testing of CB weapons in 1969. No one had translated the CANE information of effects on troops into war games or quantified how the inclusion or exclusion of chemical defensive equipment would impact casualty results. There was no consideration given to the effects of CB agents on the physiological or psychological state of personnel, or to the effects of contaminated equipment on the units' combat readiness or operational tempo.[4] The logistically intensive tasks of resupplying protective clothing, decontaminants, and medical treatments also could not be integrated. Logistics offices had some consumption rates, based on older scenarios and outdated protective clothing, but nothing as well developed as for ammunition, fuel, or other more common general supplies.

In short, since it was too hard to simulate realistic tactical/operational use of CB agent munitions or NBC defense logistics, military war gamers chose not to include CB warfare. A certain game might include an intelligence brief that the enemy had the capability to use CB weapons, but that did not mean the enemy would use them. If the enemy did, it was usually seen as the desperate response of a defeated side and a trigger for massive US retaliatory response, often leading to tactical nuclear strikes. In the 1990s, war games still did not feature CB warfare. The same problems remained unsolved. Where models that reflected cloud behavior were used to reflect realistic CB agent movement, war games often stopped as this "special event" drained computer power due to its massive memory requirements. Needless to say, CB warfare was rarely welcomed at the war games.

"Internal Look" had been an opportunity to examine which chemical defense units might deploy to CENTCOM in support of this scenario. By updating the deployment roster with active and reserve chemical defense units, a plan was made ready for delivering decontamination assets into the theater. The chemical staff infrastructure could also practice requesting and planning retaliatory chemical weapons use. Although the binary chemical weapons program had just been halted in July 1990 after producing a limited quantity of 155 mm binary chemical agent projectiles, there still was a retaliatory capability available in the form of the older, unitary chemical agent weapons. There was also the option of reinitiating the binary weapons program. Given the threat of chemical warfare in the Middle East, the option of retaliation in kind (in line with national policy) might have to be exercised.[5]

General Schwarzkopf briefed President Bush on Plan 1002-90 at Camp David on August 4, 1990. He described the gamed deployment of the XVIII Airborne Corps, Marine units, and accompanying Air Force and Navy units as the "Internal Look" plan had detailed. Schwarzkopf pointed out that the majority of the Iraqi army was not of high caliber; the main threat would come from the eight divisions of Republican Guards, the South African 155 mm artillery guns, which outranged the US 155 mm self-propelled howitzers, and chemical weapons delivered by artillery, aircraft or Scud missiles. The Iraqi military's main weaknesses included feeble logistics and strongly centralized command and control. An effective defense would lie in the deployment of over a quarter of a million soldiers, a call-up of reserves, and air superiority which Lieutenant General Chuck Horner had promised could be established in a matter of days. If President Bush wanted Iraq out of Kuwait, it would take an offensive with twice the number of troops, built up over eight to ten months.[6]

When the order to go was issued (9 p.m. EST on 6 August), the 2d Brigade of the 82d ABN DIV—as Division Ready Brigade 1—began operations to load and depart within thirty-six hours. The 1st Brigade and 3rd Brigade were recalled immediately. Each deployed with a platoon "slice" of the 21st Chemical Company (Smoke/Decon). In seven days, the entire division ready brigade, the division combat aviation brigade, a Multiple Launch Rocket System (MLRS) battery and the 2d platoon, 21st Chemical Company were on the ground in Saudi Arabia. All three airborne brigades were in Southwest Asia by August 24. The 7th Marine Expeditionary Brigade (MEB) at Twenty-nine Palms, California, received the word to deploy on August 8 to fly its troops to the Gulf. They would meet their five Maritime Prepositioning Squadron (MPS) steaming up from Diego Garcia in the Indian Ocean; the MPS vessels held an entire Marine brigade's equipment. The first three met the Marines in al-Dammam on August 14, and rolled out the only heavy tanks (M60A3s) that would be available to CENTCOM until September.

The 24th IN DIV (Mechanized) had started moving even before Major General Barry McCaffrey officially received his marching orders; as commander of the only heavy division of the XVIII ABN Corps, McCaffrey knew the orders were coming, and got his brigades moving toward the Savannah ports. The 197th IN BDE (Mech)(Sep) would join the 24th IN DIV as its roundout unit (a reserve or National Guard unit designated to join an active duty division for wartime deployment) in lieu of the division's National Guard brigade. The 24th IN DIV supplied to the XVIII ABN Corps the heavy punch of M1 tanks, able to counter the Iraqi T-72s. General Schwarzkopf's planners called Fort Hood, Texas, to activate the 6th Combat Aviation Brigade (CAB) with its sixty Apache helicopters. It was expected to deploy to the Gulf within ten days, but it was not ready: the unit was low on spare parts; all its Hellfire missiles were in storage at Anniston Army Depot, Alabama; its pilots had just come off a training exercise; and it was low on CB defense equipment. CENTCOM turned to the 11th CAB from the 2d Armored Division (AR DIV) (Forward) in Germany to deploy in their place. The 1st Cavalry Division (CAV DIV), the 3rd Armored Cavalry Regiment (ACR), and the Tiger Brigade from the 2d AR DIV at Fort Hood would deploy to offset XVIII ABN Corp's lack of armor. (Initial plans were for the Tiger Brigade to replace the National Guard roundout brigade of the 1st CAV DIV).[7] The 101st ABN DIV had units spread out from West Point to Panama and Honduras when alerted to the deployment. The 2d Brigade, 101st ABN DIV, began deployment on August 17, but the division would not "close" in Saudi Arabia until October 6.

Schwarzkopf's headquarters moved to Riyadh, Kingdom of Saudi Arabia, on August 24. Already, US intelligence had begun reporting signs of Iraqi chemical warfare preparations. Intelligence sources had reported chemical decontamination equipment near two Iraqi artillery battalions in Kuwait. Admiral Frank Kelso, Chief of Naval Operations, had activated the Navy's hospital ships, the USNS *Comfort* and USNS *Mercy*, to prepare to provide immediate treatment to thousands of expected chemical casualties. General Schwarzkopf's planners issued orders to deploy fourteen fully staffed hospital units to the Gulf.[8] VA hospitals in the United States prepared to receive airlifted chemical casualties. Even at this early stage, the military leadership was deeply concerned over the political and morale-shaking consequences should US forces be exposed to chemical warfare.

IMMEDIATE CHEMICAL DEFENSE SUPPORT

Lieutenant Colonel Kenneth Silvernail and Major Patrick Fogelson arrived in Dhahran as the CENTCOM NBC Defense Division of J-3 (Operations) on August 9, with the CENTCOM advance party. Silvernail, designated as the Theater Chemical Staff Officer, would receive seven more Army chemical officers by mid-September to form the CENTCOM NBC Center (NBCC).[9] His initial priorities were to develop the chemical unit infrastructure and coordinate the entire coalition's CB defense logistics. CENTCOM would recommend that all soldiers deploy with three unopened sets of protective clothing, a protective mask, three Nerve Agent Antidote Kits (NAAKs) and M258A1 skin decon kits, and a set of replacement mask filters. Army units would discover this goal could not be realistically met, nearly all units lacking adequate quantities of protective clothing and masks. The Marines, upon inspecting their prepositioned stocks, found their protective suits damaged by heat and petroleum, their protective masks dry-rotted, and mask filters aged past their shelf life. All the Marine Corps's M8A1 alarms were in an Albany depot supposedly because they had not instituted a radioactive control program (required for the americium isotope inside the detector). The Air Force and Navy were having similar difficulties, finding severe shortages in both protective suits and decontamination supplies. Lieutenant Colonel Silvernail began immediate discussions with the Joint Chiefs of Staff (JCS) and the Army Office of the Deputy Chief of Staff for Operations and Plans (ODCSOPS) over options to increase or accelerate the delivery of any recently fielded or about to be fielded chemical defense equipment to include the M1 CAM, the XM21 RSCAAL, and the XM93 NBCRS. The top priority was increasing the quantities of protective masks, protective clothing, and medical antidotes.

The next CENTCOM responsibility was to coordinate NBC defense operations for all coalition forces. Within the first week after the NBCC's establishment, Lieutenant Colonel Silvernail was tasked to assist the Saudi Arabian Ministry of Defense and Aviation (MODA) to form a Saudi joint-level NBC staff. He and Captain Paul Schiele conducted a three-day refresher training class (the first of several) for the Saudi NBC School located at King Khalid Military City (KKMC); it was attended by fifty Saudi, Syrian, Egyptian, and Kuwati officers. Saudi Army NBC defense stocks proved to be woefully low—not that there was any shortage of contractors offering to supply the desert nations. The US government was in no shape to assist the Saudi military logistically, barely having enough protective equipment for its own soldiers. The Saudi government did ask CENTCOM's NBCC for support in evaluating the capabilities of the many commercial offerers, relying on it to get the best value for the money.

Initially, Headquarters Army Component, Central Command (ARCENT), had a small NBC staff cell, composed of one lieutenant colonel and one master sergeant. The ARCENT NBCC would be augmented with the 63rd Chemical Detachment (JA) from III Corps in September. The JA teams were five-person staff units designed to work one twelve-hour shift, as opposed to the JB teams of ten soldiers. Both augmented division, corps and army headquarters staffs to provide NBC expertise around the clock. Until then, the two soldiers would be sorely stretched to handle the many requests for assistance in chemical defense matters. One of the ARCENT NBCC's first duties was to train the rest of the ARCENT staff on basic NBC defense skills, while assisting XVIII ABN Corps in its logistics challenges.

It fell to Colonel Ray Barbeau, the XVIII ABN Corps Chemical Officer, to organize the initial Army chemical defense preparations at corps level and below. Colonel Barbeau, Master Sergeant Zachary, the corps top chemical NCO, and the XVIII ABN Corps advance party arrived in Dhahran on August 8. Initial estimates showed a severe shortfall of decontamination assets, especially water-hauling trucks and the battalion-level M17 Lightweight Decontamination System (LDS) "SANATORs." The Army was in the process of accepting an initial delivery of a thousand M17s when troops began deploying to the Gulf in August, but only a few had been issued to his corps. Individual defense equipment (one unopened set of BDOs, a M17A2 protective mask with fresh filters, one M258A1 decon kit, three NAAKs per soldier) was available to support the initial deployment, but it would not support a sustained chemical warfare environment. The total number of M1 CAMs was only 150 for the entire XVIII ABN Corps. Many units were short their allotment of M8A1 chemical agent point detector alarms. By the end of August, the Corps NBC Center, manned by the 1st Chemical Detachment (JA), was operational and ready to operate. The 82d Chemical Detachment (JA) would support the corps support command (1st COSCOM) and rear area. The immediate priorities were supporting individual NBC defense training to sharpen forgotten skills, and obtaining additional NBC defense equipment (both consumable protective supplies and hardware).[10]

The troops' immediate survival prospects would increase in proportion to how fast they could increase their individual NBC defense expertise, especially Common Task Training and leadership training tasks. All divisions deploying to the Gulf were required to train their soldiers on thirteen NBC defense skills. These skills included the basics of how to put on, take off and maintain the protective mask, how to use the medical autoinjectors and how to use of the M258A1 decon kits and M256A1 chemical detection kits. Every soldier used a training set of chemical protective clothing to practice the various MOPP levels, rather than opening their contingency stocks. Most training was conducted in the early morning or evening, allowing soldiers a chance to acclimate gradually to the heat. Chemical officers commented that, for once, soldiers were paying very close attention to CB defense training. Besides enlisted soldiers and NCOs, officers attended the courses, from second lieutenants up through colonels. One chemical officer remarked that the individual CB defense skills were better among the lower-rank soldiers, and an individual's prior knowledge and expertise in this area actually worsened as the rank climbed. This reflected the difference between soldiers who had joined the Army prior to 1980, and those exposed to the "new" Chemical Corps doctrine and training after 1985.

Once individual training had raised the soldier's expertise to an acceptable level, battalions and brigades would move on to practicing unit missions in CB warfare scenarios, using their attached chemical defense units. Each deploying division had its own organic chemical company; the 21st Chemical Company (Smoke/Decon) deployed with the 82d ABN DIV, the 91st Chemical Company (Heavy Division) with the 24th IN DIV, and the 63rd Chemical Company (Smoke/Decon) with the 101st ABN DIV. XVIII ABN Corps had the 101st Chemical Company (Decon) as the corps general support chemical decontamination unit, deploying with 1st COSCOM. These chemical units, in conjunction with the chemical staff soldiers of combat arms companies, battalions and brigades, supplied a large source of trainers for both individual and unit NBC training, both of which would continue through September and October.

Chemical defense units designated to support the XVIII ABN Corps originally included the 415th Chemical Brigade (a reserve headquarters unit without assigned units) and two chemical battalions. The 415th Chemical Brigade was cut in favor of other units, although two chemical battalions did make the deployment schedule.[11] FORSCOM decided to deploy the 2d Chemical Battalion from Fort Hood and the 490th Chemical Battalion, a reserve headquarters unit at Anniston, Alabama. The 2d Chemical Battalion was alerted to deploy on August 10, while the 490th Chemical Battalion would wait for the president's official reserve call-up.

The number-one request for chemical defense unit support in the Gulf was for additional decontamination capability, given the high threat, perceived low training status and the lack of M17 LDSs within XVIII ABN Corps. Colonel Rick Read, chemical division chief in ODCSOPS's Space and Special Weapons Directorate, received a number of majors and lieutenant colonels from the US Army Nuclear and Chemical Agency to augment his small staff.[12] They began scouring the Chemical Corps force structure for units eligible to deploy quickly. The first two units tapped included the 59th Chemical Company (Smoke/Decon) from Fort Drum, New York, and the 761st Chemical Company (Smoke/Decon) at Fort Ord, California. Both companies had high readiness levels and were stationed near major airfields; they had the capability of being dual-purpose smoke and decontamination units. They were to be followed by the 11th Chemical Company and 51st Chemical Company, both theater decontamination units from 2d COSCOM, VII Corps, Germany. Chemical troops in III Corps that would deploy with their divisions included the 68th Chemical Company under the 1st CAV DIV, the 89th Chemical Company (ACR) under the 3rd ACR, and the 44th Chemical Company (Heavy Division), divided between 1st CAV DIV and the Tiger Brigade, 2d AR DIV. The 181st Chemical Company (Decon), a non-divisional chemical unit at Fort Hood, would deploy with the 2d Chemical Battalion at the end of September.

ODCSOPS next turned its attention to the reserves, where nearly 60 percent of the Chemical Corps's strength lay. Under President Bush's initial reserve call-up on August 24, HQ DA alerted a number of decontamination companies, staff detachments and a battalion headquarters unit to report to Fort McClellan. They included the 490th Chemical Battalion, 318th Chemical Company and 907th Chemical Detachment (JB) from Alabama; the 433rd Chemical Detachment (JB) from Georgia; the 327th Chemical Company from Texas; and the 371st Chemical Company from South Carolina. All reserve chemical units stationed east of the Mississippi River would mobilize at Fort McClellan beginning in early September. As each decontamination company arrived at Fort McClellan, its soldiers refreshed their individual and crew training through the CDTF. The two detachments (907th and 433rd) were scheduled to arrive into theater at the end of September, with the decontamination companies due into Saudi Arabia by October.

The XVIII ABN Corps, being primarily light infantry, had one chemical reconnaissance platoon authorized for the entire Corps (within the 24th IN DIV's chemical company).[13] With the 1st CAV DIV and 3rd ACR joining the Corps, the total would rise to three platoons. These recon platoons were equipped with M113A2 Armored Personnel Carriers (APCs), whose crews were not protected from chemical agent vapors and could not perform reconnaissance on the move. Given the size of the theater and its limited decontamination assets, it was important to have a recon capability to locate and isolate chemical agent contamination quickly. The Fox NBCRSs were officially two years from fielding, and there was little hope that these new vehicles would rush through US production lines. Lieutenant General Frederick Franks, Jr., VII Corps commander in Europe, offered his divisions' mechanized chemical recon platoons to supplement XVIII ABN Corps's forces. ODCSOPS, the USAREUR chemical officer, and the Seventh Army chemical officer selected several NBC reconnaissance platoons to deploy immediately.[14]

ASSESSING THE RISK

US military planners had known of Iraq's successful use of chemical weapons, especially during the 1988 campaigns against Iran. In August 1990, the Defense Intelligence Agency (DIA) and Central Intelligence Agency (CIA) released a number of assessments of Iraq's capabilities to wage CB warfare against the coalition. (While DIA was aware of the Iraqi nuclear program, there was no suggestion that Iraq had developed any nuclear munitions.) Analysts identified the major Iraqi chemical warfare agents as mustard gas and the nerve agents tabun (GA), sarin (GB), and GF (cyclosarin, a chemical agent similar to but more persistent than GB). Chemical agents in development included soman (GD), persistent nerve agent VX, and the hallucinogen agent BZ. Iraqi chemical weapon systems included Soviet-purchased 122 mm multiple rocket launchers (with Iraqi rockets sporting larger-than-normal chemical warheads), helicopter-launched 90 mm rockets with chemical warheads (another Iraqi invention), the more conventional 250/500 kilogram aerial chemical bombs, and chemical projectiles for 155 mm artillery guns and 120 mm mortars. Israeli intelligence also reported the existence of Scud chemical warheads. The weapons of choice would be the 155 mm artillery batteries. DIA pointed out that Iraq had reached the point of self-sufficiency for "precursor" agent production, and did not require foreign purchases to develop their agents. Estimates of the chemical stockpile ranged between one and four thousand tons of nerve agents and mustard gas, with a monthly production capability of 150 tons of mustard, five to ten tons of tabun, and twenty tons of sarin. The main complexes of coalition concern were the Muthanna production lines and the three weapon-filling facilities at Habbiniyah.

There were a number of suspected chemical weapons storage bunkers. The two closest to the border were the An Nasiriyah ammunition storage facility and the Ash Shuaybah ammunition storage depot. By the end of August DIA had noticed a flurry of activity as Iraqi forces prepared suspected CW storage bunkers at many of the southern airfields, the nearest ones being at Tallil and al-Jahrah. Decontamination sites were appearing at over half the Iraqi artillery batteries, including those throughout Kuwait. CIA and DIA analysts had not, however, detected any actual movement of chemical munitions to those southern sites.

DIA predicted that Iraq had "weaponized" anthrax and botulinum toxin, and was interested in doing the same with clostridium perfringens (which causes gas gangrene), staphylococcal enterotoxin B (SEB) and cholera. Candidate biological weapon systems included 250 kilogram aerial bombs, 250/500 kilogram cluster bombs, 90 mm air-to-ground rockets, mortar shells and artillery projectiles, Scud missile warheads, and ground and aerial spray systems (although DIA had no confirmed knowledge of any weaponization). Special concern was raised by the reported acquisition of a number of Italian truck-mounted agricultural sprayers, which could be adopted for biological warfare (BW) agent dissemination. Employment of biological agents in Saudi Arabia by Iraqi special forces could not be ruled out, but there was no proof that they had been trained to do so. There were three identified primary nodes of the BW program: the Salman Pak CBW Research, Production and Storage Facility; the Taji suspected BW pilot plant in the northwest suburbs of Baghdad; and the Abu-Ghurayb clostridium vaccine plant a few kilometers west of Baghdad. The Abu-Ghurayb "infant formula" plant was suspected of being a backup production plant, given its unusually high security and its state-of-the-art fermenters and driers. The research and development centers at Samarra and Tuwaitha were suspected of supporting the BW program. The offensive BW program was a relatively new aspect of Iraq's CBW program—still growing as its government purchased biological material, fermenters and other equipment from Western nations as late as 1989.

There were a number of suspected BW bunkers with the environmental control characteristics necessary to preserve BW agents. DIA counted as many as thirty-four of them at seventeen different locations, including the ones at Salman Pak. All were located near general munitions storage facilities, and all but one had been built in the late 1970s. As such, they could have had the primary purpose of protecting electronics, fuel-air explosives or "smart" weapons from the heat; then again, they would also be ideal for storing biological or chemical agents. No one had any real evidence to indicate one way or another.

The official intelligence assessment was that Iraq was "likely to use CW as an integral part of tactical operations to protect key political, military or economic strategic areas." DIA estimated that Iraq was not prepared to launch an immediate offensive into Saudi Arabia supported by chemical weapons but that Saddam could use such weapons to defend against a coalition attack. The weather and temperature through the fall and winter of 1990 would favor Iraq, since the prevailing winds (blowing east to southeast) and the heat would work against US chemical defense preparations. If the CW production facilities were attacked, Iraq might respond with its chemical munitions capability immediately, in an effort to "use it or lose it" before its poor-quality chemical stocks (estimated 20 to 50 percent purity) lost their potency. Then again, the Iraqis might save the munitions for the expected coalition attack. Potential threats included the use of aircraft and Scuds armed with persistent chemical agents against Saudi airfields and ports, and special forces/terrorist use of CB agents or other specialized weapon systems in the rear areas.

The coalition was assessed to be at significant risk if Iraq undertook biological warfare. There was no reliable information as to how Iraq might employ its biological weapons, since the Iraqi military had not used them in the war against Iran. No intelligence agency was bold enough to predict or talk about exact details as to the results of an actual biological agent attack against the coalition. The official assessment was that while Iraq had the capability tactically and strategically to deploy BW munitions, they would not be ready to take advantage of any vulnerabilities created by a biological agent attack. The more probable threat was clandestine BW agent use prior to hostilities, as opposed to overt BW attacks conducted by planes or Scud missiles.

While DIA, CIA and other agencies felt certain that Iraq would employ CB warfare against CENTCOM, a number of issues remained unresolved. There was no information on Iraqi CB agent munitions markings, or exactly where the stocks were located; no one could guess as to effects of biological munitions employment against CENTCOM's forces; no one could say of how covert employment of CB agents might occur, how effective such an attack would be, or what steps CENTCOM could employ to combat this possibility. Also, no one knew if there would be any significant CB agent dissemination if a Patriot surface-to-air missile hit a Scud high in the atmosphere. Would the chemical agents disseminate harmlessly into the jet stream or fall immediately to the ground? Chemical warfare experts at DIA and Edgewood had no idea and were unwilling to guess. If Saddam ordered chemical warfare against a CENTCOM force driving into Kuwait, the expected casualties would be high.[15]

As the deployment continued, everyone became convinced that Saddam would use CB agents against the US forces. The US military and political leadership realized how extremely vulnerable its forces were, given the shortages of chemical defense equipment and the poor level of training. There was a fine line being drawn here. The American government had to respond to an Iraqi chemical attack or face possible future Third World adversaries encouraged by Iraq's success. On the other hand, excessive or massive retaliation (read: nuclear) would drive Arab coalition partners from the force. Because of the delay in getting chemical defense units into the Gulf and the acknowledged vulnerability of the soldiers, CENTCOM had to rely on two actions to dissuade Iraqi NBC attacks.

The first action was a massive media focus on CENTCOM's defensive preparedness, beginning with training demonstrations showing soldiers donning their protective masks and getting acclimated to the protective clothing in the desert. News footage showed brand-new Patriot launchers bristled around Riyadh and Dhahran, ready to knock out potential CB agent warhead Scuds. Military spokespersons at the Pentagon, in CNN studios, and in the Gulf spoke confidently of their readiness against Iraq's CW capability. Media interest was particularly highlighted by such notable speakers as Colonel (Ret.) Harry Summers and Sam Donaldson describing military NBC defense preparedness. This show of "expertise" would, it was hoped, impress Saddam that the use of CB agents would have little or no effect on the military force assembled.

The second action was to retaliate heavily against Iraqi military, industrial and civilian centers in and around Baghdad if any use of chemical agents against US forces was detected. Air Force Component, Central Command (CENTAF), developed a plan titled "Punishment Air Tasking Order" outlining the massive retaliation options if the Iraqis did use chemical agents. Lieutenant General Chuck Horner laid out seventeen targets, including the presidential palace, to be hit by allied bombers. His assistant, Brigadier General Buster Glosson, proposed targeting three dams, whose destruction would cause a flood that would destroy much of Baghdad's industrial base. General Schwarzkopf proposed that US politicians should tell Baghdad that if chemical weapons were used, the response would be nuclear—not that it actually would be, he explained, but the forcefulness of the message might strike fear into the Iraqi leadership. Eventually, it was agreed that a combination of political threats and a public show of expertise would be the best option, combined with a broadened conventional air campaign against industrial and military targets if the bluster and showmanship did not work.[16]

Early planning to attack the CBW storage sites brought additional fears. DIA warned that the coalition had to consider a number of probable outcomes, ranging from no release of agent to the liberation of hundreds of kilograms. This could result in significant collateral loss of life unless there was total and complete destruction of all agent at the site. The many factors, including type of agent, wind speed, temperature, inversion conditions, and explosive characteristics, made it too difficult to estimate the results. Ironically, the abandoned US BW program and open-air simulant tests conducted prior to 1969 would offer a basis for further DIA/CIA analysis of these scenarios.

CHEMICAL CORPS SUPPORT BUILDS

Phones began ringing all over the chemical defense community. Major General Louis Del Rosso, director of the Space and Special Weapons Directorate within ODCSOPS, pushed his Chemical Division into overdrive. Colonel Rick Read's group included Dr. Bob Boyle, a champion of institutional knowledge on BW programs, Lieutenant Colonel Howard Willhoite, a long time sage of chemical defense programs, and Major Ted Newing. Other staff officers from the Assistant Secretary of the Army (RDA) (ASARDA), ODCSLOG, CRDEC, AMC and other agencies began working with ODCSOPS to accelerate chemical defense equipment provisions, set priorities for what was needed, commit resources to make the purchases, and update the Army's policies on chemical defense equipment. Major Newing called Army warehouses to clear out the one thousand M17 SANATORs awaiting for instructions to ship to field units, directing them to XVIII ABN Corps units instead.

Probably the most important chemical defense effort was the Fox program. Lieutenant Colonel Willhoite had won support for the effort to acquire 48 German Fuchs vehicles on a limited procurement urgent acquisition prior to August. Because the US Army's Fox NBCRS program was still in research and development, he and Major Newing talked with Brigadier General Joe W. Rigby at ASARDA to negotiate with the German government for the immediate delivery of 30 Fuchs systems, based on the operational analysis and vision of who would be deployed. Unknowing to them at the time, the German government would be "prodded" by the Bush administration to contribute to the war effort by the US government, and this was one avenue that they were more than willing to assist.

In Germany, shortly after midnight on Sunday August 5, 1990, Major Walt Polley's telephone woke him up. Brigadier General Robert Orton, the Army Chemical School Commandant, was on the other end. He said, "Sorry if I got you out of bed, Walt. You have heard of the invasion of Kuwait by Iraq. Well, the German Army does not know this yet, but the German government is going to give the United States thirty Fuchs NBC reconnaissance vehicles, and will provide training for the operators at the NBC Defense School (ABC-SeS) in Sonthofen. Tell *Oberst* [Colonel] Fluegel [the German NBC Defense School Commandant], but also let him know that he can't 'know' this until the German government tells the German Armed Forces, who will then tell him. The ABC-SeS will train at least four American NBC recon platoons. The first two platoons will arrive in two weeks on 20 August. Can you do it?"

Asked if this was for real, Brigadier General Orton assured Major Polley that it was. The German military's NBC reconnaissance course was over three months long, but Orton instructed Polley to shorten the American version to three weeks maximum. He told Polley to notify *Oberst* Fluegel of his phone call later Sunday and also to work closely with USAREUR for logistics and administrative support. When Major Polley called *Oberst* Fluegel later that day, his son answered the phone; the Commandant was not at home. After apologizing for intruding on the weekend, Polley asked that *Oberst* Fluegel call him about a matter of extreme urgency whenever he returned, no matter what time it was. Early that evening, *Oberst* Fluegel called and was told Brigadier General Orton's message. After asking "Is this for real?" he promised the full resources of the ABC-SeS and asked Polley to come in to his office Monday morning to plan the work for this project.

On Monday, *Oberst* Fluegel began quietly to recall selected critical people off their leaves to Sonthofen.[17] *Oberstleutnant* (Lieutenant Colonel) Volker Schmitt (the school S-3 officer, who had overall responsibility for all training courses at the ABC-SeS) and Major Polley pared down the three-month German NBC recon course to a three-week long course, a two-week classroom session and a one-week field session. Once they had identified the critical and essential elements and extracted them from the longer program of instruction, the team began translating the lesson plans into English. Polley contacted Colonel Jan Van Prooyen, the USAREUR Chemical Officer, to coordinate the transport of NBC recon vehicles from the production lines in Kassel to Ramstein Air Force Base (AFB) and onward to Dhahran. Colonel Guenther, head of the Training and Doctrine (TRADOC) Liaison Office at the *Heeresamt* (German General Army Office) was also notified and made aware of the "Germans can't know until officially told through their chain" requirement.

August 8, a holiday marking the Assumption of the Virgin Mary, was spent working on the translations and fitting the selected blocks of instruction into a logical sequence. The *Heeresamt* called *Oberst* Fluegel's home with an urgent message; his wife said he was in the office. Called at the office and asked why he was at work on a holiday, the Commandant said that he had a little work that needed catching up, but that he was planning on returning home soon. Why was the Army Office calling on a holiday? The answer was what *Oberst* Fluegel had been told on Sunday; he was asked if he thought the German General Army Office should ask the Americans to delay starting their training for one or two weeks past the requested date of August 20. *Oberst* Fluegel replied that if he could have authority to recall selected personnel from leave and to relax overtime and travel budget restrictions, there would be no problem meeting the start date. He was given those permissions.

On August 7, Brigadier General Rigby called the PM NBC Defense Office to inquire how many Foxes they had, where they were, and how soon could they be deployed. The Army had five "Nunn" NBC reconnaissance vehicles;[18] two of these were at Fort McClellan for doctrine development, one was at Dugway Proving Ground, one at Aberdeen Proving Ground, and the last was at the General Dynamics Land Systems (GDLS) plant in Sterling Heights, Michigan. On the next day, Colonel Ron Evans, the Project Manager for NBC Defense, was directed to accelerate the plans to field the "Nunn" Foxes. His deputy, Lieutenant Colonel Mike D'Andries, as the Product Manager for the NBCRS, suddenly had a change of fortune: after battling a recent loss of project funds, he was struggling to meet demands for as many Foxes as he could push out the door. The Chemical School immediately "Americanized" the two Foxes on site with M60 machine guns, US communications equipment, appropriate US NBC defense equipment and air conditioning, while two crews received ad hoc training at the GDLS facility. Some in the Army Staff questioned the air conditioning, but it was vital to operating the mass spectrometer (the German MM-1) within the vehicle in the desert heat; one hour at 120°F would cause the MM-1 to fail.[19]

There was no time to initiate the GDLS production line, so Lieutenant Colonel Willhoite explored the idea of buying or leasing existing Fuchs from the German Army. This had political promise, since the German government could not contribute forces to the Persian Gulf because of its constitution but wanted to support the coalition effort publicly. Brigadier General Rigby contacted Thyssen-Henschel in Germany about obtaining additional Fuchs to support Operation Desert Shield. He cited to the company president, Mr. Jurgen Massman, the urgent need for a minimum of ten vehicles by mid-August. Since Thyssen-Henschel could not accelerate its production lines that quickly, the Army offered to buy thirty existing German military Fuchs systems. The German Ministry of Defense responded immediately and favorably. The Assistant Secretary of the Army (RDA), on August 11, signed a Justification and Authorization document for the expenditure of $106 million to purchase Fuchs from the German government. Work began at Thyssen-Henschel on August 14 to "Americanize" the thirty German Fuchs.[20] As negotiations continued between the two governments, the German government considered a no-cost loan of the vehicles as part of their nation's support for Operation Desert Shield; on September 4, it offered to lend 30 Fuchs vehicles to the US military.

On August 12, the two "Nunn" vehicles at Fort McClellan were shipped to the 24th IN DIV to deploy with the 91st Chemical Company. Captain Vince Hughes and seven NCOs from the Chemical School linked up with the two Foxes at Fort Stewart. Their mission was to deploy with the 24th Infantry Division and to train the 91st Chemical Company's reconnaissance platoon on use and maintenance of the systems. The two Foxes made it to the Gulf by August 26, and were immediately pushed out with the 2nd Bn, 4th Regt. Cavalry on reconnaissance missions to protect the 24th IN DIV's deployment.[21] The remaining three "Nunn" vehicles were sent to the GDLS plant for "Americanization," with the one change, that of adding M240 machine guns for their mounts instead of M60s (which would be the standard for the rest of the Foxes). They would be shipped to Fort Hood after their conversion to deploy with the III Corps forces.[22]

After the other three Foxes had undergone their modifications at the GDLS plant, the Army test community wanted to make sure that they could detect chemical agents in the sand. Some speculated that the liquid agents would soak too deep into the sand for the detectors to sniff out, only to re-emerge as vapor when the heat rose. One official suggested that tons of Saudi Arabian sand be shipped to Michigan on C5As returning to the United States; fortunately, five of the six types of terrain in Saudi Arabia were located naturally at Dugway Proving Ground, from sand dunes to rocky hills, and the special sand transportation was not required. One of the "Nunn" Foxes was sent back to Dugway Proving Ground to test this concern. On August 31, Dugway scientists used liquid simulants on the terrain to test the Fox's limits. In all cases, the Fox's MM-1 mass spectrometer was able to identify the agent and its location correctly. Now all the Army had to do was man the vehicles with trained operators.

After evaluating the training capabilities at the Chemical School and Sonthofen and determining the training requirements, Lieutenant Colonel Willhoite and Major Newing outlined a training program. The normal US Army program of instruction, based on a four-week period, was discarded in favor of the fourteen-hour-per-day, seven-day-a-week training schedule over three weeks. It was conducted in three phases (one per week): individual training, team training, and for US troops only, mission training. Individual instruction trained the driver and various team members on their specialized skill areas. The team training phase put the four-man crew into the Fuchs simulator, which was a full-scale mock-up in the classroom of the vehicle and its equipment, and also exercised the crew in Fuchs vehicles in short-duration missions within the confines of the post. American crews would work with Chemical School instructors on more detailed reconnaissance missions for the last phase of the training; British and Israeli soldiers, who would later train at Sonthofen, would complete their mission training on their own with their base units. After the training, the crews would marry-up to their refurbished German vehicles, literally rolling off the production lines.[23]

Back at Sonthofen, Major Polley and his German hosts continued to translate and proofread the Fox class instructions. The Germans practiced their lessons in English, set up the classrooms and stripped several Fuchs vehicles of their equipment. (There was only one Fuchs simulator available, and only the drivers needed the Fuchs for familiarization.) The equipment was moved into classroom bays so the students would have hands-on items for training. They stayed busy with training preparations until August 20, when the first two busloads of Americans showed up.

Within Seventh Army, the job of getting the chemical reconnaissance platoons to training and then on to Saudi Arabia fell to a working group tagged "Task Force Fox." This task force was formed on August 14 at Montieth Barracks, Furth, Germany, under Lieutenant Colonel W. A. Funderburg, the 1st AR DIV chemical officer, and members of the 69th Chemical Company (Heavy Division). Their mission was to expedite V and VII Corps chemical reconnaissance platoons through their training at Sonthofen, assist in receipt of their Foxes at the Thyssen-Henschel factory at Kassel and deploy them to Southwest Asia from Ramstein AFB. Colonel Barbeau had suggested forming four recon platoons of six vehicles each to equip the 24th IN DIV, 101st ABN DIV, 3rd ACR, and the 2d Chemical BN, allowing for six operational readiness floats. The first two platoons identified for training were the 5th Recon Platoon, 69th Chemical Company (1st AR DIV), and 7th Recon Platoon, 92nd Chemical Company (3rd IN DIV). These fifty-three soldiers arrived at Sonthofen on August 20 to begin their training; they would finish their training by September 7, marry-up with the first ten vehicles coming off the Thyssen-Henschel line, load and deploy to Dhahran by September 18.

The second group of soldiers arrived only a week after the first. The 5th Recon Platoon, 22nd Chemical Company (or 5/22 Chem of 3rd AR DIV) and the 5th Recon Platoon, 25th Chemical Company (5/25 Chem, 8th IN DIV) would stagger their training a week behind the first two platoons. Eight more Foxes would be ready by mid-October and would leave with the third platoon (5/22 Chem) to bring three platoons to full strength of six vehicles each. The 5/25th platoon would wait for its six Foxes to come off the lines in mid-November, and would then deploy. The first ten Foxes arrived in Saudi Arabia within thirty days of Thyssen-Henschel accepting receipt of American equipment.[24]

About mid-August, General Colin Powell, Chairman of the Joint Chiefs of Staff, called Major General Gerry Watson, then commander of the Defense Nuclear Agency (DNA) and former commandant of the Chemical School, into his Pentagon office. They discussed Iraq's CB warfare capability during the Iran-Iraq War and the possible threat to the XVIII ABN Corps. General Powell had confidence in American soldiers being able to operate in a chemical warfare environment, although it would prove difficult. His greater concerns were Iraq's biological warfare capability and the threat of chemical warheads on Scuds. The biological warfare vulnerability was a real problem, since there were no biological agent sensors in the military, and the Army's vaccine production program had essentially dried up over the last two decades.[25] General Powell asked Major General Watson to get in touch with General Schwarzkopf to talk about the situation. Schwarzkopf shared the same concerns, and asked Watson to develop a capability that would allow CENTCOM to identify a biological weapons attack.

Part of the reason why General Powell had initiated this discussion was that industry lobbyists and contractors were wandering the Pentagon halls hawking various "must have" hardwares. A Californian company, SRI, offered an off-the-shelf black box, a ground-mounted long range stand-off biological detector that used passive infra-red to detect and classify biological agents. These contractors, along with many government officials (including some from Aberdeen Proving Ground), had been on an information campaign to scare Pentagon decision makers with bold threat assessments and unvalidated opinions on Iraqi BW weaponization, warning that something had to be done immediately to avoid catastrophe. This campaign motivated the Army to dedicate over $20 million toward a crash biological detector research and development program.

Major General Watson immediately pulled together a DNA team to build a prototype detector that could sense a cloud of biological agents moving toward the force. The team identified as the best approach a flow cytometer operating within an airplane, monitoring the outside environment through airflow samplers mounted on the wings. Similar in concept to the helicopter-mounted "people-sniffer" detectors of Vietnam, it would utilize a generic biological organism sampler.[26] It would not positively identify the biological agent, but it would monitor a sharp increase in biological organisms. Samples could then be brought to a forward laboratory for positive identification. By the end of August, the team had begun to build the prototype and developed a test program to run at China Lake, the naval weapons test site. DNA hired a contractor and a plane to begin its tests, which would use biological simulant clouds to assess the effectiveness of the equipment. DNA would also test and evaluate SRI's stand-off system and other commercial options. At the same time, and in response to the same requirement, ODCSOPS directed CRDEC to see what could be resurrected from the old XM2/XM19 Biological Detection and Warning System.[27]

The Chemical School had thrown its support behind the Pentagon as well. Brigadier General Orton had established a twenty-four-hour operations center at the Chemical School on August 7, with daily war councils in the library's vault. He identified two primary missions for the School. The first was to ensure that all soldiers in the deploying units were trained and prepared to operate in a CB agent-contaminated environment. This would require the School to recommend specific training programs for deploying soldiers and their units (especially the chemical reserve units) and to develop special pocket-sized training manuals for soldiers to carry in the desert to refresh them on their defense training. The second mission was to support the necessary training for any special groups of personnel and new equipment. Any new chemical defense equipment, such as the CAMs or XM21s, would require special teams to deploy to Saudi Arabia to train the operators. Training support extended to supporting Middle Eastern countries.

On August 7, the Chemical School received a TRADOC tasking to provide an officer to deploy to Saudi Arabia to support the Office of the Program Manager, Saudi Arabian National Guard (OPM-SANG). This office was subordinate to HQ Army Materiel Command (AMC), with a mission to send technical support and training to the Saudi Arabian National Guard. Major Robert Buchanan arrived in Riyadh on August 17 to head a Mobile Training Team (MTT) that would have the responsibility to outfit and train the Saudi Arabian National Guard in NBC defense equipment. His first responsibility was to train the local government civilians, military service members and their dependents in a four-hour block of individual protection skills. This training was to provide some relief for the psychological stress felt by OPM-SANG, in addition to demonstrating the basic use of protective clothing and masks.[28] A second MTT, led by Captain David Lewis and two NCOs, arrived in the United Arab Emirates in late August to offer a similar program for its military forces. In addition to offering a "train the trainer" course, the UAE MTT reviewed the type, quantity, condition, and state of maintenance of the UAE chemical defense equipment, and recommended purchases to address the immediate shortfalls. These MTTs also instructed US citizens living in Saudi Arabia, including the embassy staff, families of the Army Training Mission and employees of Lockheed Corporation, on basic NBC defense skills.

Several other chemical NCOs and officers would arrive by mid-October to augment the MTTs, as the first items of a $12.1 million purchase of chemical defense equipment began arriving. This foreign military sale purchase would outfit thirty thousand Saudi military personnel. In addition to training the National Guard troops, the MTTs gradually increased their scope to refresher training for the MODA units. The chemical section developed a "train the trainer" program that eventually instructed over sixty thousand Saudi military personnel from October 1990 through March 1991.

CHEMICAL DEFENSE LOGISTICS ISSUES

Brigadier General Orton tapped Colonel J. Harold Mashburn, who had just arrived at the School during the previous month, and Captain Eric Riecks to augment the Office of the Deputy Chief of Staff for Logistics (ODCSLOG) in the Pentagon. This need had come about since many of the deploying units did not have sufficient NBC defense equipment, could not find their reserve stocks, or had equipment that was damaged beyond immediate repair. While the ODCSOPS chemical section was already assisting ODCSLOG in this area, Orton could see the need for a full-time, dedicated augmentation in ODCSLOG.[29] The two officers began their work on August 10. Three more captains joined them by August 18. Their mission quickly expanded to overseeing the procurement and transportation of all NBC defense equipment for all four services.

This logistics shortage was not unique to the Army. Army division commanders, Air Force unit commanders, Navy fleet commanders and Marine Corps expeditionary force commanders had the responsibility to procure quantities of individual protective clothing, expendable decon kits and detector kits that their forces required to deploy into a potential NBC warfare environment. For decades, these commanders had had to decide between spending precious unit operations and maintenance funds on chemical defense equipment that would expire before being used, or purchasing spare parts for weapon systems and vehicles being operated throughout the year. This was not a tough decision for most, and as a result the protective clothing shortages grew larger every year. The commanders assumed (wrongly) that if the need was urgent enough, someone in the Pentagon would get the necessary protective clothing to them in the quantities required, in time. Now as their units deployed, all four services screamed for protective suits, which were not available in the numbers required for sustained operations under chemical warfare conditions.

First, ODCSLOG had to determine the availability, serviceability, and quantities of defense equipment, and where exactly it was stored for all four services manually. There was no top-level visibility of chemical defense assets at the units and depots. ODCSLOG accepted the fact that it would have to dip into the wartime and theater reserves worldwide to equip the CENTCOM forces fully. Very quickly the job became a twenty-hour-a-day mission, with two officers chasing down deploying units to ask them what chemical defense equipment they needed, and two others hunting chemical defense equipment all over the world. For instance, it quickly became obvious that the 82d ABN DIV was short significant quantities of protective suits, decontamination supplies and functional protective masks.   Through a series of phone calls to Saudi Arabia, the cell gathered the information needed, and at no cost to the deploying units, directed replacement stocks to Fort Bragg from European and US war reserves. This type of detailed unit support kept the team busy throughout the next few months.

The most urgently needed expendable supplies were nerve agent antidote kits and chemical protective suits. The Defense Logistics Agency (DLA) awarded four chemical protective suit contracts in August and September for 1,050,000 suits (estimated contract value, over $83 million).   Two companies were already producing suits under contract but would not be able to expand their production lines quickly enough to support the demand. The new deliveries were scheduled for October 1990, but the four new manufacturers did not start delivering the suits until January 1991 (see Figure 2.1). They had difficulties adapting to sewing the heavy clothing required.   In the past, the Defense Personnel Support Center had awarded contracts to protective suit manufacturers on a lowest-bid basis. When these small, inexperienced and underfinanced companies failed to produce, the Army didn't get its suits. This had led to a deficit of 43 percent in prepositioned war stocks over the previous five years, with industry agreements to support only 12 to 13 percent of mobilization requirements. Compounding this problem was that the other three services used different protective suits and manufacturers, none of which were prepared to mobilize their production lines in less than three months.

As the buildup in the Gulf continued, forces using the older CPOGs and BDOs had to exchange their uncontaminated suits every fourteen or thirty days,

Figure 2.1
Scheduled Cumulative Purchases of Protective Suits versus Actual Cumulative Deliveries

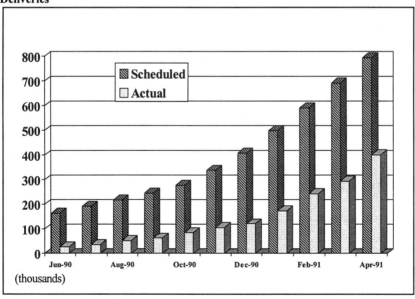

respectively, to retain full protective capability. For a force that was planned to grow to a quarter million by November, this could amount to quite a turnover rate. Reserve stocks had to be built up quickly in the event that Iraq attacked into Saudi Arabia. The Army began transferring over 1.1 million BDOs from worldwide theater reserve stocks to the Gulf. ODCSLOG requested chemical protective suits, replacement masks and other chemical defensive equipment from the Army's European and Korean theater reserve stockpiles, and that US warehouses be stripped. The Air Force quickly stripped US air bases of all older CPOGs and BDOs for shipment.

Filters were another major problem. Soldiers in the theater did not so much as walk to a latrine without a protective mask slung across their waists. Because the Army had anticipated switching to the M40-series masks, filter production for the M17, M24 and M25-series protective masks had ceased.[30]   Other NATO countries used the C2 canister, which was incompatible with the current M17A2 and M24/25A1 masks. Soon after the conflict began, the Army contracted with two manufacturers to produce 641,400 M13 filters (for the M17) and 125,000 M10 filters (for the M24/25), with initial delivery dates of March and April 1991, respectively. Filter manufacturers, however, required three months to "ramp up" their production and overcome startup problems; this set the delivery dates back to June and December 1991. Until those arrived, ODCSLOG would have to continue raiding the global war reserves for their filters. ODCSOPS asked TRADOC and AMCCOM to reexamine the serviceability criteria and change-out doctrine for filters and protective suits to make them more realistic. Because the tendency had been to err on the safe side with respect to suit and filter shelf lives, older but still useable items could presumably be safely issued, saving literally millions of suits and filters and extending the very short supply on hand.

The average temperature for Saudi Arabia in the late summer was consistently above 110° F, resulting in a number of equipment problems. The M258A1 skin decontamination kits, filled with alcohol-based liquids, swelled to three to five times their volume, bursting their packets. The BA3517/U batteries for the M8A1 alarms were similarly affected by the heat. Because of low training demands, many batteries were several years old and had been pulled out of warehouse storage for the deployment. Some had a performance life of only two hours, while many lasted only thirty-six hours of the expected seventy-two. Low battery levels were causing the detectors to give false alarms, leading to a sharp increase in stress as soldiers leapt toward their protective clothing and masks. The divisions would rapidly run out of batteries, already in short supply, at this rate. While the batteries were not difficult to produce, no one had anticipated the volume requested, and industry was not prepared to respond to the demand. Many units began requesting power cables, so as to run M8A1 alarms off their vehicle batteries.[31]

Many soldiers owning M24 and M25 protective masks reported cracked lenses and peripheral delamination of the facepiece (translation: the one-piece, chemically laminated eye lens popped off). While M17 masks were less vulnerable, many were wearing down and breaking under the heat and the stress of soldiers pulling the fitting-straps tighter. Desert sandstorms could quickly clog the filters, rendering them useless and requiring more frequent changing. When the soldiers began to examine the protective mask technical manuals, they noticed a recommendation to change mask filters every two months in a hot desert climate. The Corps NBCC quickly saw a potential shortage in protective mask filters as well as masks and called its AMC logistics representative in Fort Bragg to confirm this estimate. HQ AMCCOM quickly saw the same concern, and adjusted the filter change-out rate to once per year.

Then, of course, there were the protective suits themselves. Few soldiers were acclimated to the desert heat in T-shirts, let alone in a heavy charcoal-impregnated suit. The butyl rubber gloves and boots caused soldiers' hands and feet to soften due to the profuse sweating, making them vulnerable to mechanical injuries and trenchfoot. Sweat also decreased the effectiveness of the overgarments. Hot as they were, however, the suits were the only protection available, and no one would travel far without knowing where his or her chemical suit was. The intense heat limited the soldiers to training in the early morning or late evening hours, while during the day the contingency suits remained close at hand. The leadership had to acknowledge that overreacting to the chemical threat was worse than underreacting. Hard work in the hot BDOs could quickly exhaust the soldiers. Leaders had to accept lower MOPP levels to ensure their soldiers were able to accomplish the mission, which meant balancing the risk of chemical attack against workload and weather.

At least military personnel were protected; the enormous amount of supplies and numerous maintenance support facilities were unprotected from CB agent contamination, other than in the few warehouses available at the ports and airfields. Covering the supplies with protective sheets would greatly reduce the decontamination required if CB agents were used. The XVIII ABN Corps NBCC requested the Natick labs to accelerate their development of the NBC protective covers then undergoing test and evaluation.[32] The program was not ready for production, but procurement officers could purchase mylar and polyethylene sheets to accomplish the same objective. To augment decontaminant supplies, procurement officers also began local buys of tons of high-test calcium hypochlorite (HTH) bleach. These critical issues drove the corps NBC center to develop a more detailed logistics support request for the NBC defense equipment National Inventory Control Point (NICP) at AMCCOM, Rock Island, Illinois.

MEDICAL ISSUES MOUNT

Because of the projected requirement for nerve agent antidote kits, DLA immediately awarded a $2 million emergency contract order for the NAAK autoinjectors to Survival Technologies, Incorporated (STI), a medical supply company based in Maryland. The very fact that there were no fielded biological detectors placed an immediate urgency on vaccines and biological agent antidotes.

Since the soldiers would not know when they were being hit with BW agents, they would require medical attention both before (in the form of vaccines) and after (for post-treatment of BW agents) the attack. Vaccines were in critical supply, because of past policy decisions within NATO not to stockpile biological warfare vaccines. As a result, the US Army only made enough vaccines for medical personnel involved with the limited biological defense research effort. Now the military was faced with an adversary that might use BW agents, and there were not enough vaccines. The immediate critical issues were: what BW agents CENTCOM should protect its troops against; how the medical community was to get Food and Drug Administration (FDA) approval to use anthrax vaccine and botulinum toxoid to inoculate the troops; and how enough of the vaccines could be produced prior to an Iraqi BW attack.

On August 11, Armed Forces Medical Intelligence Center (AFMIC) analysts briefed Army officials from the Office of the Surgeon General (OTSG) on the Iraqi BW threat; the brief resulted in medical CB defense stockpile assessment and planning. By August 19, the Surgeon General had a good picture of the current status and briefed the four services' logistics chiefs on needs and issues. A Tri-Service Ad Hoc Medical Working Group met and recommended immediate immunization of the force against anthrax, procurement of more anthrax vaccines and botulinum toxoid and placement of two special analytical laboratories in-theater. On August 23, the Army OTSG discussed with FDA officials the medical emergency needs arising from biological agent threats. The Army Surgeon General recommended to General Carl Vuono (Army Chief of Staff) and Schwarzkopf that the entire force receive anthrax vaccine, and those at the greatest risk receive the botulinum toxoid. Producing more vaccines became a top national priority.

The US military had one source for botulinum toxoid, manufactured at the Michigan Department of Public Health at Lansing, Michigan. Two old horses (previously employed by Arlington National Cemetery) which had slowly built up their resistance to the toxoid, supplied the few thousand doses of vaccine needed annually for academic research and food handling. The Army immediately bought additional horses to build up a stock, although these new horses could not be exposed to the same level as the first two had been and therefore, could not immediately produce as much vaccine. The botulinum vaccine had been given to more than 3000 people at the Army's Medical Research Institute for Infectious Diseases (MRIID) over the past twenty years as a result of potential exposure to the bacterial toxin. The Center for Disease Control in Atlanta had also given the vaccine to thousands of individuals whose work in industry exposed them to this threat. The vaccine protected against five of the seven known botulinum neurotoxins (type A, B, C, D and E) and was therefore named pentavalent toxoid. Neither agency had reported any serious long-term side effects.

While these vaccines were proven safe for medical researchers, there was no proof that it protected against botulinum toxin used as a biological warfare agent on a real battlefield. This lack of efficacy data was an issue with FDA officials. Under the Food, Drug and Cosmetics Act, all vaccines and products must be proven safe and effective if sold and distributed in the United States or used by US troops. Under this law, unapproved vaccines and treatments could only be used for healthy individuals only under an Investigational New Drug (IND) procedure. Any individual who is given an IND must give informed consent—that is to say, told the potential risks and benefits of the product, orally and in writing, and choose freely whether or not to participate. In addition, the IND procedures call for a controlled environment where safety and effectiveness can be monitored. (Cancer and AIDS research clinics can request such authority to test new experimental drugs on rapidly deteriorating patients.) The only problem was that the military could not perform human test trials to determine if the vaccine worked against people exposed to BW agents.

The status of anthrax vaccine was similar. There was not enough vaccine stock immediately available for all of CENTCOM's forces. Other than for the British allies, there was no large-scale production source for anthrax vaccine. In addition, full immunization against anthrax requires a series of three shots two weeks apart followed by boosters at the six, twelve, and eighteen-month marks. This would effectively immunize 85 percent of the force, but the program had to be initiated quickly to build up the inoculations. The FDA decided not to make a fuss about the efficacy of anthrax vaccine. The FDA acknowledged that while the anthrax vaccine had never officially been approved for use as a BW vaccine, it had been used safely on humans in the civilian and military medical field for decades (especially for veterinarians and animal handlers working among sheep and cattle herds). The Army OTSG had to conduct the necessary safety and efficacy trials for both vaccines while searching for producers, determining a vaccination policy, and delivering the necessary products all prior to any Iraqi BW agent employment.

Getting a license to produce medical chemical and biological defense products was one thing; finding a domestic pharmaceutical company to produce them was another. Despite the United States' premier position as an international leader in health industries, no US firm would take the millions of dollars offered to produce the vaccines and pretreatments. Because the items were still technically (and legally) "experimental," the malpractice insurance required to cover the firms was astronomical, even with government promises of indemnity. Not one trusted that it would be free of lawsuits after the conflict if the vaccines were thought unsafe, whether or not the treatments did their job safely and efficiently. Also, there was little profit in these medical treatments; while other military medical treatments held a dual purpose in public and military health benefits, there was not much call for anthrax and botulinum toxin vaccines outside of the military. Too much risk and too little profit meant no participation from the US pharmaceutical firms.

Overall, the deployment went off as well as could be expected, especially given CENTCOM's initial low readiness status. Because Iraq did not immediately attack US forces entering Saudi Arabia, it appeared that CENTCOM would have a chance to build up its strength. There was a mountain of challenges ahead. There weren't enough chemical protective suits, masks or decontamination supplies for more than one large-area chemical warfare attack, let alone stocks for extended operations. The real defense would come from the chemical decontamination units at Fort Hood and other locations in the United States, but they would not arrive until late September at the earliest. The only thing CENTCOM did have was thousands of chemical defense specialists interwoven throughout the force, who would be juggling urgent training, operational and logistics requirements simultaneously. With no modern reconnaissance systems, limited individual defense equipment and a very low level of CB warfare training, combat leaders suddenly realized they had to rely on their chemical soldiers more than ever.

CHAPTER 3

Building Up the Defense

> If there was one absolute hole in our repertoire of capabilities, it was chemical reconnaissance. . . . Getting the Fox into the field was a tremendous confidence builder and ended up being a major factor in how we task-organized for battle.
> —Major General Barry McCaffrey, 1992

As September began, Pentagon military planners were increasingly concerned about the fact that no one knew the exact numbers of protective clothing, masks, medical autoinjectors, and agent detectors; where all this equipment was located; and how quickly it would be consumed. Since the Army had been appointed the lead DoD executive agency for NBC defense in 1976, DoD expected the Army to assist the Air Force, Navy and Marine Corps to prepare for chemical warfare. The other services were also in the dark due in large part to their traditional reluctance to spend funds on NBC defense, and they had difficulty determining their NBC defense logistics status. While the Army could use its Chemical Corps officers to track units' readiness and logistics, the other services did not have a similar resource. They saw this as the combat unit commander's, rather than one central agency's, responsibility; these unit commanders, for their part, had never seriously considered preparing for the immense logistics burden that came with a chemical battlefield.

To provide ODCSLOG with an immediate action office, the Joint Chiefs of Staff J-4 (Director for Logistics) appointed a Joint Service Coordination Committee for Chemical Defense Equipment (JSCC-CDE). Its mission was to assist in NBC defense equipment logistics prioritization and allocation of resources, maintain all DoD CDE inventory, and coordinate CDE transactions relating to the industrial base. While two other joint NBC defense panels existed (the Joint Panel for Chemical-Biological Defense and the Joint Service Review Group), this organization was formed strictly for the management of fielded CDE during the Persian Gulf conflict. This committee reported to the Assistant DCSLOG, who in turn reported on CDE readiness through the DCSLOG to the Joint Staff. Colonel

Harold Mashburn became the deputy chair for this panel, which was officially established in the first week of September.

One of the JSCC's first actions was to identify the current stock levels of CDE and the potential consumption rates of that equipment in a modern conflict. While the logistics agencies within the four services scrambled to inventory their CDE, the Institute for Defense Analysis developed a computer model to determine the consumption rates in a conflict in Southwest Asia. Gradually, a picture formed. The JSCC discovered that there were inadequate stocks of protective clothing, large vehicle protective filters and mask filters, and NAAK autoinjectors to sustain a conflict in a CB agent-contaminated environment over thirty days. The JSCC began coordinating transfers of Army protective clothing and decontaminants to the other services and tracked CDE shipments from warehouses throughout the world to the Gulf. It became a daily exercise to deal with specific logistics issues.

Some were fairly easy to resolve: for instance, the Navy wanted more of the old "fishtail" chemical protective boots and butyl rubber gloves from the Army; the Air Force and Navy requested bulk decontaminants such as DS-2 and STB from Army stocks. Also, marketers began calling ODCSLOG, sometimes hundreds of them each day. They had everything to offer, from lightweight microclimate cooling vests to mini-chemical detectors. Many were just get-rich-quick schemes, although all had to be reviewed in the event that one good product was available. There were a number of tougher policy issues to face, such as who should provide for civilian protection in Saudi Arabia, when there were not enough suits for the soldiers. The Israeli and Saudi governments were requesting protective clothing, specifically US military protective clothing, and had the money to buy it. Because US military needs took priority, Colonel Mashburn had to turn their requests over to the British and German governments to be filled with their Mark IV and Saratoga suits, respectively. Although not referred by ODCSLOG, the Russians sold several million sets of their chemical protective clothing to Middle Eastern nations. Other nations, some as far away as South Korea, offered their chemical defense equipment to the Middle Eastern nations. It was a seller's market, and no requests were being turned away.

Saudi government procurement of other than Army protective suits (and later the Marine Corps's similar actions) were interpreted by reporters (and other so-called military experts) to mean that the US protective clothing was inferior to the British and German brands, which was not the case. The British Mark IV, as Army validation reviews showed, was lighter in weight but less durable (making it better for heat stress but not as resistant or long-lasting to heavy concentrations of agent). The German Saratoga suit, on the other hand, might have been equal to or superior to the American clothing in many respects, but it cost nearly twice as much per suit, and there were only two producers that could manufacture the suits. The US production problem continued to be a nagging issue for the logistics planners, but the sturdy and cost-effective BDO remained the standard for all four services. The shortage of chemical protective suits was a concern throughout the war, even with the promise of suit deliveries by January 1991.[1]

Prior to their deployment to the Gulf, soldiers suddenly began carefully inspecting their masks. Many soldiers, for instance, had preferred large protective masks that gave easier and more comfortable fits during peacetime training exercises. Now everyone wanted smaller, tight-fitting masks. Those who found their masks inoperative had difficulties replacing them. On top of the natural wear and tear, more masks were breaking down in Saudi Arabia due to soldiers tightening their mask straps beyond the failing point; everyone wanted to cinch their masks as close to their faces as possible to minimize the chance of leaks. Pine Bluff Arsenal stepped up its mask repair and began a massive refurbishment line. Before the conflict, Pine Bluff Arsenal repaired 1,100 protective masks per week. During the conflict, ODCSLOG asked Pine Bluff to increase that to 5,000 masks per week (it would manage an average of 3,570 a week).[2]

With the deployment of several thousand government civilians, defense contractors and media crews to the Gulf, the question of protecting American citizens in theater arose. Prior to Operation Desert Shield, the Pentagon had no policy about equipping civilians or contractors with CB defense equipment. This was a new concern, arising from the increased sophistication of military equipment and the American public's desire for instantaneous news reporting. The difficulty was where the Pentagon's obligation ended. Did the government bear a responsibility to protect all the Americans in Southwest Asia, including those working for the Saudi government prior to hostilities? If so, why not all civilians who resided near military areas? The shortages of protective suits and masks forced DoD to draw the line, supplying protective clothing and masks only to American military and authorized civilians in theater. This increased the pressure on Pine Bluff Arsenal to repair as many masks as it could, twenty-four hours a day, seven days a week.[3]

Aviator protective masks across all services were at a critical juncture. The Army had just re-awarded a production contract for its M43 protective mask in 1990, but none were being produced yet. As noted, Mr. Rick Decker and Captain Ernie Nagy at CRDEC would produce and deliver 264 M43 masks for Apache crews in the Gulf before November 1990, largely out of developmental masks and spare parts at Edgewood. Mine Safety Applications would add another 658 M43s to that total, which would cover the Apache pilots in the Gulf. The Air Force issued urgent contracts for the immediate procurement of the MBU-19/P aircrew masks. By releasing funds to be directly channeled to air logistics centers, the Air Force was able to begin production of pilot masks quickly. The Navy had developed a separate program to modify the British AR-5 aircrew mask, but it would not be able to meet the demand in time. The Naval Air Systems Command (NAVAIR) borrowed 250 AR-5 masks from the Canadian military and modified them for Marine fixed-wing and Navy helicopter aircrews, the two most likely aviation candidates for chemical agent protection over land.[4]

Collective protection equipment filters became a critical issue. Army units did not often use the collective protection systems (CPS) in the M1A1 tanks, or the M20 and M51 collective protection equipment (CPE) shelters, during field training exercises. This had led to a pattern of very low peacetime requirements and consequently a shortage of wartime filters. This was a concern more for the many M1A1 tanks' collective protection system, than the fewer mobile collective protection shelters available for command and control units. Most XVIII ABN Corps units had left their M51 shelters in the United States. These aging systems (first issued in the early 1970s) had not held up well. The generators which kept air circulating in the semi-rigid walls broke down often, and many units could not afford to dedicate a five-ton truck to move each M51 shelter. Between September and October, forty-nine older M51 CPS shelters were refurbished from depots, shipped to the Gulf and set up for medical units throughout the corps. CENTCOM forces sent more than eighty backorders for the M51s, but it would be six months to a year before the manufacturer could deliver them.

The newer M20 Simplified Collective Protection Equipment (SCPE) was not working out much better. Designed for the interiors of European buildings, they were not suitable for the military or Saudi-furnished tents in the desert. Mounting tent poles within the plastic liner without rupturing it was difficult; trying to inflate an M20 SCPE in the open left it vulnerable to the elements (and hostile fire). While some of the over 300 M20s remained in Dhahran, al-Dammam, and Riyadh, combat units in the field abandoned them. Warehouses and US civilians in the cities (and their families in the theater) could and did use the M20 systems to protect against chemical attacks. Over a thousand would be shipped to Saudi Arabia, with 128 going to the Navy for its personnel in the ports. A small number of the experimental XM28 Tent Extendable, Medical Personnel (TEMPER) SCPEs were rushed through production. Four XM28s eventually were produced, of which one made it to the Gulf during the crisis.

The few Navy ships equipped with shipboard CPE filters did not practice their collective protection any better than the Army. Far worse off were the Air Force bases; while this service had made fixed site collective protection a priority in Korea and Germany, transportable CPS was still in the laboratories. While the Marine Corps had invested in portable CPS, there were few available for the MEF. As a result of low annual peacetime consumption, large filters had been ordered only to stockpile them in depots as war reserves, which led to a very small manufacturing base. While small stocks existed, it was clear that industry could not "ramp up" quickly enough to produce the large filters. Only one company had produced this type of carbon for military filters, used for both individual protective mask filters and the larger filters for vehicles and shelters. Calgon Corporation was stretched to its limits over the next six months to produce the special activated carbon for US forces and allies. This production effort still fell short, and only a limited number of large CPE filters made it to Southwest Asia prior to 1991. This made the hundreds of Abrams tank crews vulnerable to nerve agents if the filter inventory ran out, and the rear areas very vulnerable to Scud attacks due to the lack of shelters.

DEFENSIVE BATTLE PLANS

On September 3, CENTCOM practiced its mobile defense-in-sector under a plan known as "Desert Dragon III," which would later be modified as the Desert Shield defense. The plan called for the 101st ABN DIV and 3rd ACR to fight the initial covering-force action and soften the initial edge of an invasion. The 24th IN DIV would fight and halt the Iraqi army in the main battle area, and the 1st CAV DIV would counterattack from Assembly Area Horse to destroy the enemy. The 82d ABN DIV would protect the ARCENT rear area and the oil fields at Abquaiq against terrorist actions, while the Marines held the coastal regions. The operations plan assessed enemy use of chemical weapons as "likely." Since this was a defensive operation, all of Iraq's air force, ballistic missiles, and its South African artillery systems (which could outrange their US counterparts) were assumed to carry both chemical and conventional munitions. Intelligence reports had noted possible chemical munitions being loaded near Iraqi artillery batteries in Kuwait. For war-gaming purposes, the military's prime targets for persistent chemical agent included the coalition ports at al-Jubayl and al-Dammam, the airfields at Dhahran and Riyadh, and military logistics depots.

The chemical recon/decon plan to support this defense-in-sector counted on a number of reserve and active duty units that would not arrive until October (or later). XVIII ABN Corps NBCC identified hundreds of potential decon sites for the defending units. The 3rd ACR covering force would rely on its 89th Chemical Company. The 101st ABN DIV would receive the 761st Chemical Company and the 7/92d Recon Platoon in support as well as its organic 63rd Chemical Company. The 24th IN DIV had its 91st Chemical Company and the 5/69th Recon Platoon prepared for the main defensive effort. If the Iraqi army meant to use chemical munitions to soften up the US forces, the 24th's mechanized units were the best able, within the XVIII ABN Corps, to absorb it. The corp's 101st Chemical Company provided general decon support for the artillery batteries. The 1st CAV DIV with the Tiger Brigade had the 68th Chemical Company (and elements of the 44th), plus the 5/22d Recon Platoon, waiting in Assembly Area Horse as the counterattack force. The 82d ABN DIV had its own 21st Chemical Company, and, being in the rear area, could call on the 101st Chemical Company. The 2d Chemical Battalion was in general support to XVIII ABN Corps, covering the main logistics areas and ports with the 59th and 181st Chemical companies, the 5/25th Recon Platoon (when it arrived), and the first reserve decon unit due in-theater, the 327th Chemical Company.

"Desert Dragon III" offered the planners the option of retaliating against Iraqi chemical use with US chemical weapons. Although the option of deploying chemical weapons to the Gulf had been war gamed in Internal Look-1990, there had been no further guidance for the real event. Official US policy was to reduce the likelihood of enemy chemical weapons use by threatening retaliation with similar munitions, but no one had made that policy call for CENTCOM's battle plan. Colonel Rick Read suggested two courses of action for DCSOPS to recommend to the Joint Chiefs. First, the Army was preparing to remove the US chemical weapons from Germany to Johnston Island (Operation "Steel Box") in November 1990. Instead of shipping them to Johnston Island as planned, they could reroute the chemical munitions to Saudi Arabia. If the Saudi government protested the presence of nerve agents on their soil, there was a second course of action. Binary production had ceased, but the binary projectile shells themselves (minus the second component) could be shipped to the Gulf to fool the Iraqis into thinking there were US chemical munitions available for retaliation. Both of these options were ultimately rejected as politically too controversial. While the munitions would have offered a substantial counter to the Iraqi threat (as US military policy intended), President Bush had committed himself to the bilateral chemical weapons disarmament treaty between the United States and Soviet Union. Deploying chemical weapons to this conflict would seem contrary to that policy, on the global political stage. Later in the month, ODCSOPS officially confirmed to CENTCOM that there would be no chemical munitions deployment to Saudi Arabia. No plans were developed for US retaliation using chemical munitions.[5]

On September 14, the German government surprised the PM NBC Defense office by revising the terms of the Fuchs loan to make it a gift, which included the tools, parts, transportation assistance and follow-on training. In the last days of September, the German government increased the gift to a total of sixty Fuchs vehicles. This was especially magnanimous due to the fact that many of these came out of the German military's own 140 Fuchs (to be replaced later by the German government). The German military had one request: that the frantic pace of training and production be slowed down to accommodate the British and Israeli requests, as well as their own. Unless the US government was declaring war against Iraq, the training would have to expand to a six-day, ten-hour, four-week course, which would allow the trainers a less grueling schedule. Also, Thyssen-Henschel would not work through Christmas holiday unless war was declared. Since the Army had its initial recon capability en route, the US government agreed to relaxing the training demands. As for the second thirty-Fox offer, HQ DA initially refused it, despite clamoring from the PM NBC Defense office. With one corps's worth of Foxes inbound, some within the department felt that there was no need to incur additional training, supply and maintenance costs. There was a concern that additional Foxes would overload the training and employment program, and that thirty were enough for one corps. Based on that decision, Thyssen-Henschel stopped any plans to modify a second batch of thirty Fuchs vehicles. This decision would have a profound implications when it came time to develop a second corps's reconnaissance capability.

Two Fox platoons from Europe arrived in Saudi Arabia on September 20, just as the Fort Hood units began to "close" in the theater. The 5/69th Recon Platoon took four Foxes to the 24th IN DIV, marrying-up with the two "Nunn" vehicles for full platoon strength. The 7/92nd Recon Platoon took the remaining six Foxes to the 101st ABN DIV, with its covering force mission out front. The 5/22d Recon

Platoon would join the 2d Chemical Battalion in late October, with eight Foxes (six of their own and two to replace 5/69th's "Nunn" vehicles, which would become the ARCENT operational readiness floats [ORFs]). These three platoons would spend the next three months training with their division's units to familiarize them with the Foxes' capabilities. The 5/25th Recon Platoon was to arrive in Dhahran in mid-November, allowing the 1st CAV DIV to receive the 5/22d. Five of the last six Foxes were designated for 3rd ACR, with the last one joining the two "Nunn" vehicles as maintenance floats.[6]

Because the Foxes had been fielded two years ahead of schedule, there was no military capability to maintain them within CENTCOM. Thyssen-Henschel was unable to send German civilians into a war-crisis zone, so General Dynamics Services Company (GDSC, a GDLS subsidiary) provided support contractors to maintain the systems. The PM NBC Defense office established a Fixed Fox Facility in Dhahran, to begin operations in October; it would grow to accommodate maintenance support for two other PM NBC projects, the M1 CAM and XM21 RSCAAL. However, if either a CAM or RSCAAL required major repairs, it had to be evacuated to England (for the CAMs) or to CRDEC (for the RSCAAL), for lack of spare parts. In addition, the 2d Chemical Battalion would stay at the site, once it arrived in late October. When the 490th Chemical Battalion arrived in theater, it would take over the rear area chemical defense mission, allowing the 2d Chemical Battalion to move to support XVIII ABN Corps directly.

On September 26, the 2d Chemical Battalion's advance party deployed to Saudi Arabia to prepare for the main body's arrival. Back in Houston, the 2d Chemical Battalion's main body, the 181st Chemical Company and the reserve 327th Chemical Company began their move to the ports to stage their equipment and load onto the ships. At Fort McClellan, the 490th Chemical Battalion and three reserve chemical companies were training and readying their units for deployment. The first non-divisional decontamination unit, the 59th Chemical Company, would arrive ten weeks after the initial XVIII ABN Corps deployment. Its sister unit, the 761st Chemical Company, would be right behind, arriving at the end of October.

PROTECTING THE FORCE

CENTCOM began to have particular concerns over rumors of an Iraqi threat called "dusty mustard" agent. This was not a new agent or a novel weapon, nor was it certain that Iraq even stockpiled the agent. The Germans in World War II had experimented with the concept. "Dusty mustard" is created by coating dust-sized particles with mustard agent, increasing its persistency and ability to float into cracks, gaps and crevices. The concern was that this "dusty mustard" would float between the gaps of the two-piece BDO and the protective mask's hood rather than being soaked into the fabric. To address this concern and prevent a panic message to the field commanders, a Pentagon team under Dr. Bob Boyle addressed the validity of the threat and how to detect "dusty mustard." Edgewood, Dugway and Natick labs cooperated in determining whether the detectors would sense dusty agent and whether the suits would protect against it. Tests showed that if the suits were worn correctly, troops had little to fear and that the CAM and M256A1 kit would detect the agent. By November, ODCSOPS messages forwarded instructions on how to detect the "new" agent with existing detectors, should Iraqi forces employ "dusty mustard."[7]

In light of continuing protective suit production issues (and former dissatisfaction with the BDO's weight and heat stress), the Marine Corps announced the purchase of seventy-three thousand British Mark-IV protective suits. The Marines determined these "lightweight" suits to be more suitable for the desert. An overzealous Marine public affairs officer stated that the purchase was made because the suits were "better than the Army BDOs." In reality, the Mark-IV was less than four pounds lighter than the BDO and cost nearly twice as much (a major decision point for the Army, which would have to buy millions of suits, not thousands).[8] As the troops thought lighter meant less heat stress (which, as Natick lab tests would later show, was not the case), they perceived the Mark-IV to be the better suit. CRDEC and NRDEC were flooded with press inquiries about the quality of the Army's BDOs, requiring more lab analyses and frequent demonstrations to the press. The Air Force still sought a less bulky, nonflammable suit for its pilots, and ordered a small quantity of the experimental CWU-66/P one-piece protective suit through a single source without requesting bids, at a unit cost of nearly five times that of the BDOs. The Navy relied on its dwindling stocks of CPOG suits and purchased an additional 150 Mark-IVs for Navy SEALs in-theater. All three services would use the Army BDOs once their own initial suit stockpiles were consumed.

Until the later protective suit manufacturers began their shipments, the Army dug deeper into its warehouses of older CPOGs. The CPOGs constituted up to 20 percent of the protective clothing used in the Gulf; despite their shorter exposure life (fourteen days in comparison with BDO's thirty days), they met the same challenge level of ten grams of liquid agent per square centimeter. The Natick labs worked to toughen up the BDO design around the elbows and knees, as well as to incorporate a desert-tan camouflage pattern. They also inspected the stockpiles of protective gloves to extend their shelf life past the expected expiration date. Many of the glove lots were found adequate, and the current stockpile of over four million butyl rubber gloves was prepared for shipment to the Gulf.

The Chemical School concurred in CRDEC's proposal to push the development of ten XM21 RSCAAL prototypes into the field. Despite concerns with fielding chemical defense equipment before it was ready, Lieutenant Colonel Silvernail and Colonel Barbeau requested every available chemical defense program be accelerated and fielded type-classified limited procurement (asking industry to produce a limited number of devices without full formal test and evaluation). The XM21 program was close enough to completion to permit an initial production contract through Brunswick Corporation for ten systems. These systems would permit the Army and Marine Corps commanders a limited capability for early-warning, long-range chemical agent detection. The Chemical

School, in mid-October, sent a Mobile Training Team to Camp Lejeune to begin training Marines on the XM21 operation and maintenance.[9]

The M1 CAMs had not been fully fielded, due to production problems. The final delivery of CAMs from ETG, Inc., was due in March 1990 (thirty-one months after contract award), but ETG had difficulties getting its CAMs past governmental testing and approval, projecting a two-year delay in production of the final lot. The Army had a total of 1,029 CAMs in the field from previous production runs, with another 200 as maintenance floats. Only 150 of these CAMs were in the hands of XVIII ABN Corps soldiers, leading the Army to request 500 from the Canadian Mobile Command (army) and to order an additional 495 from Graesby Ionics in Britain. The Canadian government promised to deliver the CAMs by the end of December, with Graesby's CAMs following in January.

Preparations to deal with the biological warfare threat continued as the Army's MRIID worked with NAVCENT to establish an initial biological screening capability, using the medical expertise available on the hospital ships and at the Navy Medical Research Unit at Cairo, Egypt. A team of nine Navy medical specialists occupied an abandoned Saudi hospital in Al Jubayl with lab equipment designed to deal with biohazards. Working through October, they established and tested a courier specimen transport system between Saudi Arabia and CONUS. This capability would at least allow early confirmation of any Iraqi BW attacks, rather than waiting for MRIID's test results conducted at Fort Detrick.

Major General Watson's DNA team continued its tests of the prototype biological agent detector mounted on the airplane through September and into October. The biodetection program's goals and progress were relayed through the Vice Chief of Staff, Lieutenant General Gordon Sullivan, to General Powell in early October. In mid-October test results continued to be satisfying, and it seemed that the prototype might be ready for deployment by the end of the year. The program was promising—the team could not identify a biological agent, because of the cytometer technology, but it could tell there was an increase in background readings of biological material. This would be the first indication of a potential biological agent attack. On the final day of testing, the DNA team needed some final results as to how well the detector could do. Then, tragedy struck. The pilot flew the plane into the ground; the airplane, the pilots, crew and equipment were lost. It was a real setback; it wiped out almost any hope, given the time it had taken to pull this effort together. This completely stopped DNA's biodetection project. Major General Watson called CRDEC and asked them to take over the program.

Brigadier General Dave Nydam, commander of CRDEC, had appointed Colonel Gene Fuzy in September as the point of contact for CRDEC's technical support to CENTCOM, for both offensive chemical munitions and defensive NBC defense programs. Colonel Fuzy had been the last Program Manager for Binary Munitions and had begun closing out the program in July 1990. He now became responsible for the Army biological defense program, since, as mentioned earlier, the retaliatory chemical weapons option had been dropped. The new office, titled the Project Office for Biodefense, began with the data accumulated under the DNA program. It reviewed the past history of the center's biodefense programs and began identifying commercial programs that might be used. The best approach to CRDEC seemed to be to use the old XM19/XM2 Biological Detection and Warning System to provide CENTCOM an early post-attack indication of the use of biological agents. The drawbacks of using the 1970s-era detector were obvious, given its large size, weight, and potential unreliability.[10] Commercial industries might be able to field a similar system, although more fit for a laboratory than the field. CRDEC immediately began plans to update the XM2 samplers, modifying them to use commercial agent tickets that would indicate positive biological agent detections.

CRDEC proposed mounting the XM2 air samplers on vehicles, but the detectors could be operated only while stationary. If the biodetectors identified a possible positive biological warfare agent sample, the operators would have to transport the sample to a forward laboratory at KKMC or al-Jubayl for further culture testing, which could take several hours.[11] This system had to support the entire CENTCOM theater defense, since the other services had no biodetectors ready. The Navy and Marine Corps had no biological detectors ready for the field. Under their own independent effort, the Air Force had been working on a prototype model it called "Morning Song," which detected only anthrax spores after a two hour sampling period. Ten devices would eventually be manufactured and shipped to air bases in the Gulf region prior to the start of the ground war.

Higher-level unit training picked up after CENTCOM had developed its defensive plans in mid-October. The decon platoons of the chemical defense companies began working with the combat units on their thorough decontamination drills. Nearly every unit supported by a chemical decon platoon or company began practicing personnel and equipment decontamination. For those in the rear areas, such as in the COSCOMs, the chemical officers helped identify and train personnel to assist the medics in chemical casualty triage and decontamination prior to treatment. For instance, in 1st COSCOM, the division field bakery unit augmented the forward medical units as litter bearers and decontamination assistants.[12] In the 24th IN DIV, Major General McCaffrey ordered continuous chemical defense training. At the individual level, all soldiers would mask every day in response to M8A1 test alarms; all battalions would train in full protective clothing once a week; once a month, every battalion would conduct a decontamination exercise for persistent chemical agent decon operations. Training grew to include command post exercises testing the NBC Warning and Reporting System, from corps level down to the battalions.

XVIII Airborne Corps conducted two major command post exercises to test the NBC warning and reporting system among the corps chemical staff units. The corps rear area was especially vulnerable, for three reasons: first, all the logistics and support functions traditionally in the rear areas were textbook targets for any chemical weapons analyst. These troops held the majority of the reservists, most of whom had little familiarity with NBC defense operations. If the gasoline tankers, ammunition vehicles, maintenance trucks, and medical units could not support the fighters because of chemical contamination, the corps's offensive power would drop tremendously. Second, because of the immense distance between units in the rear area (often over fifty kilometers), communication was difficult and often spotty. Because of the large numbers of support units at the base clusters (over one hundred at each cluster), sending NBC messages to each was time-consuming and laborious. Not all these units had M8A1 alarms or CAMs, and they would receive little or no warning of chemical agent attacks. Last, because of the large distances, the dedicated decon units would be stretched to their limits to support all of these units. The lack of collective protection shelters increased the demands on the decon units. The exercises identified these shortfalls, and enabled the NBC elements to develop expedient solutions to keep their soldiers aware of any threats.[13] The other divisions held their own command post exercises to test and develop familiarity with the NBC Warning and Reporting System.

The many doctors and medics deploying to the Gulf had little practical knowledge on the diagnosis and treatment of NBC-related casualties. Even the most recent references relied on data documented in the 1970s; certainly, these doctors had more experience with gunshot wounds than, say, chemical agent burns. While the active duty medical units required some refresher training, the reserve medical units were initially even less prepared to deal with CB agent casualties. This wasn't exactly what doctors saw in their civilian practices. The Army's Medical Research Institute for Chemical Defense (MRICD) responded by sending its military doctors to the deploying active and reserve medical units to provide training in a five-day Medical Management of Chemical Casualties Course (M2C3). From October through November the M2C3 instructors traveled through Southwest Asia, providing a three-day version of the course to Army, Air Force, Navy and Marine Corps medical units, in addition to training doctors from Saudi Arabia, the United Kingdom, France, Canada and the United Arab Emirates. In all, they trained over 1,400 health care providers in theater. In November, when it was announced that VII Corps was deploying, they traveled to the US Army hospital in Neubreucke to train those medical units deploying from Germany to the Gulf.[14]

CONTINUING CONCERNS ABOUT READINESS

Colonel Barbeau had received a status report on XVIII ABN Corp's defensive equipment preparedness in late September, and the picture was not a pleasant one. The entire corps was still short just about everything—common items such as BDOs, masks, and BA3517 batteries, in addition to such more specialized needs, as additional M8A1 alarms, CAMs, and M17 SANATORs. He headed off the initial requirement for water haulers by leasing water trucks from the local community and had initiated purchases of HTH bleach to augment the DS-2 and STB supply. However, AMCCOM's National Inventory Control Point at Rock Island had rejected most of the requisitions for additional chemical defense equipment. AMCCOM had not been prepared for the magnitude of the requirements, could not meet them immediately, and canceled the requests it could not fill. Worse, AMCCOM was not providing any information on what items were in short supply and which ones were just not available, and when these shortages might be resolved. AMCCOM's focus was on multi-branch commodities such as ammunition, weapon systems, and maintenance and repair equipment. There was no priority on chemical defense equipment at AMCCOM, despite CENTCOM's voiced concerns.

The M8A1 battery shortage was particularly vexing since the batteries were essentially military-version D-cells in a large plastic container, not hard to manufacture. There had been insufficient quantities prior to hostilities, and now the Army could not make up the shortages. Using the batteries too long led to false alarms, which no one appreciated. These false alarms made troops increasingly reluctant to stop operations and jump into MOPP, but if they didn't respond to the real attacks. This became a real stress-builder. Communications and Electronics Command (CECOM) responded to the battery shortage by designing and manufacturing a 450-foot cable to power the M8A1 detectors from engine batteries.

Their requests for the urgent procurement of NBC protective covers and Suit, Contamination Avoidance, Liquid Protection (SCALP) suits had been heard, but none were due in any time soon. The corps NBCC requested eight million dollars to purchase plastic sheeting as a field expedient to cover the supplies; without buildings or even trees to cover the supplies against CB agent contamination, the rear area logistics bases remained very vulnerable. CENTCOM J-4 (logistics staff) denied the request, stating that there was no requirement from the logistics units to support this.[15] To confuse issues more, ODCSLOG directed that all protective mask filter elements be changed every six months instead of the previously mentioned annual requirement set by AMCCOM. These flip-flops, combined with other unresolved logistics issues and concerns over the biological agent problem, hurt the credibility of all chemical personnel throughout XVIII ABN Corps.

On October 1, Lieutenant Colonel Vicki Merryman arrived in-theater to replace the ARCENT chemical officer, who had unexpectedly left in late September. She listened to ARCENT commander Lieutenant General John Yeosock's philosophy of providing the corps with the capability to fight and acknowledged the difficulties chemical soldiers were having getting requisitions filled by the wholesale logistics system. She approached the ARCENT G-4 with the NBC defense logistics problems; he responded by identifying a Quartermaster officer on his staff as the NBC logistics specialist. This arrangement ensured that division logistics cells submitted requisitions correctly, and responsiveness to their inquiries was improved. The ARCENT NBC Cell and the G-4 NBC logistics specialist began identifying theater shortages and submitting requisitions. Supplies were transferred from Europe until the Seventh Army began having reservations about the rapid depletion of its theater reserves; overgarment requisitions shifted from the stripped-down European theater reserves to the Pacific theater war reserves.

Medical officers in the United States had a busy few months as well. Existing topical skin protectants against blister agents were old and not stocked in sufficient numbers to support the forces in the Gulf in September. MRDC accelerated its research to find an effective skin protectant, narrowing in on two promising treatments that were under development and also a commercially available protectant. After testing the three candidates, MRDC shifted the two government treatments to full development and recommended production of all three. DLA issued an order in the fall for about one million tubes of the commercial protectant, with the majority of the shipment due to arrive in early February 1991.[16] MRDC also accelerated the development of its diazepam autoinjectors. A nerve agent attack, even if the soldier used atropine, could be vulnerable to convulsions that could cause brain damage. The diazepam autoinjectors would reduce the incidents of those convulsions. Since this drug was already available to Army medics as valium, the FDA had fewer reservations about authorizing the use of this drug, even though its efficacy had not been absolutely proven (that is to say, it had not been tested on soldiers suffering from nerve agent exposure).

In early September, General Powell and the Joint Chiefs of Staff had listened to the Surgeon General's medical recommendations and forwarded the recommendations to Defense Secretary Dick Cheney. The decision was to surge vaccine production, delay the start of immunizations, and review the status of the vaccine program every two weeks. The tri-service task force began investigating both domestic and foreign production sources. Because US firms still did want to produce the medical products, even with offers of indemnity, the group began to look at European firms (as Europe's military forces had similar concerns). A Danish company, Solvay-Duphar, was approved to produce diazepam auto-injectors, based on its past autoinjector production for European nations and an inspection of its plant.

On October 3, Secretary Cheney directed the Army to increase its vaccine production capability. By October 11 MRDC had identified the need to obtain FDA efficacy waivers for the topical skin protectant, the diazepam autoinjectors (Convulsant Antidote for Nerve Agents—CANA), hepatitis A, the botulinum toxoid, J-5 monoclonal antibody and Ribavirin. DoD was not about to suggest human-volunteer agent tests to prove the efficacy of CB agent pretreatments, treatments and vaccines. By mid-October, the Joint Chiefs had agreed to request a waiver of informed consent and had began to express concerns about the stockpile size and the time needed to immunize and develop immunity. MRDC submitted to the FDA an Investigational New Drug application for the botulinum toxoid and a New Developmental Drug application for the CANA. By the end of the month, the CINCCENT Surgeon had outlined an immunization plan for the delivery and use of vaccines in the theater.

The Office of the Assistant to the Secretary of Defense for Health Affairs (OASD/HA) sought a waiver of the FDA requirements for informed consent of both the botulinum vaccine and pyridostigmine bromide (PB) tablets, on the basis that initial testing had been good; that there was established prior human use in other medical cases (although not specifically for CB agent treatment); that there were no medical alternatives; and that the need to protect the troops was a national security issue. The FDA was still concerned about soldier safety, product liability and the need to follow well-thought out and practiced regulations. However, congressional regulations would not permit testing the vaccines and antidotes on human volunteers afflicted with CB agents. DoD did not want to go ahead with unapproved products, but given the nature of the threat, was prepared to do so.

The FDA agreed to test the botulinum vaccine for safety prior to the end of the year. DoD requested and received approval to conduct an immediate study of four men to evaluate the effects of PB tablets. These tests would provide at least some indication of any health issues prior to their use by soldiers in the Gulf. But the bottom line was plain for the political and military leadership—it could not afford to ignore any possible medical solutions to the CBW threat. The leadership was aware of the intense scrutiny of the media and the American public and their concern to minimize American casualties over all else. If DoD held back on developmental vaccines and pretreatments to troops in the Gulf, and Saddam initiated CB warfare, the outcry would have been deafening. DoD had to take the risk that these drugs would save lives if CB agents were employed.

BATTLE PLANS FOR DESERT STORM

CENTAF's air power concept, "Instant Thunder," had made Iraqi NBC production and storage facilities one of its highest priority targets. The designers of this plan likened the strategic campaign to a dartboard. In the bulls-eye were the command, control and communications targets, the decision-making capability of the military. In the first ring around the bulls-eye the targets involved military production and storage capability, to include factories, electric power grids, power plants and oil refineries—and NBC munitions factories. The next ring held transportation infrastructure targets: the railroads, bridges, main highways, airfields and ports. The third ring held the population centers and food sources. The outmost ring contained the least important targets—the enemy's military forces.[17]

Through September and into October, CENTCOM began planning for a possible one-corps offensive into Kuwait. General Vuono had sent four graduates of the School of Advanced Military Studies, the "Jedi Knights," as they became known, to Saudi Arabia in mid-September to assist the CENTCOM headquarters with possible war game scenarios. After two weeks of planning and discussing options, the group settled on an up-the-middle attack that began just east of the Wadi al-Batin and two left-hook options that began just west of the wadi. The left-hook options left the outnumbered corps vulnerable to counterattacks by the more numerous Iraqi mechanized divisions, which could sweep around the US Army and cut off its supplies. Potential US casualties for the favored option, the up-the-middle approach, ran to two thousand dead and eight thousand wounded troops. Schwarzkopf was also concerned about the impact of chemical weapons use and the mass casualties that might result, but were impossible to estimate. Their recommendation was that another corps was necessary to defeat the Iraqi force.[18]

On October 11, a CENTCOM team flew to Washington to brief President Bush, Secretary Cheney, General Powell and other advisors at the White House. Brigadier General Buster Glossen briefed the Air Force strategic plan first, including its targeting of CB weapon sites at Karbala, Samarra, and Salman Pak. The plan listed eight chemical and biological main targets. Major General Robert Johnston, Schwarzkopf's chief of staff, briefed the one-corps ground offensive concept. The plan stressed the risks of significant casualties: the danger of extending the offensive from the logistics rear area, the lack of a theater reserve, and the threat that Iraqi chemical attacks would slow the tempo of combat operations. The plan called for an effective air campaign against the Iraqi ground forces, and for quick execution, before counterattacks would threaten the rear area. General Schwarzkopf's personal assessment pointed out that the one corps, as promised, had a solid capability to protect Saudi Arabia, but that an additional heavy corps was needed to guarantee the success of an operation to liberate Kuwait.[19]

After he received feedback on the one-corps offensive plan, Schwarzkopf told his Jedi Knights to plan a two-corps operation. They began on the assumptions that strategic and tactical air campaigns would wear down the air defense, ground, and command-control-communication units in the Kuwaiti Theater of Operations (KTO) and that Iraqi forces would use chemical weapons during the ground attack. On October 22, General Powell flew to Riyadh to discuss the one-corps versus the two-corps concept. Based on discussions with the CENTCOM staff, he brought the two-corps concept to a National Security Council meeting; the concept included activating VII Corps in Europe, bringing additional Army and Marine combat units from forces in the United States, adding three more carrier groups, doubling the Air Force units, and calling up additional reserve forces. A second corps was on the way, with large implications for the logistically-sensitive NBC defense community.

With the arrival of the 59th Chemical Company on October 15 and the 2d Chemical Battalion advance party on October 19, the XVIII ABN Corps could finally institute detailed and realistic plans for decontamination support throughout the theater. On October 21, the Corps NBCC conducted a corps-wide decontamination assessment. This meeting highlighted a defense strategy of contamination avoidance, reconnaissance, decon sites, and the use of weathering to defeat contamination. The chemical officers discussed the strategies available, given the massive shortage of M17 SANATORs (less than 500 in-theater), the water-hauling issue, and the critical shortage of water points. Originally, the Corps NBCC had planned hundreds of decontamination sites throughout the theater. Because of the limited resources available, the 2d Chemical Battalion operations officer, Major Mike Brown, suggested that the corps change this plan to allow the battalion to mass its assets at designated priority sites.

The anticipated arrival of the 2nd Chemical Battalion and the active and reserve chemical decontamination companies allowed the CENTCOM, ARCENT and XVIII ABN Corps NBCCs to breath easier. On October 26, Colonel Barbeau held a conference of all chemical staffs and units to discuss the more critical NBC defense issues. This conference allowed the chemical officers throughout the corps to meet one another and share training ideas and lessons learned on CDE problem areas. One of the prime issues was an update on the Fox platoons' training and deployment. For perhaps the first time since the deployment, the division chemical staffs were briefed in full on the NBCRS Fox fielding plan and the emerging reconnaissance strategy for the corps. Three chemical reconnaissance platoons were in theater, but there were no spare parts or maintenance facilities. General Dynamics Land Systems contractors were arriving to help support the Fox (as well as other GDLS equipment, such as the M1A1 tanks).

The officers also discussed the lack of a standard NBC threat warning system throughout the theater. With assets from three Army corps present (XVIII, III and VII), no one had designated which field procedure would be used. Colonel Barbeau suggested that they build from the III Corps threat warning system. This system had been developed to guide the necessary leadership actions to prepare for a potential NBC attack but not to replace the commanders' delegation of MOPP levels. The NBC threat condition (THREATCON) had Red, Amber, Green, and White levels to define imminent, probable, possible and nil enemy attack probabilities respectively, and indicated what protective actions, other than changing MOPP levels, should be taken. This system was easily adaptable to all units' standard operating procedures, and eliminated confusion over what states of readiness should be maintained and minimum actions required.

The main party of the 2d Chemical Battalion and the 181st and 327th Chemical companies arrived in al-Dammam on October 28 and began precombat operations in a nearby marshaling area. The 490th Chemical Battalion and 318th Chemical Company arrived in Saudi Arabia on the same day. The 761st Chemical Company joined the 101st ABN DIV on November 2. On November 5, the 2d Chemical Battalion received orders to move forward to support the XVIII ABN Corps with the 181st, the 327th and the 59th Chemical companies, allowing the 101st Chemical Company to move from supporting the corps rear area to supporting the XVIII ABN Corps artillery. The 490th Chemical Battalion would provide general support to the Army's echelons above corps units in the Support Command area of responsibility. It took the 318th Chemical Company under its control, with other reserve chemical units due to join in November. Rear area support mission included decon for troops, equipment, logistical stockpiles, facilities, ports, airfields, terrain and main supply routes, on a priority basis.

Initially, there was a debate over how the rear areas would receive decontamination support. Major General Gus Pagonis, as the theater army support commander, and the XVIII ABN Corps support commander had mixed combat support units in and around the Saudi airfields and ports. Both commanders expected the two chemical battalions to offer support to their respective units; the two initial non-divisional chemical companies, the 59th and 761st, only had three of their four authorized decon platoons. The continued lack of M17 SANATORs meant that XVIII ABN Corps also needed general support above and beyond its capabilities in the forward areas. Supporting the CENTCOM and ARCENT rear areas, in addition to the XVIII ABN Corps main area, would disperse the few decontamination assets available over a large area, straining their operational capabilities.

On November 9, the two chemical battalion commanders and Colonel Barbeau conferred and agreed to a division of labor. The 490th Chemical Battalion would have the responsibility for all soldiers at the King Abdul Aziz Port and Dhahran's airport. The 2nd Chemical Battalion would support the XVIII ABN Corps Rear Command Post area of responsibility in the Dhahran/Dammam complex in addition to ARCENT's rear area. The rest of the decon capability for XVIII ABN Corps would have to come from the divisional chemical companies and the promised SANATORs, which had still not arrived.[20]

Two more decon companies, the 371st and 413th Chemical Companies, were due on November 18; they would join the 490th Chemical Battalion for rear area support. While the CONUS chemical units were arriving, the 11th and 51st Chemical companies had been held back in Europe. With the recognition of VII Corps's deployment needs, the VII Corps staff had noted that when the XVIII ABN Corps deployed into theater, it had emphasized "teeth" over "tail" (or combat power over logistics sustainability). As a result, the combat units would have been vulnerable if they had had to sustain combat operations immediately. Cognizant of the need to avoid that vulnerability, VII Corps would deploy the two chemical companies with their COSCOM in early December, just after the 2d ACR (the first VII Corps unit in theater). Appendix A details the task organization for the chemical units within Saudi Arabia as of the beginning of November.

Approval of the two-corps offensive meant another call to the PM NBC Defense office. Just when the PM shop was about to congratulate itself for a strong (and very busy) supporting effort, it got the news that it had to equip another corps with Foxes. CENTCOM NBCC informed Colonel Evans and Lieutenant Colonel D'Andries that the new goal was to provide two corps with NBCRS Foxes by mid-January.[21] By the end of October, less than twenty had arrived—about enough for two-thirds of one corps. And to make it more interesting, VII Corps chemical recon units were already in the theater, supporting XVIII ABN Corps! Now, one month after the German government had offered a second gift of thirty Foxes, the Army accepted the vehicles. Initially, the Army was reluctant to accept more than 50 systems, as the original initial procurement was planned at 48. ASARDA had told ODCSOPS chemical division that a Marine commander in the Gulf had heard of this capability and wanted some as well. Lieutenant Colonel Willhoite and Major Newing quickly contacted the Marine Corps offices in Quantico, Virginia, and Saudi Arabia and got the committment for ten more systems, matching the German offer of 60 systems. The delay would cost a month, since Thyssen-Henschel had not committed resources to the program until the US government agreed to the gift. The first thirty vehicles would be "Americanized" by the end of November as planned; the second thirty would be fielded as four batches—five systems in December, ten each in January and February, and five more in March. This would permit an additional five platoons of Foxes to be deployed to the theater.[22]

Lieutenant General Franks wanted a ready reconnaissance capability prior to sending his forces into the overcrowded Gulf ports and airfields. The 2d ACR's chemical recon platoon from the 87th Chemical Company bumped 3rd ACR's 89th Chemical Company on the training list, and would enter training after the 5/25th Recon Platoon in November, receiving its six NBCRS Foxes (the last of the initial thirty) in early December. While this represented an initial NBC reconnaissance capability for the deploying VII Corps, the main issue remained—how to get the VII Corps recon platoons back to their own divisions in a way that let the XVIII ABN Corps divisions retain their NBC reconnaissance capability.

A second corps also meant new headaches for the medical NBC defense community. Supporting one corps with biological vaccines and atropine injectors seemed within the realm of feasibility; vaccinating two corps would mean hundreds of thousands of additional dosages, which were not available. With FDA negotiations continuing and continued reluctance from American pharmaceutical companies, the medical community had no idea how it would meet the new requirements. There was no rest for the weary.

CHAPTER 4

Move to the Offense

The one [threat] that scares me to death—even more so than attack of nuclear weapons and the one we have even less capability against—is biological weapons.
—General Colin Powell, 1992

The Pentagon officially mobilized VII Corps on November 9, 1990; certainly, however, VII Corps had begun planning its deployment much earlier. Plans had been kicked around for the past month as to which corps within the Army should deploy to augment CENTCOM. General Vuono was emphatic that the III Corps, although partially mobilized, should not be fully deployed, leaving the United States without a major Army corps. VII Corps in Europe had been planning a drawdown since the fall of the Berlin Wall in 1989, and so it seemed the logical choice. The Seventh Army commander, General Crosbie Saint, chose VII Corps headquarters, with its 1st AR DIV and 2d ACR, and V Corps's 3rd AR DIV and the US-based 1st IN DIV to deploy. On November 13, Lieutenant General Franks, as VII Corps commander, brought his commanders and primary staff to Saudi Arabia for a leaders' reconnaissance. General Schwarzkopf emphasized his desire to see VII Corps in place by mid-January. VII Corps began deploying on November 21; and it would take the rest of the year and part of January to move into the theater. There were a number of immediate issues for the Corps NBC Center to work on.

One of the first issues was to collect all available CAMs in Europe for the deploying units. As mentioned, there were not many CAMs fielded, and every one was critical to preparedness. VII Corps made a considered decision not to deploy any of the M20 SCPEs that the units already had, based on the trials conducted by XVIII ABN Corps. It seemed unlikely that VII Corps would have any more luck erecting these shelters in the desert. A team of technical experts from Pine Bluff Arsenal deployed to Germany, where they spent two weeks checking hundreds of protective masks for soldiers with abnormal face requirements. During the two-week period, only a half dozen soldiers could not be properly fitted; they were left behind in Germany.

Perhaps the greatest concern was the VII Corps's requirement that each deploying soldier have at least two unopened sets of chemical protective clothing and three NAAKs with his or her mask. While a USAREUR regulation stated that every soldier have two complete sets of clothing, there was no requirement to report their on-hand status; therefore, no one had checked. As the Cold War ended, most protective suits remained in warehouses throughout Germany rather than with troops. No one knew exactly where the suits were or how many there were, but everyone knew that there were not enough. Most suits in storage were primarily the older CPOGs. Despite the known threat in the Gulf and their potential deployment in that theater, many units had neglected to identify their shortages and request replacements. Several units had packed their extra protective suits in military containers for shipment, which took several weeks to move from Europe to Saudi Arabia, while the troops arrived in days. Last, several military units that would augment VII Corps came from CONUS; unfortunately, many were told that they would receive protective suits once in Saudi Arabia. Of course, there were no extra suits, increasing the overall shortage. As a result, the majority of VII Corps units deployed with only one set of overgarments, as had the XVIII ABN Corps.[1]

This is not to suggest that VII Corps had been as unprepared in November as XVIII ABN Corps had been in August. The level of chemical training of forces in Germany was generally good, and probably much higher due to the past Soviet threat and constant REFORGER exercises. VII Corps medical personnel had the opportunity to undergo refresher training in chemical agent casualty operations. Their familiarity with French and British forces in NATO would allow them to integrate these divisions' NBC defense operations smoothly. Because XVIII ABN Corps had established a theater warning system, VII Corps and its attached units would adopt it as their standard while in the Gulf. Overall, they would deploy in a somewhat better posture, which was good for one main reason—they would not have six months, or even much more than three months, to equip and train their forces.

Very much on the minds of Lieutenant General Franks and his division commanders was that three of their chemical recon platoons were already in Saudi Arabia, with a fourth on the way in mid-November. Two of those belonged to units remaining in Europe (3rd and 8th IN DIV), but the other two, attached to the 24th IN DIV and 2d Chemical Battalion, belonged to the deploying 1st and 3rd AR DIV, respectively. As the Foxes had been one of the earliest VII Corps contributions to CENTCOM, Franks had visited the Sonthofen training and seen his NBC recon platoons off. The XVIII ABN Corps's divisions had become very comfortable with the Foxes, had made extensive plans on the assumption of retaining these vehicles, and now had to find out how to replace them.

Complicating Fox distribution were demands from the Marine Corps for a similar capability for its two divisions. In October, General Schwarzkopf had made the concession that the first ten NBCRS vehicles in-theater in January 1991 would go to the Marines (as per the earlier ODCSOPS negotiation with the Marines). No arguments from the Army commanders to redirect the vehicles could sway him. The two platoons gave the two Marine divisions a specialized NBC reconnaissance capability equal to the Army divisions. Although the Marines had never developed specialized chemical units and had turned down initial procurements of Foxes, they were not about to turn down this capability in the hour of their need.[2]

Part of the solution would come from the Chemical School. The remaining three "Nunn" Fox vehicles that had been shipped to the GDLS facility in Michigan for refit were ready in September and were shipped to Fort Hood for deployment with the III Corps units. Since the German government had made its initial thirty Foxes a gift, the Chemical School requested the three "Nunn" Foxes be sent to Fort McClellan to support training of chemical reconnaissance troops. The Chemical School did not have an NBCRS simulator like the one in Sonthofen and had submitted a critical-needs statement to HQ DA to acquire two Fox simulators (with two mass spectrometers, navigation systems, and a supporting chemical laboratory), at a cost of $6.1 million.[3] However, these would not arrive until November 1991. In the meantime, they could make do with classroom training and the three Fox vehicles on hand.

On November 3, the 1st IN DIV's chemical recon platoon from the 12th Chemical Company attended the first three-week NBCRS training course. Another chemical company would send its recon platoon to Fort McClellan in December (training as potential replacements). One USMC platoon would arrive just before Christmas, returning prior to the beginning of the air offensive, followed by a third Army recon platoon. The 1st IN DIV's recon platoon returned to Fort Riley to deploy with its division in early January, while the two Marine recon platoons would return to Southwest Asia. All three platoons would wait for orders to pick up their Foxes from the factory at Kassel, Germany, where they were being "Americanized." The XVIII ABN Corps's release of two recon platoons back to VII Corps would balance both corps at three recon platoons each in January, with two platoons going to the Marines.

The recon training program in Germany continued on track. Major Polley had left the German school to join the 1st IN DIV as its division chemical officer and had had an opportunity to stop by Fort McClellan to see his division's chemical soldiers' training on the Chemical School Foxes. Major Jeff Adams replaced Polley as the liaison officer at Sonthofen to continue the training. The recon platoon from 87th Chemical Company (2d ACR) arrived at Sonthofen for its training in early November. 3rd ACR's reconnaissance platoon from the 89th Chemical Company would train with it, but would deploy with its own Foxes from the second batch of thirty vehicles after the 2d ACR received its Foxes.[4] As these troops arrived, the 5/25th Recon Platoon from 8th IN DIV was preparing to deploy to Saudi Arabia with its six Foxes (arriving on November 16).

Major General Watson had an opportunity to talk to General Schwarzkopf again in November; Schwarzkopf referred him to Major General Burt Moore, US Air Force, the J-3 (operations) on the CENTCOM staff. Watson suggested to

Moore that CENTCOM needed a one-star general officer to help coordinate the NBC defense requirements for the four services, especially in light of a second corps coming into the theater. The original CENTCOM deployment plan had a chemical brigade (which would have been commanded by a brigadier general or promotable colonel) that would plan, coordinate and support the non-divisional chemical defense units' actions as they moved to support one division or another or across the two corps. That had not materialized. In the minds of many senior chemical officers, the situation to date had not been fruitful, since the two corps had colonels as their chemical officers as compared to the lieutenant colonels at the higher ARCENT headquarters (Vicki Merryman) and CENTCOM headquarters (Ken Silvernail).

The two lieutenant colonels had done their best to stay abreast of growing chemical defense requirements, requisitions, and related issues of a huge force. But in a climate of general officers running the ARCENT/CENTCOM policy in the various staff offices, a lieutenant colonel did not have the horsepower to recommend and execute timely decisions. This issue had been a significant source of friction between XVIII ABN Corps's, ARCENT's and CENTCOM's NBCCs and NBC defense organizations in the United States, with respect to obtaining the timely support that XVIII ABN Corps thought it needed. A chemical general officer would have sat in on the two corps commanders' war councils, enabling closer operational and logistical support and presenting a single, authoritative voice to the United States. Regardless, Major General Moore was not convinced; he told Watson that he did not see that much work for a chemical general officer in CENTCOM. This decision would affect the Army chemical defense staff and units throughout the war, denying General Schwarzkopf valuable advice and contributing to delays in assigning chemical defense units to and from the divisions.[5]

Major General Watson did convince ODCSOPS to allow DNA to develop an Automated Nuclear, Biological And Chemical Information System, or ANBACIS. This was a computer software package that could take data concerning an enemy CB munitions strike, such as munition type, agent used, number of munitions, and combine it with local weather information to create a "footprint" of the downwind CB agent contamination hazard. This effort had begun in 1982 as an Apple program for the 9th Infantry Division in Fort Lewis, Washington—a simple computer exercise to practice crude NBC agent contamination plots. It had never become more than a training tool until 1989, when the right amount of synergy between software development, program funds, and modern Army communications came about to develop it into a planning tool for military units in combat.

Major General Watson was able to authorize several million dollars to refine the ANBACIS model at DNA. In early November, he gathered his modeling team; its members included a Navy officer (with a biological warfare agent model), Dr. Clyde Replogle from Wright-Patterson AFB (supplying a weather information model), and a small group of scientists from CRDEC (in the chemical warfare agent modeling and simulation area). Members from Los Alamos National

Laboratory, contractors from the SAIC, Mitre, and JAYCOR firms, and a representative from the Air Force Global Weather Center joined the team. Over a period of about forty days they were able to develop a model that, using the Cray supercomputers at DNA, could use real-time Middle East weather information and enemy munitions data to develop footprints of the predicted contamination area quickly. The model integrated three chemical agent models (NUSSE4, PARACOMPT, and Plume) into one model (ANBACIS-II), which provided an improved depiction of CB agent collateral effects. This was light-years ahead of the current NATO ATP-45 method, which an individual manually consulted wind speed charts and a simple hand calculator to develop an (overly conservative) contamination prediction within a half hour, if the analyst was well trained.[6]

CONTINUING CB DEFENSE PREPARATIONS

Logistics units under Major General Gus Pagonis used the time given to them to bring in every materiel advantage they could to improve the combat units' odds in the upcoming desert battle. One possible improvement was to upgrade the many M1 Abrams tanks in Southwest Asia to the M1A1 standard. The majority of tanks in CONUS divisions were M1s, armed with a 105 mm main gun and using the same ventilated facepiece protective system as the M60A3 tanks used. US Army divisions in Europe were equipped with M1A2 tanks, armed with a 120 mm main gun, advanced targeting electronics, and hybrid collective protection that included an overpressure system with the ventilated facepiece. This meant that the later model tanks could keep chemical agent vapors out of their interior. They also featured micro-climate cooling vests, which were worn under the crew's protective clothing; the hybrid system would pump cool liquid through the vest, keeping the crew comfortable despite the protective clothing and fierce desert heat. Overall, this enabled the crews in M1A2 tanks to fight with a lower physiological and psychological burden than those in M1s or M60A3s. The combined bonus of increased lethality and better protection was a strong incentive to upgrade the M1 systems before the ground war began. HQ AMC began the upgrade of 1032 M1 tanks in early November, with the final tanks receiving their modifications only days prior to the start of the ground war. As these tanks were upgraded and repainted to desert schemes, the 490th Chemical Battalion was tasked to support AMC by providing decon systems to wash the tanks prior to painting them.

Fox vehicles continued to roll into Southwest Asia. By establishing liaison offices at the Thyssen-Henschel site at Kassel, the Sonthofen NBC defense school, and Dhahran's King Fahd International Airfield, the PM for NBC Defense office was able to monitor and troubleshoot the production and deployment process continuously. Thyssen-Henschel produced ten additional systems in October and November, and five of the second thirty in late December, raising the projected total end-year figure to thirty-seven modified NBCRS vehicles. There was concern that the Fox's profile resembled the Soviet-built BTR-60 (used by the Iraqi Army). To avoid fratricide, the Fox crews raised "Jolly Roger" flags or American flags on their radio antennas and taped large inverted Vs with florescent infrared reflecting tape on the vehicles' sides. The PM NBC Defense Office issued thousands of vehicle identification cards, meant to familiarize CENTCOM soldiers, marines and aviators with the new vehicle's silhouette.

Thirty-five General Dynamics Services Company contractors joined the AMC maintenance facility at Dhahran, where the Army had established a limited repair depot in October. The Fox facility in Dhahran grew to include a small fleet of vehicles (for the mobile organizational maintenance support of forward combat units), a second facility site at KKMC, and seven organizational maintenance teams for around-the-clock operations by February 11, 1991. The seven teams included two with the USMC, one with the British forces, two corps-level direct-support sites, and two fixed facilities.[7]

To have another corps in-theater called for another chemical battalion to support its CB defense operations. Under the November reserve call-up, ODCSOPS tapped the 457th Chemical Battalion and 413th Chemical Company from South Carolina, the 323rd Chemical Company from South Dakota, the 340th Chemical Company from Texas, and the 496th Chemical Detachment (JB) from Alabama. The 496th would arrive in Saudi Arabia the day after Christmas; the rest would follow in the first week of January. All the companies were decontamination units. Although concern over insufficient decontamination assets was now not as great as it had been in August, there still was a large corps rear area that would require these additional units if chemical strikes occurred.

In early November, an advance military group from the Czechoslovakian Ministry of National Defense visited Saudi Arabia to offer assistance in the form of a Czech "anti-chemical" team. The unit would be stationed in the rear support area about 160 kilometers from the Iraqi border. Its main function was to detect and identify chemical agents delivered against the Saudi military's rear area and the Saudi population. This support was accepted by the Saudi government, with the deployment of the Czech troops scheduled to begin in December.[8] Officially, these units would not report to CENTCOM but were directly contracted to the Saudi government, to support Saudi forces *only*.

The 5/25th Recon Platoon joined the 2d Chemical Battalion on November 16 to begin a rear area support mission, allowing the 1st CAV DIV to receive the 22d Chemical Company's platoon. The 87th Chemical Company's platoon (from 2d ACR) would take the last six vehicles of the initial thirty back to Saudi Arabia in mid-December. Having accomplished the mission of reorganizing, training and equipping the four initial NBC reconnaissance platoons, Task Force Fox stood down. After all, its soldiers had to deploy with 3rd AR DIV to get into the war. The training at Sonthofen went on, however, as it did at Fort McClellan. Since two "float" vehicles remained available, the 490th Chemical Battalion (which had arrived in late October) saw an opportunity to provide NBC reconnaissance for the ARCENT rear area. Eight chemical soldiers (five from the battalion headquarters and three from the 318th Chemical Company) traveled to Sonthofen on November 17 for the three-week course; they would arrive back in Saudi Arabia after

Christmas. A Marine platoon would follow in early January, about two weeks after their colleagues began Fort McClellan's NBCRS training course. Platoons from 13th Chemical Company and 95th Chemical Company (both from 3rd COSCOM) were scheduled to enter Sonthofen training on February 8 (to be ready by mid-March) as replacements prepared to replace casualties once the ground offensive began.

President Bush and a party, including Barbara Bush, Secretary of State George Baker, Chief of Staff John Sununu, National Security Advisor Brent Scowcraft, Senators George Mitchel and Bob Dole, and Representatives Tom Foley and Bob Mitchell, arrived in Saudi Arabia on November 22 for Thanksgiving. The Secret Service, understandably worried about protecting the president against Scuds and CB agent attacks, ensured that the president and his party all carried MCU-2/P protective masks. Aboard Air Force 1 during the overseas flight, chemical officers had shown President Bush how to don a mask. His entourage traveled to within seventy miles of the Kuwaiti border to eat Thanksgiving dinner with the 2-18th Infantry Battalion. Three Fox NBCRS vehicles from the 5/69th Recon Platoon joined the protective phalanx of gunships, fighter planes and bodyguards. In the event of a chemical attack, the president and his group would have been whisked away in the NBCRS back to Riyadh.[9]

On November 26, one Fox vehicle from the 92d Chemical Company hit a washout in the road during high-speed training operations, rolling several times before breaking its left front wheel and damaging the front axle. It could not be repaired in-theater and was shipped back to the depot in Kassel in December. This would leave a total of thirty-one Foxes in theater by the end of December—four recon platoons with XVIII ABN Corps (one with five vehicles and one with a "Nunn" vehicle), one platoon with 2d ACR, and one "Nunn" vehicle as the ARCENT ORF.[10]

NO TIME FOR CAUTIOUS DECISIONS

Many normally accepted, day-to-day operations were complicated by the CB agent threat, raising special concerns at CENTCOM that had to be answered quickly. At Dugway Proving Ground, scientists had increased their test activities to accommodate them. CENTCOM was concerned about a report that the Iraqi government had purchased forty Mistral-2 aerosol generators, which could be mounted on flatbed trucks, aircraft or boats. This agricultural sprayer consisted of a motor, a pump, a cannon-type blower assembly and storage areas for liquid and solid materials. These sprayers were designed to disperse either liquids or powders (i.e., insecticides), or both liquids and solids simultaneously. They had a military potential to disperse CB agents against the coalition if driven along the Iraq-Kuwait border, or against Navy ships and Marine forces in the Gulf if employed by small boats along the shore. DoD purchased two of these sprayers, transported them to Dugway, and used biological simulants to study their effectiveness. Other studies examined various terrorist chemical attack scenarios against command, control, communications and intelligence operations within CENTCOM. These studies remain classified to this day because of the implications of their potential applications.[11]

One of the more sensitive issues was the disposal of contaminated bodies of US troops. The Quartermaster Corps, which has responsibility for the graves registration units, realized that mere body bags might be insufficient to seal in CB agents that might emanate from a contaminated corpse. Possibilities were to leave the corpses in Saudi Arabia or cremate the bodies prior to shipping the remains home. These were not seen as politically viable solutions. The Army Medical and Quartermaster Schools worked with Dugway Proving Ground scientists to find ways to decontaminate the bodies, check for excessive contamination, seal the remains in double body bags, and ship them back in sealed coffins to the United States. Prior to releasing the remains, the coffins would be checked again with sensitive laboratory chemical agent detectors for any leaking contamination. The details of this macabre procedure had to be tested and validated prior to its use, which meant months of careful evaluation.

A similar situation arose in shipping back formerly contaminated equipment. There was no question but that soldiers would continue to fight in their aircraft and vehicles, contaminated or not; that was a staple of chemical doctrine, to "fight dirty." However, when it was time to return the equipment back to CONUS, there was the possibility that contaminated tanks, helicopters and other major systems would require refit and repair by civilian and government depots. Before unprotected maintenance workers could safely handle equipment that had once been contaminated, the equipment had to be proven clean to a degree that military field detectors could not register. To achieve this very low agent level, soldiers would have to expose the equipment to intense heat for a period of time that would effectively destroy it—those $3 million tanks and $35 million helicopters—as well as the suspected contamination. Dugway Proving Ground scientists worked on procedures and laboratory equipment to screen the suspected contaminated equipment in Southwest Asia before it was loaded onto ships for the ride back, and again once the equipment arrived in the United States.[12]

At the end of November, the UN Security Council adopted Resolution 678 by a 12–2 vote, calling for the United Nations to act against Iraq unless its forces withdrew from Kuwait by January 15. The British, French, US and Russian representatives took the opportunity to warn Iraq against "initiating the use of chemical or biological weapons." This resolution initiated increasing diplomatic pressure to warn Iraq about the consequences of using these weapons against the coalition.[13] For the military members of the coalition, however, the fact that there was a resolution against CB warfare meant about as much as the Geneva Protocol of 1925 had meant to the Iraqis in the 1980s.

In the early morning hours of December 2, Iraq launched three Scud missiles on a test flight within its own boundaries, causing XVIII ABN Corps to institute MOPP-0 levels (chemical protective suits within reach). This sent a clear signal

Figure 4.1
Suspected Iraqi NBC Warfare Targets

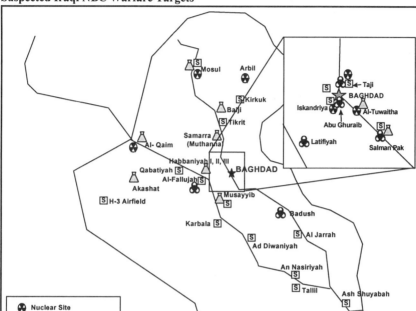

to the coalition that its readiness would be tested. Colonel Barbeau sent messages throughout the corps to re-examine operating procedures and defensive equipment status in preparation for any Scud attacks that might initiate CB warfare.

CENTAF targeting lists swelled with the additional fighter and bomber wings brought in by the November call-up. Targeted NBC sites grew in number from eight to twenty in the fall, and finally to thirty-four (see Figure 4.1). Target and weapons analysts worked with DNA to predict the possible collateral hazards of destroying facilities that housed radiological, bacteriological and hazardous chemical solvents. The nuclear targets were the least worry; the idea was to bury the enriched uranium under debris rather than completely destroy the reactors. In addition to weapons production and storage sites, planners targeted the specific airfields where Iraqi forces had built chemical weapons bunkers. These included airfields at H3 (an oil-pumping site in the west), Mosul, Qayarrah West, Kirkuk, al-Taqqadum, Ubaydah bin Al Jarrah, and Shuaybah (a helicopter base). The two airfields at Tallil and an-Nasiriyah were targeted because of their proximity to the front and ability to launch air attacks into Kuwait.

DNA computer modeling showed a very small chance of any chemical agent traces traveling downwind far enough to threaten any allied troops.[14] Basic physics explained that high concentrations of chemical agents eighty kilometers away would dissipate to sub-lethal levels long before reaching CENTCOM forces. Biological agents, however, scared the target analysts. Because any small sample of biological agent can, under optimal conditions, quickly cover a large area, there were serious and long debates over the possibility of causing an anthrax epidemic by bombing a biological weapons site. British and American troops had not begun their inoculation programs, and there was not enough vaccine for all the troops, let alone the civilian population. Biological warfare experts suggested that the risks of causing an epidemic were grossly overstated, given the extreme desert environment and distance the agent would have to travel.

Politicians and military leaders in London, Washington and Moscow were still wary. The analysts offered up three options. First, they could mine the area around the bunkers with cluster bombs, denying access to the weapons. Second, they could guarantee that all the spores would die, by raising the temperature of the immediate area up to 20,000° F in three seconds—through tactical nuclear weapon employment. Some suggested that it might be morally correct to use one weapon of mass destruction to destroy another. Scientists at Yuma Proving Grounds examined the effects of fuel-air explosives against bunkers holding simulated biological weapons. Last, F-117s could drop two thousand pound GBU-27 bombs on the bunkers right after dawn, followed by cluster bomb runs. This option would deny access to the sites while the sun's ultraviolet rays killed the spores that had escaped the bunker. CENTCOM's final position was to attack the biological weapons storage sites using the third option, hitting the sites with GBU-27 bombs followed by cluster bombs.[15]

As more government civilians and defense contractors deployed to Saudi Arabia to help maintain military equipment, all had to be prepared for working within range of CB agent delivery systems. The majority of government civilians traveled to Aberdeen Proving Ground, Maryland, or Fort Jackson, South Carolina, to undergo a two-week predeployment staging. All deploying civilians had to take their immunization record, list of current medications, and their most recent eyeglass prescription (for the optical lens insert of the protective mask) to their medical screening appointment. The physicians assessed their ability to wear full protective equipment in the heat. This included identifying any history of heat stress, medical conditions that would limit the use of a mask, hearing problems that would prevent their reacting to a chemical agent alarm, and evidence of physical stress from other medical tests. Government civilians drew protective masks and protective clothing. In addition to some basic training, they attended a one-day course on proper wear and maintenance of the protective mask, how to wear protective clothing, and how to administer medical antidotes. This predeployment training was vital if they were to respond properly to the expected gas alerts, especially for individuals who had never been exposed to such exercises in the military. One AMCCOM civilian commented later, "When you first hear over the radio the words 'GAS, GAS, MOPP-4' that is so frightening.   And you're struggling, and all of a sudden you feel yourself breathing, and you have to count one thousand one, one thousand two, so you don't lose it."[16]

BIODEFENSE TEAM PREPARATION

The CRDEC biodetection development team had received $20 million directly from Congress to develop and test a biological agent detector, with a deadline of January 15. The existing biodetection programs there were too immature to rush into development. CRDEC had identified two possible approaches—to see what industry could provide, or rely on the XM19 biological agent detector of the 1970s era. It narrowed down the choices to four systems. Two relied on point aerosol sampling—the previously abandoned XM2 biological agent air sampler and a commercial aerosol sampler, the PM10 Biological Aerosol Sampler/Cyclone. These systems would concentrate air particles into a saline solution. Another commercial item, Sensitive Membrane Antigen, Rapid Test (or SMART) tickets, would selectively identify biological materiels in the concentrated medium through antibody reactions, indicated by a bright red spot for "positive."   Both the commercial and military detectors required manual operation and fifteen minutes per test after forty-five minutes of aerosol collection.

The other two biodetector concepts were stand-off systems developed by Los Alamos National Laboratory (LANL) and SRI, which had begun their development under the DNA effort. LANL had developed an aircraft-mounted laser system to test alongside SRI's ground-mounted passive infrared system. A stand-off capability was desirable, since commanders wanted early warning of biological agent clouds rather than an indication that the ground that they were standing on had already been hit by BW agents. The Project Office for Biodefense transported the four systems (the two stand-off systems and the two point detectors) for testing at Yuma and Dugway, and arranged for a special environmental permission to use biological simulants and an active laser system (which involved eye-screening concerns). Ms. Donna Shandle, then the Assistant Technical Director for Testing at CRDEC, became the PO Biodefense coordinator for the testing at the proving grounds, given her past experience with the Dugway Proving Ground test program.[17]

While the theater biodetection concept was still forming, CENTCOM had designated the Navy Forward Laboratory as the theater medical lab for biological agent testing. Based on their collaborative work, the Army and Navy would share all incoming samples, with the NAVCENT Surgeon offering initial results to CENTCOM, and USAMRIID confirming the results at Fort Detrick. The Army planned to deploy its own forward lab from the 996th Medical Laboratory in December, equipped with advanced diagnostics equipment.

ASARDA ordered the low-rate initial production of the XM2 and commercial PM10 biological aerosol samplers on December 3, 1990. There had been no final word from CENTCOM about when or even if the systems would make it to the

Gulf. Because of the pressure to get VII Corps to the Gulf and the looming deadline of the air war, CENTCOM had in January instituted strict guidelines on who was permitted to enter the theater. Even the Fox maintenance support teams had run into difficulties expanding the number of personnel at the Dhahran facility to support two corps' worth of NBCRS systems.

Initially, in late November ARCENT's G-3 had refused the biodetectors. Lieutenant Colonel Merryman distrusted the biodetectors; they were untested, previously rejected programs with no tested doctrine to back up their employment, no tried procedures on the collection, transportation, and identification of biological agents, and required 45 minutes to sample the air for one test.[18] The point detectors would not provide early warning for treatment; it would be hours after the fact before the operators knew that they had indeed been hit with biological warfare agents. There was just no strong indication that these teams would be a real asset to the NBCCs. Lieutenant General Dennis Reimer, DCSOPS, pressured Brigadier General S.L. Arnold, the ARCENT G-3, to give his immediate support to the concept; there had to be a biodetection capability to give the military and political leadership some indication of the threat employment, if Iraq choose to use BW agents against CENTCOM.

In the bowels of the Pentagon, Colonel Read virtually locked Major Newing and a small group of Army, Navy and Air Force CBW specialists in a room to develop the doctrine to provide that capability. The group brainstormed to develop a doctrine using airborne stand-off biological agent detectors, the XM2 point samplers and the forward laboratories to alert CENTCOM to a biological agent attack. With the limited detectors being built (roughly a dozen), should they deploy in front of the divisions to allow an early warning capability? Or what about the rear area, which was probably more vulnerable than the front lines? How would they confirm the biological agent attack? And upon confirmation of a biological warfare agent, how should they alert CENTCOM, and what then? How would they determine when it was safe to unmask after a biological agent attack? There were many thorny issues, and little time.

After three days, the group emerged with what is still today the most accurate prediction and threat analysis on employment of anthrax and botulinum toxin. They had analyzed weather windows of opportunity, possible weapon delivery systems, triggers for employment, and war-gamed several scenarios. The result was a one-inch thick operational concept that laid the threat, provided point detection sampling and detection operations, and described the splitting of samples to theater medical labs (for immediate analysis) and CONUS labs (for international evidence if needed). It included an airborne stand-off option using a dedicated C130 to employ the detector and an AWACS for command, control and communications. As Major Newing briefed this concept in the Pentagon's briefing rooms, he sensed the Air Force's reluctance to commit these planes to a fly-by-night, ad hoc effort. Passive defense (detection) was still not favored over active defense (attacking the CW/BW sites), no matter the low battle-damage assessments.

ODCSOPS had selected the 9th Chemical Company (Motorized) from Fort Lewis, Washington, to take the biological agent detectors and XM21 RSCAALs into the Gulf (at the time, the 9th IN DIV was being deactivated). Two chemical officers and forty-three soldiers from the 9th Chemical Company at Fort Lewis would travel to Edgewood in mid-January to begin training and receive vaccinations. Two CRDEC officers, Captain Gerald Minor and Captain Lloyd Plume, would join them as technical representatives and advance party for the 9th Chem's biodetection teams. The deployment concept was to send an initial liaison team after the New Year, followed by area CB sampling teams using XM2s and XM21 RSCAALs and fixed-site teams using PM10 commercial detectors. CRDEC began to train their Biological Detachment Teams, in the hopes that ARCENT would accept them prior to the ground offensive.

ARCENT agreed on December 19 to request formally deployment of the biodetection teams. They would host the teams under the Foreign Materiel Intelligence Battalion (FMIB), attached to the 513th Military Intelligence Brigade, rather than with one of the chemical battalions (or the missing chemical brigade). The FMIB had the mission of collecting foreign military equipment, providing some on-site analysis, and shipping the equipment back to the United States for further intelligence analysis. As such, it was ideal to support the biodetection teams, although it had never worked with chemical soldiers before. One of its technical intelligence teams and the S-3 cell was already in the theater. The FMIB planned to deploy and establish a Joint Captured Materiel Exploitation Center (JCMEC) in theater by mid-January. Its operations and logistics cells had already left on December 10 to lay the foundations for the JCMEC.

The JCMEC had a technical intelligence mission. It would conduct battlefield exploitation of captured enemy equipment to determine its capabilities, limitations and vulnerabilities. Its new mission was to oversee CB agent and medical sampling to verify first use of CB agent weapons, in order to support national-level introduction of countermeasures. The 9th Chemical Company would conduct biological air sampling and provide a chemical stand-off detection capability at strategic locations across the theater front in two and three-man teams. The Army's Technical Escort Unit (TEU) would conduct the battlefield processing and packaging of suspected CB agent samples, and escort the suspected CB agent samples back to CONUS. If a biodetection team "hit" on a possible positive chemical or biological agent sample, it would send it to one of the labs—the Naval Forward Laboratory at al-Jubayl, or later, the Army's Forward Medical Laboratory at KKMC—to produce an initial analysis for CENTCOM.[19]

While the in-theater labs began their analysis, the TEU team would seal the sample in commercially-available medical hazard handling containers and send it from Dhahran to the United States on the next available flight. If the sample was suspected to be a chemical agent, it went to the CRDEC labs at Edgewood; if a suspected biological agent, it went to the USAMRIID labs at Fort Detrick. Once the sample was positively identified as either a false alarm or a real agent, the results would be forwarded to the Pentagon and CENTCOM. This was the same procedure that the Fox teams, medical preventive medicine units and special operations teams would follow if they had CB agent samples.

At least, this was the theory. In practice, a number of challenges lay ahead. No one was exactly sure how this would work, since this was the first time this sort of military sampling analysis had actually been put into operation. The equipment had been slapped together from commercial and antiquated military designs, and the operators were unfamiliar with them. There were not enough organic radio or vehicle assets to maintain twelve mobile teams across two corps and the corps support area. The forward labs required a minimum of six hours to analyze the samples after however long it took to get the samples back to the labs. To transport the samples back to CONUS, the TEU teams had to throw peacetime Army and Air Force transportation regulations about hazardous materials out the window. Last, even if CENTCOM was aware of a large-area biological attack, it had no way of knowing if a contaminated area could be cleared and rendered safe for troops after the attack. There was no way to declare "all clear" to the soldiers, as was done with the M256A1 kits for chemical agents. The whole concept had no precedent, making it difficult to estimate how quickly and how accurately it could provide answers on suspected CB samples.[20] Yet they would be the basis for any presidential decision and CENTCOM's reaction to Iraqi CBW attacks.

CHAPTER 5

Tensions Rise in the Gulf

Anti-chemical protection is essential today, when the possession of chemical weapons is not prohibited by international law and when several nations possess stocks of chemical weapons. Moreover, chemical defense will remain essential after entry into force of the Chemical Weapons Convention.
—Dr. Matthew Meselson, November 1990

The FDA formally approved the Army's New Drug Application for the CANA autoinjectors on December 5. It seemed like the CANA would be available in limited quantities in time for the air war. All of the soldiers might have them by the ground offensive, if the production lines kept to schedule and training programs to use the CANAs were accomplished as planned. The forecasted numbers for biological vaccines were less clear. The FDA and DoD had wrangled over the question of biological vaccine and chemical agent pretreatment Investigational New Drugs (INDs) for months. As General Sir Peter de la Billiere would point out later, there really was no need for a trial-tested decision, in the end. He noted, "We should be entirely blameworthy if we didn't use it [the vaccines] and Saddam delivered biological."[1] To supplement the troops' ability to resist infections, the Armed Forces Epidemiological Board agreed to the CINCCENT Surgeon's recommendation to issue antibiotics to all troops. At a special Biological Warfare Defense Review hosted by ODCSOPS on December 18, Major General Louis Del Rosso reviewed the biodetector employment scheme and the biodefense vaccine plan. The results went the next day to Secretary Cheney, who approved the immunization plan for anthrax and botulinum toxin, the immunization team travel, the use of antibiotics and other treatments.

General Powell authorized a warning order to CENTCOM on the biological vaccine distribution. CENTCOM was to initiate plans to receive the bio detection teams, 500,000 individually packaged antibiotic kits plus enough bulk-packaged ciprofloxacin and doxycycline for one million troops for thirty days, 3,500 doses of botulinum toxin vaccine, and 100,000 doses of anthrax vaccine. This would require additional refrigeration and vaccination teams to distribute the doses.

Finally, the FDA published regulations on waivers of informed consent. OASD(HA) submitted the waivers for informed consent for the topical skin protectant, the PB tablets, and the botulinum toxoid. On December 31, DoD and FDA officials agreed that the botulism vaccine would be administered by trained individuals with a health care background, and that the inoculated soldiers would be briefed orally at a minimum, and if feasible in writing. DoD pointed out that this information sheet would not be available to all troops, depending on where in the theater of operations they were; but at the least, the soldiers would receive a verbal brief. The FDA granted the informed consent waiver, concurring that obtaining the informed consent during wartime was not feasible in a specific military operation involving combat, and that it appeared there were no other medical alternatives to PB tablets or botulinum vaccine. Time was running out—if Saddam was planning to launch BW-armed Scuds, the coalition needed time to distribute the vaccines and begin the inoculations.

The House of Representatives held hearings within the Armed Services Committee on December 10, 1990, to discuss the "Crisis in the Persian Gulf." The committee heard conflicting views on the potential effectiveness of Iraq's CB arsenal. This began with the CIA assessment from Director Judge William Webster, estimating that Iraqi military forces had a stockpile of at least 1,000 tons of various chemical agents loaded into munitions. Intelligence sources had identified these munitions entering Kuwait, including stockpiles of CW warheads for FROG-7 missiles. General Ed Meyers, former Army Chief of Staff, admitted that chemical defense was one of the major problem areas of the military. Admiral Elmo Zumwalt, former Chief of Naval Operations (once involved in decisions about employing Agent Orange in Vietnam), cautioned the committee to take the threat of CB weapons seriously, given evidence that the Iraqi threat of CB weapons against Tehran had had a significant impact for the ending of the Iran-Iraq War. General George Crist, the former CENTCOM Commander-in-Chief, echoed the assessment of skilled Iraqi chemical warfare operations, adding his opinion that CB warfare should be expected against US troops. Edward Heath, former British prime minister, had met Saddam to arrange for the release of British hostages in Iraq. He recalled the president's determination to use CB weapons if the allied coalition used nuclear weapons against Iraq.

Several other military experts countered these views with far more dismissive attitudes. Colonel (Ret.) Trevor DePuy, a noted military analyst, argued that historically an antagonist armed with chemical weapons had never used them against a force that could retaliate in kind or worse. Colonel Michael Dunn, commander of the Army's MRICD, stressed that the Iranian chemical agent fatalities during the Iran-Iraq War were about 3 percent for mustard gas and 5 percent for nerve gas. His naval medical colleague, Commander Thad Zajdowicz, echoed the assessment that poison gas was not a "particularly effective or efficient way to make war." Julian Perry Robinson, Seth Carus, and Professor Matthew Meselson, all civilian experts in CB warfare, downplayed the effectiveness of the Iraqi stockpile. They felt that given the level of chemical defense equipment and training of the allied coalition, the (relatively) small Iraqi chemical stockpile would be operationally insignificant.

Two other testimonies, given by Brad Roberts and Lieutenant Colonel John Pitman (former division chemical officer, 24th IN DIV), pointed out that no one was considering CB weapons as an overwhelming decisive capability for Iraq; nor was it a war-winning factor against the coalition. These weapons could, however, be used as a force-multiplier during specific military operations. For instance, chemical agents could protect weak flanks of the armies, upset logistical operations in the rear areas (slowing the tempo of combat operations), disrupt assembly areas or planned drop zones for airmobile forces, affect aircraft pilots' vision (by low levels of nerve agent causing miosis over several days), and so on.[2] This would enable temporary tactical advantages to the side using chemical agents, allowing attackers to overwhelm disorganized defenders fumbling around in their protective clothing. Using chemical weapons in conjunction with other conventional weapon systems was a lesson the Iraqis had learned in their struggles against the Iranians.

Notably absent from the train of experts invited to the Congress were the many former Chemical Corps chiefs of latter years, such as Major General (Ret.) John Stoner, Major General (Ret.) Jack Appel, Major General (Ret.) Pete Olenchuck, Major General (Ret.) Jim Klugh, Brigadier General (Ret.) Pete Hidalgo or chemical general officers still on active duty (Generals Gerry Watson, Walt Busbee, and Bob Orton). In part, this may have been due to Congress's exposure to senior chemical officers testifying in the 1950s and 1960s on issues such as the potentially devastating effects of NBC warfare, the military's need for chemical binary weapons, and the public concern over the chemical demilitarization program. As a result of the overselling of the need for a Chemical Corps in the past, no one in Congress (except for a select few) believed these general officers would be able to express their expert opinions without personal bias.

MORE CHEMICAL DEFENSE EQUIPMENT ARRIVES

The Marine Corps decided to purchase a number of ETGI's Individual Chemical Agent Detectors (ICADs) to offset shortages of M8A1 chemical agent detectors. These small, cigarette pack-sized individual alarms allowed Marines more freedom of movement, but possibly less warning time, thus representing a higher chemical agent casualty risk in favor of increased operational capability. Congress questioned why the Army had not invested in the ICAD program, which appeared on the surface like a good idea, a low-unit cost, lightweight chemical agent detector. Rather than try to explain the Army's concerns that the ICAD was a high-risk detector prone to false alarms, ODCSOPS ordered one thousand for ARCENT forces.[3]

The Canadian CAMs were distributed as planned in December 1990. There would never be enough CAMs to go to every line company, as had been intended. In fact, the 500 CAMs had to be split among the four services (despite their previously expressed disinterest in the CAM). The immediate scheme of issue gave medical units and decontamination companies the first priority for CAMs, which pretty much consumed the Army's share in a very short period of time. The Chemical School sent over a CAM new equipment training team from December 11 to January 15; it trained 670 operators in all four services. All units were running short of the unique lithium batteries required to power the CAMs. This was in part due to attempts to convert them to automatic chemical agent detectors by jamming on the power switch, and in part due to using the same battery for the hand-held Global Positioning Systems that proved so valuable in the desert. Complicating the issue was the fact that the Canadian and British CAM loan did not include lithium batteries. Because US industry was unable to "ramp up" the production of the expensive and complex lithium batteries quickly, CRDEC developed an alternative battery pack for training, using D-cell sized alkaline batteries. These would not last as long, but could somewhat alleviate the units' shortages. Two thousand battery packs were shipped by the end of December, with another 3,000 on the way in January and February.

The issue of maintaining what was already a small stock of protective masks kept chemical soldiers busy inspecting their units' masks. Ever since the XVIII ABN Corps had requested maintenance support on the heat stress problems of the M24/25 masks (and related issues for the M17 masks), Pine Bluff had been accelerating its efforts to repair and rebuild all the masks it could. VII Corps had a requirement for 5,000 masks, yet came into the theater with less than two hundred masks in reserve. Representatives from both corps NBCCs met with representatives of CRDEC, AMCCOM, Depot Support Command, and Pine Bluff to discuss requirements for repairing and supplying protective masks. Pine Bluff officials observed early on that it would be more cost-effective to check and repair the masks in theater than to ship them back to CONUS (given that most masks needed only minor repairs). There had been no opportunity to create this capability until HQ AMC established on November 17 the US Army Support Group-Forward (USASG) in Dhahran, Saudi Arabia, to keep up with the constant demand for logistical support for all Army equipment. A group of Pine Bluff Arsenal technicians volunteered to join the USASG. They packed and palletized their test equipment and repair parts, shipped the equipment to Dhahran, and were operational by December 10.

The original intent of the Mask Maintenance Facility was to inspect, repair and test theater M17-series masks assets turned in as unserviceable by the units. Upon successfully repair and tests, the facility would return them to theater stocks for reissuing. This would entail about an eight-day turnaround on most masks. It was not originally meant as a casual "drop-in" service shop for passing soldiers. While this facility did provide some immediate relief to the mask shortage, walk-ins increased through December and into 1991. The problem was that soldiers wanting to have their masks inspected had not allowed their units' chemical officers and NCOs to inspect them first. Many of the masks were rigorously challenged at the Mask Facility, as the Pine Bluff Arsenal personnel held the inspected masks against new inventory acceptance standards. During the first three days of operation, 160

M17-series masks were tested. More than 40 percent failed standard quality assurance tests, most problems centering on the voicemeter assembly or one of its subcomponents, which a soldier's unit NBC or supply NCO might have been able to fix at their level. As more soldiers heard of the high number of "rejects" by word-of-mouth, the number of walk-ins increased, as many soldiers questioned their masks' fitness. None of these masks were shipped back to Pine Bluff Arsenal, which meant that these rejects would shorten the already low supply. The facility's intentions were good, but it was sending the wrong message to the soldiers.

In response to the increased concerns, CRDEC released a number of protective mask fit validation systems (PMFVS), the XM41, a spinoff of a commercial mask testing device. The PMFVS compared the pressure inside and outside the mask through a series of tubes, electronically compared the two, and digitally displayed a confidence factor that would judge the mask's fit on an individual. The Marine Corps and Army were both very interested in this system and purchased 128 PMFVSs starting in late November to test soldiers' masks prior to their deployment. Teams deployed to the division deployment sites in the US and in Europe to test and validate hard-to-fit individuals. The PMFVS teams deployed to the USASG mask maintenance facility in December to augment their staff. The personnel who could not use an M17 mask were fitted with one of the 426 M40 masks available; if that didn't work, they didn't deploy.[4]

CHEMICAL DEFENSE UNIT PREPARATIONS

The 2d Chemical Battalion held a smoke demonstration at King Fahd International Airfield (KFIA) on December 13–15. CENTAF had always been concerned about the chance that an Iraqi air attack might sneak in with CB munitions. The AirBase Operations office at Eglin AFB suggested using fixed smoke generators to obscure the airport; they would act as a survivability countermeasure to keep Iraqi pilots from acquiring and hitting targets with chemical (and conventional) munitions. The 2d Chemical Battalion controlled the 761st and 59th Chemical company's smoke generator platoons to generate both a covering smoke haze over the airfield and a smoke curtain before the airfield. Seventy-two smoke generators gushed thick white smoke from thirty-six High Mobility Multi-purpose Wheeled Vehicles (HMMWVs). Smoke screens, rolling horizontally over the ground, would work best early in the morning or late in the evening, while smoke curtains, rising vertically from the generators, would be better in the midday heat.

CENTAF tested the smoke screens with A-10 aircraft from the 354th Tactical Fighter Wing acting as the Iraqi air force. The smoke generator platoons had fifteen minutes warning to make smoke. On the first morning run, the A-10s found that was the only thing that their weapon systems would lock onto was the control tower, jutting out of an immense sea of white smoke. On the second run, the low-flying A-10s came up against the smoke curtain, which was located just before the pilots' munitions release point. The A-10s had to climb to get over the curtain (not knowing what was on the other side) and ran directly into the sights of an air defense Stinger missile team. The one-to-two-second disruption gave the Stinger teams time to lock on and "kill" the attacking A-10s before they could lock onto the airfield targets. The smoke demonstration worked so well that the 59th Chemical Company had to leave its smoke platoon in place at the airfield for the air war's duration.

Colonel Bob Thornton arrived at VII Corps HQ early in December to assume the corps chemical officer position, having been heavily involved in the Chemical School's preparations for the military operations between August and November. The VII Corps NBCC deployed to Saudi Arabia on December 18, after the 2d ACR had arrived and the VII Corps COSCOM was unloading.[5] Along with the COSCOM came the 51st and 11th Chemical companies, which had originally been designated to arrive earlier in XVIII ABN Corps's deployment. VII Corps would have immediate reconnaissance and decontamination support for its deploying forces, which were very vulnerable as they arrived at the jam-packed ports and airfields.

Decontamination units no longer held the urgent priority that they had had in August. Now the Army needed smoke generators to cover the breaching of the berms and minefields. ODCSOPS called on three mechanized smoke generator units to provide front cover for the armored and mechanized divisions that would lead VII Corps into Iraq. ODCSOPS tagged the 46th Chemical Company from Fort Hood, the 84th Chemical Company from Fort Polk, and the 172d Chemical Company from Fort Carson to mobilize and support smoke operations in Southwest Asia. They were scheduled to arrive by the end of January. These smoke generator units would require a substantial amount of fog oil, having one-third more capacity than the HMMWV versions. Obtaining fog oil for the smoke generators was one of the few materiel success stories of the Chemical Corps. Military supplies of fog oil were delivered in fifty-five-gallon drums, and because no other military unit within CENTCOM required fog oil, divisions were not used to procuring and prepositioning large quantities of it. The Saudi government could supply petroleum products in huge quantities, and there would be no difficulty in supplying smoke generator units with all the fog oil they could haul. Local procurement of fog oil began on December 18.[6]

Saudi Arabia had formally invited Czechoslovakia to send the previously mentioned "anti-chemical" detection unit on November 7. Its deployment of sixty-one vehicles and 170 personnel began on December 11 with the assistance of US military transport in Germany. The Czech detection unit, as noted, would be stationed in CENTCOM's rear support area (around KKMC) about 160 kilometers from the Iraqi border.[7] By December 14, it was in-theater, setting up shop. The Saudi government positioned one platoon at KKMC, one at the Saudi Army's field hospital near Hafar al-Batin, and one each with the Saudi 20th Mechanized Brigade and 4th Mechanized Brigade. Each platoon carried an AL-1 Mobile Laboratory, three ARS-12M decontamination vehicles, and one UAZ-469 NBC recon jeep.[8]

As the CENTCOM force doubled in size, managing the logistics became twice the headache. Unit requisitions and supplies became misplaced or lost, or were given to the wrong units in the constant loading and unloading of ships and planes. Often, if a unit received supplies that did not belong to it, its logistics cell would hoard the CB defense supplies rather than returning them to the already overburdened supply channels. This resulted in the original unit sending another requisition to AMCCOM, and another shipment being shipped out. This congestion of supplies severely taxed CB defense logistics, since there was a shortage of items in the first place. VII Corps did not have the luxury of making local purchases to augment their CB defense supplies; the local supplies of HTH bleach, for instance, had long been depleted by XVIII ABN Corps. There were several orders for drums of HTH due in over the next few months. At least the mechanized nature of VII Corps meant that it did not require the use of local water haulers, also all taken by XVIII ABN Corps.

Just after Christmas a special Fox briefing was given to the division and corps commanders during an operation plan update. The two corps agreed to transfer the two borrowed VII Corps platoons back to their original units after the New Year, equalizing the distribution of Fox assets at three platoons each (with the 3rd ACR returning to Saudi Arabia on December 27–28), but depriving the 24th IN DIV and 1st CAV DIV of their assets. Of the remaining twenty-five vehicles, the Marines would take ten, leaving fifteen for the Army. ARCENT had evaluated the proposed two-corps attack plan with the intent of evaluating the CBW threat and deciding which units would benefit the most by adding Foxes to their chemical companies. Their proposal was to equip the incoming 1st IN DIV with one platoon and use the second platoon for ARCENT rear area reconnaissance, leaving three for floats. ARCENT's staff argued that if the theater rear area were attacked with persistent chemical agents, the results would impact on both corps' sustainment and operational tempo. As a result, the 490th Chemical Battalion would man the last Fox platoon under ARCENT Support Command. This would leave a total of four Foxes as theater floats.

Other options were to field the second platoon to either the 24th IN or the 1st CAV DIVs. The 24th IN DIV claimed that its soldiers had worked closely with its attached Fox platoon. While their chemical company had not deployed their recon platoon to Sonthofen for formal training, they had acquired adequate "on-the-job" training to operate their own Fox platoon. Giving the 24th IN DIV an organic Fox platoon would have freed the 5/25th Recon Platoon to protect the XVIII ABN Corps's vulnerable rear area. If the XVIII ABN Corps did not receive the additional Fox platoon, it would have to decide whether the 5/25th would support the 24th IN DIV, the rear area, or both. Major General McCaffrey asked for a waiver to allow his division to receive the Foxes without training.

As for the 1st CAV DIV, it had become the theater reserve for the ground offensive. Because the 1st CAV DIV would have a prominent role in feinting up the Wadi al-Batin and might be called on to counterattack the Republican Guards, there was an argument that they should get a Fox platoon (either from XVIII ABN

Corps or ARCENT's second platoon option). These Foxes would help the two combat brigades negotiate their way through chemically contaminated areas much faster than the M113 APCs currently in the 68th Chemical Company's recon platoon. Both the ARCENT G-3 and Lieutenant General Gary Luck, XVIII ABN Corps commander, disagreed with giving up one of XVIII ABN Corps' Fox platoons. They argued that the Foxes should not serve in a reserve role but rather be in general or direct support of front line units (similar to the use of artillery). In addition, the 1st CAV DIV's chemical company had never received the Fox recon training nor had they the benefit of Chemical School trainers and would not have been able to operate and maintain the new systems properly.

General Schwarzkopf sided with ARCENT's recommendation, stressing the need for school-trained chemical recon platoons. The division and corps commanders discussed the allied nations' needs for reconnaissance vehicles. The British force had eleven Foxes, eight of which were outfitted for NBC recon, and three for electronic warfare. The French and Arab forces had decontamination assets but no NBC recon vehicles. One section of the 82d ABN DIV's Fox platoon (now the 92d Chemical Company recon platoon) would be under the operational control of the French division (as would one brigade from the 82d) as of February 16, through the initial ground offensive. CENTCOM considered giving two Foxes to the Egyptian forces next to the Marine divisions, but no division commander felt comfortable giving these assets up. It was decided that if chemical agents were used against the Arab military forces, the nearest Fox platoon to the area would assist them in marking the contaminated areas.

These discussions demonstrated the blind faith and lack of understanding by the senior leadership regarding the role of NBC reconnaissance systems. These commanders saw the XM93 NBCRS as a lucky charm against chemical contamination, rather than realizing that their predecessors, the M113-equipped chemical recon platoons, had the same essential capabilities with trained chemical soldiers and tested equipment (albeit in a slower-moving package). While the XM93 NBCRS had several important features that made it superior to the M113, commanders overemphasized the system's potential and ignored the lack of crew experience operating and maintaining the NBCRS. They wanted the latest, state-of-the-art system to minimize the effects of CB munitions against their operations, and who could blame them?

After Christmas, the 2d Chemical Battalion staff worked with the two corps to identify ways to support the planned movement west. The commander's intent was to hold the enemy's attention to the area of the Wadi al-Batin and eastward while the forces moved west. A ground maneuver force from the 1st IN DIV, mixed liberally with realistic tank and APC decoys, would move near the front lines east of the wadi. The 59th Chemical Company would provide large-area smoke to cover the force and decoys, confusing the real size and location of the force. Their deception operation would begin between January 5 and 10 and continue until the XVIII ABN Corps had enough time to move safely past the wadi.

As the end of the year approached, all the services continued high-level defense exercises. ARCENT's divisions conducted large-scale decontamination exercises, mass chemical agent casualty exercises, and the command post exercises. CENTAF tested disaster preparedness plans at its air bases, and readied its decontamination equipment. NAVCENT exercised its chemical agent casualty handling process through the two medical ships, and practiced decontamination training in shipboard and in the ports. The Marines conducted a division-wide decontamination exercise to assess the effects of a large-scale CB agent attack and their ability to defend against it. SOCCENT prepared its teams to hunt for chemical and biological weapons bunkers and the mobile Scud delivery systems hidden in the Iraqi desert.[9]

INTO THE NEW YEAR—PREPARATIONS MOUNT

The vaccination teams arrived in the Gulf on January 2, followed closely by the advance liaison for the Biological Detection Teams. CPTs Plume and Minor arrived in Dhahran on January 3 with XM2 samplers and a meteorological sensor, ready to set up operations and test their equipment. One of their primary goals was to establish background readings prior to employing the biodetectors. After getting established in the theater, the biodetection teams found that they had to rent vehicles to get around. Auto rental prices had skyrocketed, but they were able to rent a number of British Land Rovers to augment their transportation. The Army's 966th Medical Laboratory established its forward base at KKMC, bringing advanced laboratory equipment and supplies for the Naval Forward Laboratory and for the KKMC site.

When Lieutenant General Calvin Waller, Deputy CINC for CENTCOM, was briefed on the final biological defense concept on January 10, he formally approved deployment of the point detection systems. The stand-off biological detection systems would not be deployed. The SRI ground infrared stand-off system had failed its testing at Yuma and Dugway, and it was scrapped. The LANL aerial laser stand-off system was ready to be mounted on a C130 aircraft and deployed to Saudi Arabia, but there was a concern about the availability of hanger space there. Due to the crowded airfields throughout the theater, General Schwarzkopf had laid down the law on any additional planes due in after January 1. If the aerial stand-off system was to enter the theater, CENTCOM had to make room for two fixed-wing aircraft and one helicopter to support the system. Unwilling to give up any aircraft spaces prior to the air offensive, Lieutenant General Waller refused the stand-off system, preferring to rely solely on the point biodetectors.[10]

Some military and civilian personnel in CONUS fought that decision into mid-February, stressing the need to deliver anything that might aid the biodetection effort. However, one aerial stand-off system would only cover a very small area of the overall theater, and definitely could not stay airborne continuously. Combined with its inability to positively identify suspected biological agent clouds, the eye-laser hazard out to ten kilometers, and the lack of tested doctrine, it was better left behind.

The first thirty soldiers from Fort Lewis arrived at CRDEC on January 15 to initiate their training on XM2 samplers and XM21 RSCAALs. The remaining soldiers would arrive four days later to train on the PM10 samplers. All would have less than two weeks training prior to deploying to the desert, becoming the only force that could positively indicate to CENTCOM headquarters whether the force was under biological agent attack or not.

As the orders to move west arrived, the 2d Chemical Battalion received orders to switch its support to VII Corps (as the main effort) effective 10 January. Several other chemical units arrived in January, adding to the strength of the force. The 457th Chemical Battalion would support XVIII ABN Corps, taking the 59th Chemical Company (after the deception operation was executed), the 327th and 340th Chemical companies under its control. The 413th Chemical Company joined the 490th Chemical Battalion, while the 323rd Chemical Company reported to 2d Chemical Battalion upon its arrival.

The order moving the 2d Chemical Battalion to VII Corps also initiated the return of two VII Corps recon platoons to their original parent companies. All the Fox platoons commenced to play "musical chairs" as they rotated to new commands. The Foxes in 1st CAV DIV returned to the 22d Chemical Company in 3rd AR DIV (due to the 3rd AR DIV's expected arrival in theater). The 24th IN DIV gave up the 5/69th Recon Platoon to its original division, the 1st AR DIV. The 5/25th Recon Platoon rotated from the 2d Chemical Battalion to the 24th IN DIV. The 101st ABN DIV transferred the 7/92d Recon Platoon to the 82d ABN DIV. The 101st would have no replacement, given its planned air assault mission, but would retain the 761st Chemical Company (Smoke/Decon). The remaining twenty-five Foxes earmarked for CENTCOM had not yet arrived. With the British, Israeli and Turkish armies and the Marine Corps all demanding their Foxes, Thyssen-Henschel had a very busy month.

Serious logistics issues still remained on the eve of the air war. The Mask Maintenance Facility had the entire theater stockage at Dhahran, 2,000 M17A2 masks. In the forward logistics bases of VII Corps 800 kilometers away, the entire corps stock consisted of 147 M17 masks. This would maintain the normal wear and tear of combat, but would quickly be consumed if chemical warfare broke out. XVIII ABN Corps was not much better off in its mask status. Both corps had a zero balance of extra M256A1 detector kits and had just received the British CAMs. XVIII ABN Corps received 260 CAMs, while VII Corps received the balance of the 500-CAM order. As it appeared, each combat division would have less than fifty CAMs each, with six detectors given to each brigade. The medics and decontamination companies would have a few extra CAMs, given their potentially larger exposure to chemical agents.

New BDOs began arriving as the four new suit contractors delivered the first 8,000 of their emergency contract. Roughly 100,000 protective suits had been delivered over the past six months under the old contract (in place before the war), which helped divisions to start reaching for the recommended goal of three protective suits per soldier. It appeared feasible that at least two suits would be available to each soldier in CENTCOM, and five suits for each decon company soldier. The Marine Corps was still unsatisfied with the shortfall of BDOs and ordered an additional 135,000 lightweight Saratoga suits from a US clothing producer. These were not due to be delivered before March 1991.[11] The Marine Corps also finalized a procurement contract for 100 M21 RSCAALs from Brunswick in January (none of which would be delivered before the ground offensive).

By the end of January, one thousand M17 SANATORs would be in the Gulf—one-third distributed to Marine Corps units, and two-thirds sent to the Army's two corps. Air Force and Navy facilities units continued to rely on the larger (and older) M12A1 decontamination apparatus as did many Army units; but M12A1 decon systems were increasingly breaking down due to the heat, and spare parts were not readily available for the ancient system. The M17 SANATORs would ease the challenge of having to maintain the M12A1s. DS-2 decontamination solvent eventually became plentiful, and thousands of gallons were stockpiled in the Gulf. The German government made another equipment gift, this time of 150 Kärcher decontamination apparatuses that closely resembled the M17 SANATOR. Half of these went to VII Corps, and half went to XVIII Corps. When Army units discovered that the M1 CAM gave a false alarm when used near the M258A1 or M290 decon kits, the Medical Research and Development Command released its M291 personal decon kit for production. Many of these kits (but not enough) were in the Gulf in time for the beginning of ground combat. The Navy complained of another problem with the CAM—it was false-alarming due to the organic compounds in the fire-fighting foam aboard the ships. It continued to ask for the CAMs, however, to allow a detection capability for their port facilities.

Military and political leaders still had concerns over bombing the biological and chemical weapons production sites. While DIA suspected that Iraq's last major chemical agent production run had ended in October, there was evidence of increased activities in mid-December through mid-January. Late that month, trucks carrying suspected Scud warheads were observed entering and leaving the Muthanna facility, whose activity had increased significantly. This might confirm both the existence of Scud chemical warheads and a continued weaponization program. These sites had to be hit soon to knock out Iraq's production capability, but predictions of possible contamination were still sketchy.

DNA had successfully developed ANBACIS-II into a highly sophisticated contamination prediction package by January 1991. It detailed weapon effects with a real-time satellite weather input and digital raster maps, together with a user-friendly, interactive graphical interface. Given the appropriate weapon data and release height, it could draw a map overlay contour with different agent dosage levels. By incorporating the ANBACIS-II software into Crays, DNA teams could develop a contamination footprint inside of three minutes. In addition, for a given map scale (from 1:50,000 to 1:2,000,000), the program could automatically adjust the contamination prediction. The target analyst could then print the footprint on a transparency, place it on the appropriate map, copy the two together, and end up with a complete contamination prediction, ready for transmission. The only drawback was that the model could not determine the effects of terrain on the CB agent cloud, resulting in flat-earth predictions; this would not become a critical issue in the desert, but it meant the predictions would not be 100% accurate.

Since the ANBACIS-II system relied upon the DNA Crays for computational power, Major General Watson devised an operational plan for the NBCCs to use their resources from Southwest Asia. He purchased twenty-one STU-III phones and facsimile machines, and proposed to set these up at the CENTCOM HQ, ARCENT main and alternative HQs, and corps and division HQs. When the NBCC reported an NBC attack, they would fax the information to the waiting DNA teams in their Ops Center. The team would develop the information, copy the map, and fax a complete contamination prediction directly to the requester within ten minutes, worst case. Because the analysts had pre-determined 11,000 footprints of various weapons releasing either chemical or biological agents, the actual time of the analysis could be cut down even further. The DNA Operations Center would run three shifts of operators twenty-four hours a day, with a minimum of six computer operators available on each shift to conduct multi-tasking, simultaneous calculations as needed. They would use ten Sun computers interfaced with the Crays.

DNA displayed their capability to the CENTCOM J-3 on January 11. The only catch was that Major General Moore, CENTCOM's J-3 operations officer, did not think CENTCOM needed the ANBACIS-II system. The Air Force was completely comfortable in manually charting contamination predictions, by the official but "safe-sided" Allied Technical Publication-45 prediction method. On the other hand, many people inside and outside Southwest Asia were questioning exactly how far would CB agents travel downwind if a CBW production facility blew up; they did not trust these hand calculations after seeing the potential of a more accurate ANBACIS-II plot. CENTCOM NBCC and DNA's Operations Center assisted Air Force planners by providing advice on the potential for bombing missions on all of the CBW production and storage sites creating a downwind collateral CB agent hazard.[12]

The British Ministry of Defense and the US DoD both publicly announced the beginning of the biological vaccine program at the end of December. Only 8,000 individuals could receive the botulin toxin vaccine. The anthrax vaccine situation was similarly perilous: because of the limited supply and inability to find additional sources of vaccine, only 150,000 military personnel in the Gulf would receive this vaccine. If it had had until May 1991, the entire US force would be protected, but time had run out. The question was, which part of the theater would be protected?

CENTCOM had to decide whom to vaccinate, as Washington officials did not want to make the call. War game studies postulated a special forces/terrorist attack with biological agents in Riyadh and Dhahran, while others thought the front lines the obvious target. CENTCOM staff recommended that the special operations forces, the armored units that would lead the assault, and the important rear area targets (such as the CENTCOM headquarters staff) should receive the vaccines.

This decision became a very serious and stressful one for the division commanders. No one wanted to choose who should and who should not receive the vaccines. Who was to say who the more critical individuals truly were? The final decision for the anthrax vaccinations would be to prioritize the areas at risk, starting with Riyadh, Dhahran, and Bahrain, where the most critical command and communications and supply bases lay. KKMC and the major logistics bases (Alpha through Echo) were next, followed by HQ VII Corps, HQ XVIII ABN Corps, and 1st CAV DIV (in order of mission priority). Major General Binford Peay, commander of the 101st ABN DIV, later told Colonel Read that the decision to use this limited amount of vaccine was one of the greatest mistakes of the war. In his view, there should have been enough vaccines for everyone or for no one, sharing an equal risk among all troops. Lieutenant General Franks and other commanders shared this view as well.

Now that the medical community was free to implement its vaccination plans, the anthrax vaccinations began, starting on January 5. By January 13, half of all forces received their first anthrax vaccine shots. Each soldier was to read a statement detailing the purpose of the vaccinations, warning them that the fact that they were receiving the shots was classified *SECRET*. While some would later interpret this as covering up experimental vaccine testing on troops, the true intent of the classification was to conceal the extent of the vaccination program from Iraqi intelligence sources.

The safety test on the botulinum vaccine was still not completed, however. The FDA would not complete the tests until January 24, 1991, nearly a week after the air campaign had begun. While it was known that the vaccines were in short supply, both the US and British defense departments refused to detail publicly how much they had or who would be receiving the vaccines. The PB tablets received FDA approval on January 8. All military individuals in the Gulf, and also government civilians and even news media crews, began receiving the PB tablets before the air war began.[13]

BATTLE PLANS FINALIZE

The Operation Desert Storm operations order was published on January 13. It made several assumptions about Iraqi CB weapons employment. The Marine Corps divisions would initiate the assault at 0400 hours local time, attacking into Kuwait. The Tiger Brigade would hold the left flank of the 2d Marine Division (MARDIV), with the 1st MARDIV on the right flank. Their objectives were to hold down the Iraqi divisions within Kuwait and keep the attention of the

Republican Guards on the first day of battle. Since their M60A3s could not use the mine plows designed for the M1 tanks, they would have a more difficult time penetrating the minefields. This would make the Marines prime targets for chemical munitions effects. The Marines counted on the Army MLRS battery and air support to suppress any artillery fire during the mine-clearing operation. Their Foxes would mark contaminated areas to allow the following troops to avoid most of the hazard. As the Tiger Brigade moved to replace the British 7th AR BDE as the Marine Corps heavy armor attachment, it brought along one decon platoon of the 44th Chemical Company.

The XVIII ABN Corps would initiate its attack at 0538 hours, just as the night began yielding to the dawn. The French 6th AR DIV had the main air base near as-Salman as an immediate objective (Objective White, or Rochambeau to the French). Although there were no air units there, it had been identified as a potential mobile Scud firing site, and intelligence was calling it a major chemical weapons stockpile. This airfield had been a major concern throughout the war as an arming point from which Iraqi planes could hit KKMC. The 101st ABN DIV would conduct the largest airmobile operation in history, leapfrogging forward to Cobra Base and onward to the Euphrates. This would seal off reinforcements and supplies from Kuwait. The 761st Chemical Company would join them to compensate for their lost recon assets. The 24th IN DIV had several objectives in and around an-Nasariyah, including several suspected CB munitions stockpiles. Its intermediate objective was to take the ground around the Iraqi 26th Division (Objective Grey), which was suspected of holding a chemical stockpile. The final objectives included Tallil and Jalibah air bases, which military intelligence had identified as significant chemical stockpiles. Because of the increased chance that 24th IN DIV units would cross chemically contaminated areas, it received the 327th Chemical Company for direct support, and an additional decon platoon from the corps's 101st Chemical Company for its DISCOM. 3rd ACR would protect the right flank of the corps and conduct chemical reconnaissance along with its screening mission.

While the French expected the possibility of a chemical attack at as-Salman, Major General McCaffrey was convinced that his division could be attacked several times with chemical munitions. When his division hit the Euphrates valley, it would threaten the Iraqi army's main supply route to Baghdad. It would be within range of several Iraqi helicopter landing pads and other air fields, all of which could deploy Iraqi helicopters and aircraft with chemical weapons. He and his division chemical officer, Lieutenant Colonel Schubert, concluded that it would be counterproductive to dwell on the threat. They knew their soldiers had the capability to protect themselves and that at some point they might be called upon to use that defensive capability. There was not much they could do about it other than trust in their soldiers' training and defensive equipment. Of all the CENTCOM divisions, McCaffrey's troops were perhaps the best trained and prepared for the potential chemical attacks.

VII Corps would initiate the breach operations (the XVIII ABN Corps area of operation was beyond the border berm obstacles) at 0538 hours. The 1st IN DIV would break and penetrate the berm on the right flank, allowing the British 1st AR DIV to pass through it and protect the right flank of the corps. One hour later, the 2d ACR would breach the berm on the left flank, followed by 1st AR DIV and 3rd AR DIV. Once they secured their immediate security area past the berm, they would pause to allow the "wheel" to develop prior to continuing the attack the next day. This was the most vulnerable point of the offensive. If the Iraqis reacted quickly enough, they could catch the 1st IN DIV and 2d ACR in the middle of their berm breaching operations, and attempt to slow VII Corps down with a chemical attack. If there was one thing the Iraqis knew how to do well, it was slowing down an enemy offensive with chemical munitions.

Two scenarios were envisioned. First, the Iraqis might react to the breach by a local counterattack against the VII Corps while it was passing through the berms at the fourth hour of the attack. This would include coordinated nerve or mustard agent attacks with artillery, Scuds, and aircraft. Based on computer war gaming, this might slow the VII Corps attack by as much as thirteen to eighteen hours. This would allow time for the Republican Guards either to assault the vulnerable flanks of the Marine divisions or attempt to position themselves to seal the breach. The other scenario envisioned a larger last-ditch Iraqi counterattack between twenty-four and thirty-six hours after the breach. Then the Republican Guards, as the theater strategic reserve, might reorient themselves against the western attacks and employ persistent chemical attacks to halt the coalition's advance. The first scenario seemed the more likely.

The 1st CAV DIV, with its two combat brigades, would act as the CENTCOM theater reserve. It would remain near the Wadi al-Batin to keep Iraqi forces concerned about an attack up the wadi into the Republican Guards (where the Iraqis expected the main attack) and then commit to either VII Corps or the MARCENT effort, on CENTCOM's call. To keep the Iraqi military's attention, the 1st CAV DIV would feint at the wadi's defenders. While the 1st CAV DIV did not expect to be a primary target of initial chemical weapons attacks, to be an effective counterattack force it required the capability to maneuver through wide contamination areas created by Iraqi artillery, aircraft and Scuds. The 44th Chemical Company headquarters, one decon platoon and one smoke platoon remained with the 1st CAV DIV, as well as its own 68th Chemical Company.

To support the operations plan, ARCENT moved the 2d Chemical Battalion to support VII Corps, as the main effort, and attached two mechanized smoke companies to the battalion to aid in the breaching. For the breach itself, the 2d Chemical Battalion would operate directly in support of 1st IN DIV. The 457th Chemical Battalion would support XVIII ABN Corps largely by protecting the rear logistics supply dumps and supply routes that would lead into Iraq. The 490th Chemical Battalion would continue protecting ARCENT's rear area and would borrow the ARCENT maintenance float Foxes to provide a limited reconnaissance capability.[14] The 457th was at a disadvantage compared to the other two battalions, having just arrived in the first week of January. While both the 2d and 490th Chemical Battalion had had several months to settle into the theater, the 457th would have to adjust very quickly prior to the ground offensive. Fortunately, the 59th Chemical Company, as one of its attached units, would help the battalion staff adjust to the theater's administrative and logistics procedures.[15] Each chemical battalion would have at least one reserve decon company for general support in its respective corps rear area; the 490th Chemical Battalion had three decon companies for its larger mission of theater rear area support (see appendix A). All decon companies coordinated with engineers to dig sumps for the thorough decontamination sites envisioned ahead.

Because CENTCOM and ARCENT NBCCs were more focused on supporting battle plans, the logistics flow of chemical defense equipment (especially Foxes and protective clothing), and chemical soldier personnel shortages, they could not directly support the changing task organizations. The arrival of the additional reserve chemical decon companies and staff detachments to support VII Corps caused real confusion at the division and corps as to what chemical defense units were supporting whose divisions, and what was available for future operations. While serious logistics issues continued to threaten the Army's ability to sustain operations in an NBC-contaminated environment, chemical specialists could see the light at the end of the tunnel. It was beginning to look like CENTCOM would survive a short-term, limited chemical war. Now it was time to see if all the preparations had been time and energy well spent.

The 1980s combat soldier wore a Chemical Protective Overgarment with M9 detection paper circling his arms and one leg, butyl rubber gloves and "fishtail" boots, and the M17A2 protective mask. Courtesy of the U.S. Army

M43A1 Chemical Agent Detector and M42 Alarm with BA-3517 battery (together called the M8A1 Automatic Chemical Agent Alarm) was the world's most sophisticated automatic chemical agent detector in the field in the mid-to-late 1980s. Courtesy of the U.S. Army

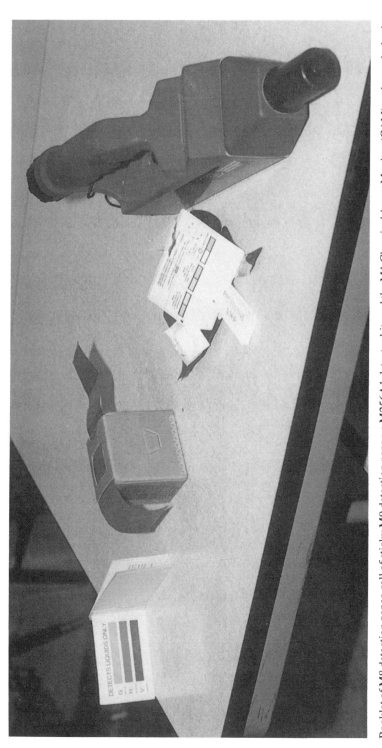

Booklet of M8 detection paper, roll of sticky M9 detection paper, a M256A1 detector kit, and the M1 Chemical Agent Monitor (CAM) make up the basic chemical agent detection tools for the small combat units. Courtesy of the U.S. Army

XM-21 Remote Sensing Chemical Agent Alarm (RSCAAL) detected chemical agent vapors up to five kilometers distant, but weighed nearly fifty pounds and could not detect agents "on the move" mounted on a vehicle. Courtesy of the U.S. Army

A trainee uses an M11 decontaminating apparatus to clean an agent-contaminated M151 jeep in the U.S. Army Chemical School's Chemical Defense Training Facility at Fort McClellan, Alabama. Courtesy of the U.S. Army

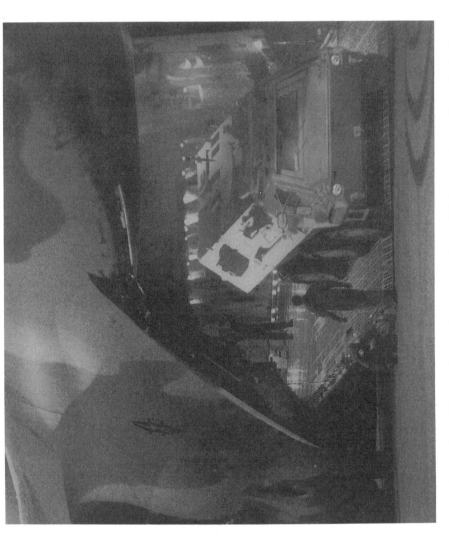

An XM93 "Fox" NBC Reconnaissance System backs into a C5A1 cargo plane at Ramstein Air Force Base, Germany, on its way to Saudi Arabia. Courtesy of the U.S. Army

Soldiers in the 1st Corps Support Command, XVIII Airborne Corps, practice deconning their individual combat gear in a makeshift decontamination line. Courtesy of Major Shirley DeGroot

Then the soldiers in the 1st Corps Support Command strip off their "contaminated" clothing in a personal decon exercise. In an actual decon drill, they would don new protective gear or move out of the contaminated area. Courtesy of Major Shirley DeGroot

XM2/XM19 Biological Detection and Warning System. Each system stands about six feet tall. Courtesy of the U.S. Army

The Army's interim biological agent reconnaissance vehicle for the Gulf War was a leased Isuzu civilian truck with an XM2 Biological Sampler strapped to its hood. Courtesy of the U.S. Army

M1059 mechanized smoke generator system lays down a dense white screen at the National Training Center, Fort Irwin, California. Courtesy of the U.S. Army

Smoke covers King Fahd International Airport, generated by seventy-two smoke generators on thirty-six HMMWVs. Notice the control tower jutting out of the blanket of smoke in the upper left corner. Courtesy of the U.S. Army

2d Chemical Battalion and mechanized smoke generator systems roll into Iraq, supporting VII Corps. Courtesy of Lieutenant Colonel Michael T. Brown

UNSCOM inspector takes a sample from one of Iraq's Scud warheads. Courtesy of the U.S. Army

CHAPTER 6

Operation Desert Storm Begins

> We got a lot of questions about why the Iraqis didn't use chemical weapons, and
> I don't know the answer. But I just thank God that they didn't.
>   —General H. Norman Schwarzkopf, February 27, 1991

United Nations Resolution 678, cast on November 29, 1990, set January 15 as the
deadline for the removal of Iraqi forces out of Kuwait; otherwise the coalition
could use "all necessary means" to oust the Iraqi occupation. Despite several
meetings between UN and Iraqi delegations through December, it appeared that the
Iraqi forces were in Kuwait to stay. Congress finally voted to support the UN
measure on January 12, 1991. CENTCOM forces were not fully ready for NBC
warfare, although individually the troops were as finely honed as they would be.
By this time, CENTCOM had thirty-six Foxes in theater. Although the ANBACIS-
II system had been proven functional, none were set up in the theater to warn
against the threatened attacks. Concerns remained over the shortages of chemical
protective suits and masks in theater stockpiles. There were insufficient stocks for
the thirty days of conflict planned, if CB agent warfare continued throughout the
conflict. Hospitals on land integrated their few collective protection systems into
their unit positions, while the two Navy hospital ships prepared for chemical
casualty treatment.

The political rhetoric increased on all levels to convince Saddam Hussein
against using CB agent munitions. During a visit to the Gulf in December, Defense
Secretary Cheney warned that if Saddam Hussein was "foolish enough to use
weapons of mass destruction, the US response would be absolutely overwhelming
and it would be devastating." White House Chief of Staff John Sununu made clear
that this did not mean retaliation with chemical weapons, contrary to the existing
policy of retaliation in kind. British Prime Minister John Major assured reporters
during a trip to Saudi Arabia on January 6 that the UK would not consider nuclear
weapons in response to Iraqi CW attack: "We have plenty of weapons short of that.
We have no plans of the sort you envisage." In Saudi Arabia, British embassy

officials began distributing protective masks out to British civilians in the area. In Israel, government officials accelerated the distribution of protective masks, atropine kits, and instructions on how to construct temporary collective protection shelters at home.[1] Israeli officials made clear to Washington that they would have to respond to any Iraqi chemical strikes against their cities, and that response would not be limited to conventional arms.

Secretary of State James Baker met with Iraqi Foreign Minister Tariq Aziz in Geneva on January 9 to allow Saddam one more chance to back out of a conflict. Secretary Baker hand-delivered a letter from the president for Saddam Hussein. In the letter, President Bush warned of the consequences of not pulling out of Kuwait and engaging in other unconventional warfare. "Let me state, too, that the United States will not tolerate the use of chemical or biological weapons or the destruction of Kuwait's oil fields and installations. Further, you will be held directly responsible for terrorist actions against any member of the coalition. You and your country will pay a terrible price if you order unconscionable acts of this sort."[2]

The deadline came and passed. At 2230 hours on 16 January (Kuwaiti time), the air phase began as air crews readied their planes for combat operations over Iraq. Tomahawks leapt out of their tubes on Navy warships at 0130 hours. At 0238 hours, Apache helicopters from the 101st ABN DIV destroyed Iraqi early warning radar stations. The strategic air campaign had begun.

PHASE I/II: STRATEGIC AIR CAMPAIGN/KTO AIR SUPREMACY

The final, approved air campaign plan focused on five military objectives. These included isolating and incapacitating the Iraqi regime's leadership and communication systems, gaining and maintaining air supremacy to permit unhindered operations, destroying Iraq's NBC warfare production and storage capability, destroying major parts of key military production and infrastructure, and rendering the Iraqi forces in the KTO ineffective. In the case of Iraq's NBC warfare capabilities, targets included the nuclear research and production facilities and reactors, the biological research and development center at Salman Pak and suspected biological storage sites, the chemical research and development centers at Samarra and chemical storage sites, and operational delivery systems such as Scud launchers and aircraft mounted with spray tanks.[3]

The biological and chemical targets were hit on the first day of bombing, as they were considered more of a threat than the nuclear targets; the coalition hit the nuclear facilities on the second day. Later press releases had revealed that three primary nuclear sites, ten biological sites, and eighteen chemical sites had been attacked. Nuclear targets included the two small reactors at Tuwaitha (including the rebuilt Osirak nuclear facility), a centrifuge production facility at Taji, north of Baghdad, and a nuclear weapons R&D establishment in Iskandariya. The Tuwaitha reactors had been hit by both Air Force fighters and Navy Tomahawk missiles. Two nuclear research sites in the north, one near Mosul, the other near Arbil, were hit later in the month by F-117s and cruise missiles, causing 95 percent destruction of the buildings. A fourth nuclear weapons plant, which processed uranium near al-Qaim, was damaged heavily by missiles and bombs. Biological targets included the main research facility at Salman Pak and support facilities at Samarra, al-Fallujah, Akashat and Badush. Fighter-bombers hit several refrigerated bunkers suspected to be biological weapons storage sites. Chemical targets focused on the major chemical weapons plants located at Samarra, northwest of Baghdad. The Muthanna complex at Samarra was hit by at least sixteen cruise missiles fired by Navy battleships, in addition to follow-up bomb runs by the Air Force. The three Habbaniyah chemical agent precursor facilities at al-Falujah, heavily bombed, were destroyed. Secondary targets included subsidiary facilities such as the ethylene oxide plant near Basrah (used in the production of thiodyglycol, a mustard precursor), two phosphorous production sites at Akashat and Al Qaim, and suspected chemical munitions storage sites.[4]

General Schwarzkopf told reporters that all Iraq's nuclear facilities had been destroyed and that half of the nation's chemical and biological munition production sites either destroyed or heavily damaged. In addition, eleven CB weapon storage sites had been destroyed. "We're going to continue a relentless attack on this very, very, very heinous weapon system," he stated.[5] Allied bombing had wreaked considerable damage: six of the ten buildings at Samarra were destroyed; all the buildings in the three Habbaniyah precursor chemical facilities were seriously damaged; one bunker of the eight targeted was destroyed, while the remaining seven were only superficially damaged; of the twenty-two S-shaped chemical bunkers at thirteen other locations, sixteen bunkers were destroyed, and the rest were seriously damaged.

The four biological agent facilities at Salman Pak, Taji and Abu Ghurayb were attacked on the first day of bombing. Eleven of the thirteen main buildings were destroyed, and the remaining two were severely damaged. All of the nineteen suspected BW storage bunkers were destroyed. In addition, CENTAF targeted the Baghdad power grid. When it was knocked out, the nearby refrigerated bunkers had lost power, and presumably their suspected biological cultures had died. The strikes on the nuclear facilities were reportedly devastating; in General Powell's words, "I think I can confirm for you that the two operating reactors they had are both gone. They're down. They're finished."[6]

The battle damage was not, however, as extensive as CENTCOM's initial assessments had estimated. In truth, only about 60 percent of Iraq's weapons of mass destruction program had been destroyed. The bombings hampered only the production capability, sparing the munitions that had already been manufactured. Later battle-damage assessment (BDA) reports in February brought this fact to light, initiating a second wave of bombing against the NBC warfare sites. In later congressional testimony, Lieutenant General Horner admitted that the seemingly inflated estimates of 75 percent or higher given during the air campaign had represented the assessments on "known" targets.[7] In truth, actual BDA assessments were not available for days later (and in some cases, weeks), and the assessments had been made on percentage of sorties and target hits. After the war, UN inspection teams got a look at the real size of the Iraqi NBC munitions program, much of which was untouched by the air campaign.

Saddam had anticipated the fierce air attack and after the raid on Osirak developed considerable deception capabilities and defensive counters to the coalition's air campaign. The DoD Report to Congress noted that Baghdad was more heavily defended than Murmansk, one of the main ports of the Soviet Navy, with at least twice the defensive density of the most heavily defended targets in Cold War–era Eastern Europe. While the reactors could not be hidden, much of the secondary equipment and research and development was concealed. Much of Iraq's nuclear program was spread across the entire country, including 2,000 foreign-trained scientists, 18,000 Iraqi engineers, a network of Jordanian front companies to procure foreign equipment, and had thirty-nine facilities at nineteen locations. Components of the centrifuges were manufactured at Za' Faraniyah, south of Baghdad, assembled at Tuwaitha and moved to locations in north Iraq. The components for the high-explosive trigger were built and assembled at Al Atheer, a facility that claimed to manufacture composite materials. It was the target of the last bomb dropped by an F-117A1 in the conflict, late in the war. Most of these facilities escaped damage.[8]

Tuwaitha had been especially well protected. As mentioned earlier, it was surrounded by SAM batteries and anti-aircraft guns, as well as protected by sand berms. Several F-117s had bombed the nuclear reactors and laboratory on the first day, but Lieutenant General Horner wanted the installation flattened. A flight of F-16s flew out to level the remaining buildings. As they approached the facility, the Iraqis put out several smoke pots, effectively concealing the buildings from view. The lack of visibility, combined with the anti-aircraft fire and SAMs lofting skyward, prevented the F-16s from bombing the targets without risking collateral damage. CENTAF would have to rely on the Tomahawks and F-117s to knock out Tuwaitha.[9]

The biological R&D center at Salman Pak was hit hard—but not before its valuable equipment had been moved to a complex at Al Hakam, a facility southwest of Baghdad whose cover was research on the production of animal feed. The Iraqis had kept the program safe by arranging equipment and supplies ordered overseas to be delivered to facilities at Taji and Latifiyah, and then moving them to al Hakam. This fooled American intelligence into targeting the facilities at Taji and Latifiyah instead of al Hakam, which remained a secret until the end of the war. This could be one of the reasons the "infant formula factory" at Abu-Ghurayd was bombed early in the air war, without any evidence being found later of biological manufacturing equipment, biological munitions or biological agents. The fighters hit BW support facilities at al Fallujahm, Akashat and Badush. The twenty-one suspected refrigerated bunkers did not hold biological agent munitions; instead, as UN inspectors learned after the war, these air-conditioned bunkers protected conventional munitions and electronics from the desert heat.[10]

The targeting of the Abu-Ghurayd "infant formula factory" had resulted from DIA analysts tracing potential biological warfare agent supplies and equipment sent to the factory over a period of years. Over the previous six months, there had been no milk transport or other commercial activities at this facility, although there had been a large presence of Iraqi military personnel. While this did not confirm it as a biological agent production site, it was enough to put it on the "suspected" list. In December 1990, Iraqi forces began painting a mottled camouflage pattern on two other confirmed biological sites' roofs and applied the same to this factory's roof. This caused analysts to immediately shift the target from "suspected" to "confirmed." This, combined with the presence of military guards at a nearby garrison and a barbed wire fence surrounding the facility, seemed to contradict Iraqi claims that the factory was an innocent non-military target.

Despite these points, this event shook many onlookers in the Arab world as well as in Washington. A French contractor who had built the factory in the 1970s stated that it was constructed as an infant formula factory. It had subsequently closed in 1980 and had just reopened in 1990 due to the UN embargo. Two New Zealand dairy experts who had worked until May 1990 in a cheese-manufacturing building a half mile from the target, also indicated that the plant was innocent. Both their cheese factory and the baby formula factory were enclosed within the industrial park, which included a pharmaceutical plant, a milk sterilization plant and a housing complex. This event, combined with the bombing of a civilian-filled bunker, would result in new orders that air targets in and around Baghdad had to be reviewed and approved by General Powell specifically.[11]

The chemical weapons targets were much more in the open, built on the same design as large manufacturing plants for pesticides and fertilizers, and thus more vulnerable to the bombers and Tomahawk missiles. The main complex at al-Muthanna, near Samarra, had been hit hard, but its heavy equipment had been already dispersed to other locations in the country. The three precursor facilities were put out of operation, but as later inspections would reveal, only two facilities had really been in operation; the munitions themselves had been dispersed to more than twenty locations including storage sites and air bases. The mobile Scuds built at Taji were moved out into the desert as CENTAF attacked the permanent Scud sites in the west. Subsidiary chemical facilities at Basra, al Qaim, Mosul and Akashat were hit. Despite the destruction of 75 percent of the chemical munition manufacturing capability of Iraq, this still left before the ground war 46,000 chemical munitions, 97,000 unfilled munitions, 750 tons of bulk nerve and mustard agents and unknown tons of anthrax and botulinum toxin.[12]

SADDAM'S RESPONSE

Iraq's military countered with salvos from mobile Scuds in the early hours of the second day of the coalition's air campaign. Twenty-eight fixed-launch sites in western Iraq had been knocked out early on the first day, but the mobile Scud teams were trained to "shoot and scoot" from one pre-surveyed launching point to the next. These points allowed the Scud teams to fire their rockets at cities and known target points using map coordinates, without having to verify if a target was there or not. Estimates on the number of mobile launchers averaged approximately thirty-six, twenty-two of which had been bought from the Soviets and the remainder built in Iraq. Contrary to what one might expect in the desert, there were a number of ravines, wadis, and other natural and man-made features which allowed the mobile Scuds to hide between missions. In addition, East German launcher decoys distracted allied planes from the real launchers. As a result, on the morning of January 18, the first of eighty-six Scuds against Israel and Saudi Arabia was launched.

In the first week and a half, Iraq fired twenty-five Scuds against Israel (Tel Aviv and Haifa) and twenty-four against Saudi Arabia (Riyadh and Dhahran). The first eight fired against Israel on that Friday morning (six against Tel Aviv) caused the most concern for the coalition, which feared the threat of Scud-delivered nerve agents. As the warning sirens wailed just after 2:00 a.m., Israeli citizens scrambled to don their protective masks and enter their "safe rooms," sealed against any intrusive chemical vapors with plastic sheets and masking tape. In the United States, as families watched the evening newscasts, moderators interrupted their field correspondents in Tel Aviv to tell them to don their own protective masks, even though the masks muffled their report's on the events.

As the missiles struck, Israeli and US officials immediately began to fear the worst. Reconnaissance teams raced to the impact sites with CAMs and other detection equipment. NBC news correspondents came on-air with the first reports from Israeli police confirming nerve agents, with CBS and CNN adding their reports of suspected nerve agent detection. As more detailed reports came in, it appeared that the CAMs had falsely identified the nitrous acid rocket fuel in the Scuds as nerve agent; further tests from M256A1 kits confirmed that the warheads had actually been conventional high explosives. The news was not enough to save three Israelis who had suffocated in ill-prepared protective masks, or the dozens that fell ill from injecting themselves prematurely with atropine autoinjectors. Ironically, not one death resulted from the Scud warheads.[13]

The second danger arising from the Scud attacks was the Israeli retaliation that Saddam had hoped to provoke. If Israel attacked Iraq, Saddam could hope for sharp dissent among the Arab allies within the coalition. In fact, as the attacks took place, reports of Israeli fighter-bombers on standby and Jericho rockets being prepared for launch soon surfaced. Defensive flights circled Jerusalem, searching for inbound Iraqi fighters. When the first reports of chemical agent from the Scuds came in, White House officials were convinced that the Israelis would retaliate. US officials were able to talk the Israeli government out of a retaliatory attack, promising to deploy two Patriot batteries to Israel.[14]

In the next few days, Scuds flew against Saudi Arabia. Satellite warnings of the launches gave a five-to-eight-minute warning to soldiers and civilians in Riyadh and Dhahran. Patriot batteries had been stationed in Riyadh and Dhahran during the deployment of the American forces. These batteries had been primarily designed for anti-aircraft roles, and secondarily for intercepting a stable ballistic missile warhead reentry. The erratic path of a disintegrating missile and its warhead were hard for the Patriot's radar to lock-on to. This led to operational decisions to err on the side of safety; for instance, on the third night of Scud attacks, thirty-six Patriot PAC-2 missiles rose to meet six incoming Scuds. Contractors from Raytheon continued refining the target acquisition software in an effort to better predict interception patterns. The Pentagon reportedly asked Raytheon to investigate the possibility of putting chemical-neutralizing agents on the Patriot missiles to counteract any chemical agents that might escape from an exploding warhead. There is no evidence that this project came to fruition. Initially, disintegrating Scuds were interpreted as successful Patriot strikes, accounting for claims of a more than 90 percent kill rate. Later studies of the twenty-one Patriot batteries in Saudi Arabia showed that actual confirmed warhead kills might have been as low as 9 percent. Still, it was used, as the Israeli military attaché in Washington stated, not because it was the best weapon against Scuds but because it was the *only* weapon available.[15]

The US military did not react well to the Scud attacks. The two Army corps NBCCs had expected some form of Iraqi retaliation, and warned their corps rear areas to assume MOPP-1 with the beginning of the air war. Since most logistics bases were at known Saudi fixed sites, they could be easily targeted, using a simple map. The forward combat units would not be as vulnerable, since the Iraqis had little intelligence information as to where they were, but most of them assumed MOPP-0. As the Scuds flew, radio messages warned of the launches through the chain of command. Because CENTCOM could not predict exactly where the Scuds were headed and what was their intended target, everyone assumed that their unit was at risk. Practically every soldier in the theater ripped open his or her protective clothing packs and went to MOPP-4, gulping down PB tablets on the way to the trenches. Without any local chemical agent alarms sounding or munitions landing near their locations, soldiers everywhere had masked and suited up, expecting their areas to be hit by chemical agents. It was a massive overreaction that no one had anticipated. Added to the Scud scare, false alarms from individual M8A1 detectors were now causing panicked stampedes for their suits. The next morning, many units realized that their newly opened chemical suits would expire in fourteen to thirty days (depending on which suit one owned—at least a third had been the older CPOGs). This left most individuals with only one suit for future chemical attacks. Commanders immediately reduced the MOPP levels to zero (removing all protective clothing) and told their units to discontinue taking PB tablets.

The big problem was that the supply of suits could not support the anticipated combat usage. Many soldiers thought that since they had opened their suit's protective packaging, they required replacement suits in unopened packages prior to the next Scud attack. In addition to troop requirements, the numerous Third World civilians driving much of the ARCENT's truck fleet deserted, in fear of exposure to chemical attacks. The only way they could be coaxed back was to give all their own chemical protective suit to keep in the truck cab with them. Other Third World nationals, serving as cooks, security guards and other positions soon began eying the US troops' masks slung at their waists. Based on the high use of protective suits during the Scud alerts and calculated projections, CENTCOM would be out of suits by April.

When the logisticians brought up these concerns, CENTCOM NBCC called the Natick labs to find whether these expiration dates were firm and hard, or what level of protection could be expected if the suits were repackaged and resealed to be used again. All the scientists had done previously was guarantee the BDO suits up to twenty-two days, extendable to thirty days; they had no data on when suits would actually expire if unused. The older CPOGs caused more concern, as they were not designed to be extended past fourteen days. These expiration dates were determined based on the concept that soldiers would be constantly moving and fighting, wearing down the suits over that time period through physical wear and tear (not because of expiring charcoal liners). Even if the CPOGs were used past fourteen days, they were certainly still better than a sweat-soaked T-shirt in protecting against chemical agents. A quick review of protective suit qualities seemed to indicate that if the suits were repackaged and not damaged or water-soaked, they might provide the protection against a ten-gram-per-square-meter challenge for a longer period of time than expected. However, no one was willing to swear to exactly how much longer or to what level of protection was provided.

As the soldiers repacked and resealed their protective clothing packs, there was a nagging suspicion in many of their minds that the "studies" were not telling the whole truth. During peacetime training, hadn't chemical officers and NCOs stressed the need to retain fresh suits? Many soldiers suspected that the leadership was fudging the data to cover for the extreme shortages of protective suits. In Major General McCaffrey's words, soldiers half-expected that some magic preserving fluid leaked out if one had torn or punctured the protective suit airtight bags, making the concept of repackaging the suits illusory. The number of walk-ins to the Mask Maintenance Facility in Dhahran soared after the first Scuds fell, as soldiers ran in to confirm their protective mask fits yet again. As later Scuds fell and the chemical agents did not emerge, soldiers gradually relaxed from jumping into MOPP suits every time an alert sounded.

While the Scud attacks alarmed many in the theater, it did have two positive aspects. First, the missiles had been armed with high explosives, not CB agent warheads. Just as with the World War II V-2 rockets, these missiles relied on shock and explosive power for terror and did not disseminate CB agents. Whether or not Saddam was reserving CB warheads for later was unknown. Second, this allowed the divisions to work out several operational issues. This "rehearsal" allowed the divisions to send out chemical recon teams and Fox vehicles to sample for CB agents at impact sites, to practice plotting and communicating predicted contamination hazard areas, to operate chemical agent detectors, to determine how to sleep in protective clothing, and how entry/exit procedures into collective protection shelters should work. This threat also emphasized the need for quick turnaround reports on Scud impact areas and predicted contamination hazard areas.

ARCENT NBCC changed its procedures so as to provide Scud warnings to subordinate units only after the Scud azimuth had been determined, and then only to sectors that were targeted. Cooperation between the ARCENT Air Defense Officer and NBCC would result in a quick report of at what height and what slant angle the Scud exploded, allowing them to identify the target area accurately. The two corps NBCCs designated high-risk areas that would "MOPP up" in the event of future Scud launches. The main and rear headquarters, the Corps Tactical Operations Centers, units in Dhahran, and the main logistics bases would go to MOPP-2 (suits and boots, no masks). No other units would assume MOPP status unless their detectors went off or there were other indications (munition explosions, agent symptoms, etc.). These steps would reduce the number of suits expended. Lieutenant General Franks was unwilling to allow his soldiers to take an unknown risk if there were protective suits available, however. Efforts redoubled to draw protective clothing from Pacific and European war reserves and CONUS stocks. Chemical officers soon were tracking the individual flights bringing protective suits into Dhahran. All Scud intercept areas were scanned by Fox vehicles, in addition to CAMs and M256A1 kits.

The threat of potential CB agent Scud warheads kept strong political pressure on CENTCOM to step up anti-Scud efforts. SOCCENT created a special 877-man Joint Special Operations Task Force of aviation and ground forces, which worked in conjunction with British special operations teams under CENTCOM to hunt Scuds. These teams searched out Scud launchers and called in Air Force support to destroy their targets. The SOCCENT task force claimed a dozen launcher kills; many of these were later found to be decoys. The Air Force responded by diverting resources to Scud-busting and mining suspected access roads of the launchers. Many of the targets attacked by F-15s turned out to be decoys or mistaken targets. Throughout the great Scud-hunt, CENTCOM could not state conclusively that one Scud launcher had been destroyed. The number of launches apparently did decrease between January 28 and February 10; only eight Scuds (five against Israel, three against Saudi Arabia) were launched during this period. This was more the result of the Iraqi crews running from the coalition's air superiority and SOCCENT teams than from the effective elimination of Scud launchers.[16]

The threat of CB agent munition attacks would keep Iraqi delivery systems a high priority target. Air bases at Tallil, Al Jahrah, Shaibah, al-Taqaddum and Balad were reported as storing chemical warheads. American intelligence had received a report that the Iraqi military had prepared to launch three remotely piloted MiGs equipped with spray tanks from Al Rashid Air Base in southern Baghdad. An F-117 nailed one MiG, but poor weather prevented attacks on the other two. A salvo of six cruise missiles were fired from the cruiser USS *Normandy* in the Red Sea against this target to destroy the planes before they were launched. This demonstrates the level of concern within CENTCOM, expending over $10 million worth of missiles to take out two aircraft capable of chemical agent delivery. The mere threat posed by potential CB agent weapon platforms redirected a substantial portion of CENTCOM's air and sea assets from conventional interdiction and air superiority missions to these special search and destroy missions.[17]

Iraqi soldiers began walking toward allied lines to surrender as soon as the air offensive began. To allow a capability to control these prisoners firmly, President Bush granted CENTCOM's request to use riot control agents (RCAs—specifically, CS and CN grenades), under strict guidelines (only for defensive purposes, only within the theater of operations, and only during the period of hostilities). Because of the media's exaggeration of the use of tear gas in Vietnam, CENTCOM's staff was told not to discuss publicly the concept of operations or any operational matters concerning the use of tear gas in theater.[18]

As the air effort shifted toward targets within the KTO, military officials sought to reassure the American public as well as their own forces that the CB warfare threat had been neutralized. In Riyadh, CENTCOM spokesman Brigadier General Richard Neal told the press that the targeting analysts had used "special bombs" on the chemical weapons plants and storage facilities in order to produce a minimum impact on the environment. In Washington, Lieutenant General Kelly told the media that "there is very, very, very little NBC production going on in that country—it ranges from zero to maybe ten percent of what they had before the war." Several days later, Kelly assured the press that some chemical weapons in storage would have lost their potency over the last month because of Iraq's poor manufacturing capabilities. He assessed the Iraqi CW threat as nowhere near as significant as it was at the outset of Operation Desert Shield.[19]

That did not reassure any of the commanders. Random reports of CB munitions attacks kept coming into CENTCOM HQ. Early in the morning of January 17, CENTCOM J-2 (Intelligence) passed a Saudi report of a chemical rocket launch on the border (later discounted). A pilot stated he had flown through a cloud of anthrax while returning from a raid; this claim was discounted by CENTAF an hour later. Incoming Scuds all had to be physically verified as having had high explosive or chemical warheads. An early morning British report on January 19 detailed a mustard agent attack at al-Jubayl, disproved by later tests. Many troops were calling in chemical agent alarms based on one detector's alarm, often without using manual and more sensitive backups such as the CAM and M256A1 kits to confirm the presence or absence of agent. When soldiers conducted second checks at the reported sites, all the alarms were proven false.

On January 19, Czech chemical units and French units reported to the Saudi military traces of nerve agents—air readings of 0.05 and 0.003 mg/m^3 lasting for about an hour at two sites 25–30 kilometers northeast of Hafir al Batin. ARCENT dispatched a Fox team to the location; it arrived four hours later. Its crew could not verify any chemical agents, nor did it find any sign of munitions (Scuds, artillery shells, or aerial bombs). Some staff officers immediately speculated that it could have been traces of agent released from the bombing of Iraqi chemical weapons manufacturing sites, or the suspect CW bunkers at An Nasiriyah.[20] Two days later, the Czech team reported low-level traces of nerve agent in the air near KKMC in the French sector; again, US chemical teams were unable to confirm their readings. On January 24, Saudi officials called a Czech unit to investigate a small area of what appeared to be wet desert soil several kilometers to the north and outside of KKMC. The contaminated area measured only about sixty centimeters by 200 centimeters. Using two separate protocols, the team determined that the area had been contaminated with the mustard agent. The Czech units filed a situation report with the Saudi forces; however, there is no record of that report being forwarded to CENTCOM, and there is no record that any other units were called to provide independent confirmation. Since there were no CB agent casualties or expended weapon systems in the area, no contact reports from other coalition forces (Egyptians, Syrians, British), and no enemy activity (other than Scud launches), CENTCOM NBCC decided the events were false alarms, at worst non-incidents. Once the media got wind of this event, they immediately began speculating about CB agents originating from the bombed munition production facilities and weapon storage sites.[21]

The CENTCOM and ARCENT staff studied the Czech reports, but the "bombed facilities" story did not pan out. KKMC is hundreds of miles from the bombed facilities. It would be physically impossible for liquid agents to travel that distance through the air in any lethal amounts. Any vapor traces of chemical agents would have evaporated long before reaching KKMC. CENTAF had been careful to attack CB agent storage and production sites prior to dawn, allowing the rising sun to begin its evaporative effects immediately. M8A1 alarms and numerous M256A1 kits (and similar sensitive detectors of other nations' forces) used to detect agents in between KKMC and the bombed facilities (where, in theory, agent concentrations should have been higher) were all reporting negative results. No CENTCOM units had reported any immediate ill effects from low levels of CB agents. The weather between January 18 and 24 had included winds pushing northward, and rainstorms, which should have prevented any vapor clouds from retaining any integrity over one hundred-plus miles.

The lack of any evidence of CB agent exposure did not stop the spread of fears as the Scud launches continued, although they were not as great as in the initial two weeks of the air campaign. Rumors continued to run wild; statements such as "a guy in the mess hall said he talked to an MP who talked to a truck driver who saw some dead camels and said they had died of poison gas. Pass it on," ran through the theater. To paraphrase a saying, no one wanted to be confused with facts.

Scud attacks accelerated the pressure to deploy the biological detection teams and to field ANBACIS-II computers in theater.   On January 19, Lieutenant General Waller formally agreed to implement DNA's ANBACIS-II system, and he approved the biodetection team concept. DNA teams began installing equipment at fifteen ARCENT and six CENTAF locations beginning on January 22, to be completed by the end of the month.[22]   On January 23, CENTCOM NBCC discovered that not all of the first wave of the 9th Chemical Company was inbound. Because of airlift constraints, only five biodetection teams (instead of the planned seven) could enter the theater as the first increment of three deployments. The personnel arrived at Dhahran on January 26, with equipment (seven XM2 samplers, four PM10s, five XM21 RSCAALs and eight HMMWVs) arriving on January 29. Five more XM21 RSCAALs were sent to MARCENT. The five Army area-sampling chemical-biological detection teams deployed on February 1 to al-Jubayl, Ras Safania, Riyadh, KKMC and Dhahran to begin immediate monitoring operations using XM2s and XM21s. The XM21 RSCAALs, not reliable during the hotter parts of the day, would operate between 0100 and 0700 hours, the most vulnerable windows for chemical agent attacks. The teams would take two biological agent samples daily, at 0600 and 1800 hours, likewise anticipated windows for biological agent attacks.

PHASE III: BATTLEFIELD PREPARATION

Fox vehicles shipped to the theater were tracked throughout their journey by the PM NBC Defense Office, both ODCSOPS and ODCSLOG at the Pentagon, the USAREUR chemical officer, and the CENTCOM, ARCENT, corps and division NBCCs. Lieutenant Colonel Willhoite and Major Newing were briefing Lieutenant Generals Gordon Sullivan (Vice Chief of Staff of the Army) and Dennis Reimer (DCSOPS) regularly on the Fox program. This personal involvement increased after the Scud attacks. In some cases, chemical officers were tracking airplane tail numbers and vehicle bumper numbers to monitor the progress of "their" vehicles. 3rd ACR's 89th Chemical Company accepted five Foxes rolling off the lines in Kassel just prior to Christmas, representing the first of the second batch of thirty vehicles, and returned with them to Saudi Arabia. There were an additional twelve Foxes due in by the end of January, raising the total to forty-eight. The first ten of those would go to the 1st and 2nd Marine divisions (whose troops would just be completing training at Sonthofen and Fort McClellan), and two vehicles would join the 1st IN DIV. Thirteen more might make the deadline of mid-February. Originally the schedule had called for the last five to be delivered in late March, but the PM office had been able to convince Thyssen-Henschel to accelerate the deliveries. Four more vehicles would pass to 1st IN DIV, six vehicles for ARCENT's Support Command, and one to replace the "Nunn" vehicle standing in for the 92d Chemical Company's loss, leaving the last two to be added to the theater "float" (for a total of four reserves). If everything went according to plans, CENTCOM would receive sixty-two Fox recon vehicles, including the one that had broken its axle in November, leaving a final tally of sixty-one NBCRS in theater for the ground offensive.

The 1st IN DIV was the last Army heavy division to receive Foxes. The division's brigades wanted its Foxes up front to monitor whether the Iraqis used chemical weapons while they were working through the border berm and minefields. As they represented the corps' main effort, their sense of urgency increased. In the event that the 1st IN DIV Foxes did not arrive on time, the division was to receive four Fox vehicles from 3rd AR DIV on the morning of January 21. The 3rd AR DIV had received its platoon back from 82d ABN DIV, but the entire division force would not close into the theater until February 6. The deal struck was that two Foxes would be returned to 3rd AR DIV after the breach operations and that the remaining two Foxes would return once the British 1st AR DIV passed through 1st IN DIV lines.[23]

Problems surfaced regarding the GDLS maintenance contract support. The British, Israelis and now Turkish militaries had received their Foxes, and this began to put a strain on the maintenance system for spare parts. Because most of the recon platoons had been careful not to overtax their vehicles, the operational readiness of the US Foxes remained above 95 percent. The contractors, however, had never been told about the possibility that they might have to go into Iraq to maintain the Foxes. As the coalition bombings began and the offensive intent of the coalition became clear, many contractors left Dhahran. GDLS had to hire new contractors, under terms that included the offensive plans. (This should reflect on the future need to pay more attention to the role of contractors in an armed conflict.) While the Navy and Air Force were more accustomed to this procedure, the Army had not as much experience; Navy and Air Force contractors, however, were never involved on the very edge of the battlefield, as the Army contractors would soon be.

On the morning of January 29, three Iraqi heavy divisions advanced against the Marine Corps lines in what was later called the "Khafji offensive." According to later analysis, this was not just a preemptive probe or quick attempt to bloody the Americans but a major attack designed to test the coalition front. The early attacks on the west side of the advance included an artillery barrage against the frontier observation points. Some explosions sounded more faint than others. Because both Army and Marine Corps troops had been warned that munitions exploding with a "hollow" sound were potential chemical munitions, the chemical agent alarm quickly ran up the chain of command. Fox vehicles scurried from one site to another, confirming the lack of any agent. Fierce air attacks and a ground Marine Corps/Arab coalition counterattack to retake Khafji on January 31 drove the Iraqi units back. Later, after the attack had been blunted, the Marines discovered there had been no chemical munitions used. This battle was seen by some to be indicative of the battle ahead, although CENTCOM missed much of the significance of the attack at the time. Attempting to stage a major mechanized attack, the Iraqi forces had been unable to coordinate a multi-divisional movement under a sky they did not own. This was not the way the battles against the Iranians had taken place.

The Khafji battle was significant in that no chemical munitions had been used. If the attack had been just a probe, that in and of itself would not be surprising. Iraq had always saved its chemical munitions for major assaults or defense missions, during the Iraq-Iran War. Later analysis showed the Iraqi attack to have been much greater than just a probe. As part of a major attack, the lack of chemical munitions use meant one of three things: either Iraqi forces did not have the chemical munitions nearby; or they were unwilling to use chemical munitions because of the threat of massive conventional retaliation; or their forces were not well enough trained to incorporate chemical weapons into the offensive. Then again, the Iraqi force in Kuwait could have had the chemical munitions nearby but had thought they would not need the munitions for a short, swift assault. Or it might mean that the Iraqis were saving it for the expected allied offensive. While the results were encouraging, no one was ready to discount the possibility of chemical attacks once the CENTCOM forces moved into Iraq.[24]

MOVING CB DEFENSE UNITS INTO PLACE

The two corps began their movements west after the air war began. The 82d and 101st ABN DIVs, as the extreme left wing of the attack, moved forward first, followed by the 24th IN DIV and 3rd ACR. VII Corps would follow as soon as the XVIII ABN Corps had cleared the KKMC area, to avoid a potential traffic jam. This was an extremely vulnerable time for both corps. XVIII ABN Corps was lined up along Tapline Road, a single hardtop road that paralleled the border. As 113,000 troops and thousands of vehicles headed west along the road, the nervous division NBCCs could only hope that the Iraqis did not get any reports of the movement. A few Scuds or FROGs spilling persistent agent on the Tapline Road would have disrupted the movement plan considerably, which would have been worse than the few casualties that might result. The 1st IN DIV task force in the al-Batin area, with its decoys and large-area smoke, mesmerized the Iraqi forces into looking for a straight-up-the-middle attack into Kuwait. Only one Iraqi division deployed west of the wadi after the deception operation.

XVIII ABN Corps would also lose a degree of its rear area chemical defense during the movement. While the corps NBCC had kept the rear area reasonably well informed with warning messages, once the corps was spread out and moving, radio communication with the numerous support units became very spotty. The majority of the chemical agent detectors and decontaminants were in the combat divisions, and the promised NBC protective covers for protecting the corps logistics had never materialized. VII Corps would be in a similar situation, but being more mechanized, it could count on speed and heavier protection for some degree of contamination avoidance. Both rear support areas would have to augment their decontamination companies and medical units with other rear-area support troops to ensure quick evacuation, decontamination and treatment of chemical casualties. The last Reserve chemical defense company, 340th Chemical Company (Decon), arrived in theater 30 January and moved to Logbase CHARLIE to join the 457th Chemical Battalion.

Once the VII Corps HQ began moving west, it decided to use the movement from the tactical assembly areas to the forward assembly areas as a rehearsal for the attack into Iraq. Each division assumed the planned distance and spacing, moving along axes that mirrored those that would be used in the actual attack. During this movement, the units were confronted with exercise scenarios that caused them to use the Fox NBCRS platoons to negotiate simulated contamination. The divisions discovered during this rehearsal that a large maneuver formation traveling in column had to plan its actions to execute upon encountering a contaminated area. There had to be a quickly executed process wherein the NBCRS vehicles would discover the contamination, mark it, and guide the following units around the area without losing their momentum. For the upcoming offensive, VII Corps decided to include military police in the forward units, so that once the NBCRS had marked the contamination, the MPs could guide the rest of the column around it (until the agent evaporated). This would allow the NBCRS vehicles to resume their point recon mission quickly. Another potential problem was that the warning markers dropped by the NBCRS were too small and too spread out; they would never be noticed in the dark hours of the morning. Fox crews would now attach chemical luminescence lights to the NBCRS markers to make them more visible in the dark.

On February 3, a second increment of soldiers, representing seven biodetection teams, arrived at Dhahran International; their eight HMMWVs with 3/4-ton trailers, two XM2 samplers and five PM10 aerosol samplers arrived the next day. The fixed-site biodefense teams had been trained primarily on the PM10 commercial biodetectors. With the additional teams in theater, CENTCOM NBCC made plans to move the five area-sampling teams to Logbases Alpha, Charlie, Echo, Al Qaisumah (near Hafar al Batin) and Ras Safaniya, focusing on the vulnerable forward deployment and logistics areas. Two fixed site teams would deploy to the Riyahd and Dhahran/Dammam areas, with the remaining three moving to Jubayl, KKMC, and Log Base Bastogne (see Figure 6.1). Because the commercial biological detectors were experimental prototypes, heavy, more fragile and highly dependant on logistics and maintenance support, they were not stationed directly on the fluid front lines.

Initial operational tests of the biodetectors resulted in a report of anthrax at Dhahran late on February 4. Team 6 using an XM2 sampler had registered the detection downwind of sheep pens, leading medics to believe it was a false positive report. In addition, samples taken west and upwind of the sheep pens were negative. False positives occurred when the biodetector detected a potential positive biological agent that was later proven absent at the forward labs. Of course, these tentative results, reacting to indigenous biological organisms, were better than false negatives (not reacting to a real BW agent).

Once the Navy Forward Laboratory matured the biological sample into a more definable culture, it proved the report to be wrong. The samples were evacuated to Fort Detrick to be sure; there the results were confirmed as relating to an organism similar to anthrax but definitely not lethal or a manufactured agent. The biodefense teams had not correctly established the natural background of biological organisms in theater; also, the SMART tickets were reacting to filter paper fibers in the liquid samples, leading to false positives. Changes in sampling and evacuation practices would lessen the chance of future alarms.

Figure 6.1
Locations of Biological Detection Teams

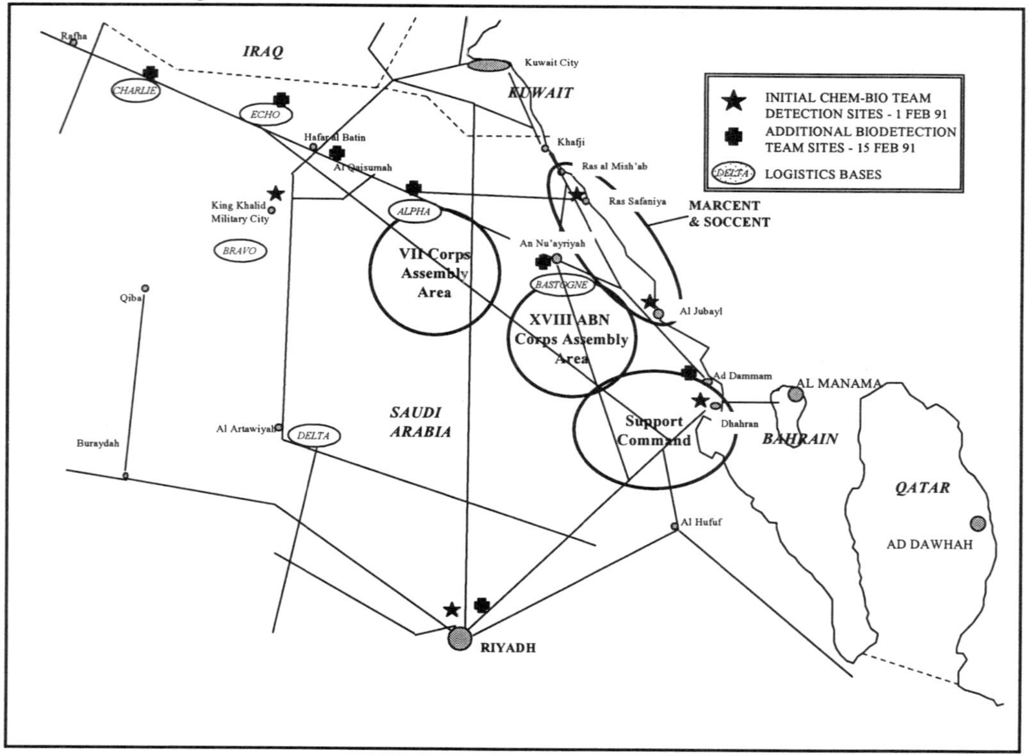

INITIAL CHEM-BIO TEAM
DETECTION SITES - 1 FEB 91

ADDITIONAL BIODETECTION
TEAM SITES - 15 FEB 91

LOGISTICS BASES

MARCENT
& SOCENT

IRAQ

KUWAIT

Kuwait City

Khafji

Ras al Mish'ab

Ras Safaniya

Al Jubayl

Al Dammam

Dhahran

BAHRAIN

AL MANAMA

QATAR

AD DAWWAH

SAUDI ARABIA

RIYADH

Al Hufuf

An Na'ayriyah

XVIIIABN
Corps Assembly
Area

Support
Command

VII Corps
Assembly
Area

Hafayd Batin

Al Qaysumah

King Khalid
Military City

Al Artawiyah

Qiba

Buraydah

Rafha

BASTOGNE

ALPHA

ECHO

CHARLIE

BRAVO

DELTA

DIEZA

The ANBACIS teams ran tests from mid-January through mid-February, using several possible scenarios of Iraqi chemical weapon attacks. This included 122 mm rocket attacks, MiG-23 aerial attacks, FROG and Scud rocket attacks, using all known chemical agents. The DNA Operations Cell in the United States returned contamination hazard footprints to CENTCOM within fifteen minutes. This quick turnaround ensured the most accurate prediction capability against any possible CB agent attack the Iraqis might deliver, throughout the theater and at all hours.

Concerns over protective clothing shortages had climbed to a pitch as the fourteen-day shelf life CPOGs "expired" at the end of January. CENTCOM and its units had been flooded with messages from CRDEC, NRDEC, AMC, DLA, medical offices and the Pentagon on what the overgarment wear life extension policy should be, in the absence of any official guidance or clarification. Not all of this advice was good; Lieutenant General Yeosock told Lieutenant General Reimer that he was well aware of the situation and did not need more message traffic to confuse the issue. ODSCOPS finally laid down the "final word" and instructed CENTCOM that ODCSLOG, as the point office for chemical defense equipment procurement, would release the official policy and that only this policy would apply. This policy confirmed that CPOGs that had been exposed to the air and resealed in their packages would still have an effective protection capability when used again. The important factor was the number of days that the troops actually wore the overgarments, not the number that the suit had been removed from its airtight bag. Reports that 130,000 BDOs were due in from Korea via air and the promised BDOs from Europe were enroute by sea gave ARCENT some hope of resolving the CPOG issue. If these suits could be distributed to the troops by mid-February, many commanders would breathe much easier.

There still were no confirmed guidelines on the handling, decontamination and transportation of contaminated human remains. The issue of contaminated casualties had been worked on throughout the DoD and up to President Bush, with the intent that no American remains be left behind because of CB agent contamination. Scientists at Dugway Proving Ground and Quartermaster School had developed a theoretical procedure, but they had not tested it. Decon personnel would use wire-mesh litters to dip the contaminated body in a high-bleach solution to clean the body, and then use two body bags to seal the remains. Medical units at Dover AFB had monitoring and transportation procedures in place and were prepared to accept the contaminated casualties. Lieutenant General Franks saw no reason to alarm the troops and commanders on this aspect of chemical warfare. He reviewed and approved a message on handling contaminated remains, a message that would have been distributed in the event of a chemical attack.[25]

In Washington, the political leadership expressed its concerns as well. Colonel Read presented a special brief to Paul Wolfowitz, Under Secretary of Defense for Policy. Paul Wolfowitz had participated in all of the high-level discussions about the CB agent threat and asked ODCSOPS how the first few days of the ground offensive would look if Saddam chose to use CB agent munitions. Colonel Read explained the expectation that CENTCOM forces would come under attack as they broke through the berms, by both Iraqi artillery and possibly aircraft using chemical munitions. Iraqi military forces would use previously identified target points, since their observation of CENTCOM forces would be severely limited.

Colonel Read described how CB agent attacks in the corps' rear areas would slow down the force's logistics and resupply. He discussed how the Fox vehicles would locate and mark contaminated areas, allowing following units to bypass and avoid them. If divisions could keep moving and avoid heavy engagements, they would avoid becoming targets for Iraqi CB weapons. Heavy casualties might be minimized by closing quickly with the enemy. The question came up again about the possibility of contaminated casualties. One solution was to leave the bodies in Saudi Arabia, seal the bodies in airtight coffins, or cremate the bodies to avoid the problems associated with transporting contaminated bodies to their families. This was unacceptable to both the civilian and military leadership in Washington—one way or another, all US troops were coming home.

CHAPTER 7

"... And Then We Are Going to Kill It"

Corps will be in MOPP-I starting at 0538 hrs, 24 Feb 91. The 1 ID will be in MOPP-II, but only for those *north* of Phase Line Vermont. DMain will be in MOPP-I starting at stand-to (0500).
—1st IN DIV NBC Center, 1820 hours, 23 February 1991

Final combat preparation against Iraqi CB agent use would include massive conventional attacks against any rebuilt airfields, facilities or delivery systems that might be able to employ CB agents. NBC weapons production and storage sites, such as a newly discovered BW facility at Latifiyah (west of Baghdad), received another barrage of aircraft delivered munitions and Tomahawks. Despite coalition emphasis on degrading Iraqi artillery, there were still more than enough artillery tubes and rocket launchers available to Iraqi forces to fire high-priority chemical agent delivery missions. Operational intelligence assets had pinpointed most of these. Artillery batteries and naval battleship guns pounded anything in range of the Iraqi border that might be able to deliver CB agent munitions.[1]

This still left the threat of Scuds and Iraqi aircraft. Saddam Hussein had built up an air force with over 600 combat aircraft. Approximately 100 of these flew to Iran before the air war, and another thirty-three aircraft had been destroyed by the air offensive. This left over 500 aircraft capable of delivering CB agent munitions. If the command and control structure could still operate, and if the munitions produced prior to the air campaign had been transported to the air bases, there was the possibility that Iraq could employ CB agent munitions against the coalition. CENTAF's air offensive had destroyed the ability of the southern airfields to support CW strikes against CENTCOM forces, but other airfields still existed. The limited number of CW warheads designed for Scuds and the intense coalition air superiority would mean only a limited capability but could not necessarily prevent any "leak through" of aircraft or Scuds in a saturation air attack.

Logistically speaking, the coalition was about as ready as it would ever be. When Defense Secretary Cheney and General Powell asked the corps commanders what would prevent them from being able to launch offensive operations by

February 21, Lieutenant General Frank's reply was, "Having two chemical overgarments for every soldier crossing the line of departure."[2] Supply centers continued distributing the protective suit shipments throughout CENTCOM. Orders had gone out that no soldiers would turn in uncontaminated suits used in January's Scud scare, unless a second set had been issued to all soldiers. LTC Merryman described the search for additional protective suits as similar to a 90 percent-off suit sale at Macy's. All the soldiers would have at least two unused protective suits, including the resealed suit opened in mid-January. The protective mask shortage had not improved; VII Corps would go in with less than 150 spare M17-series masks immediately available for replacements. The M291 skin decon kit had gone out to most of the soldiers, not necessarily in bulk, but enough to handle the first few chemical attacks.

Media attention fell on the absence of the new M40 protective masks, in part due to Scott Aviation's observations that the M40 mask could have been available had the government stayed with it as the prime contractor (now Mine Safety Applications [MSA] and ILC Dover). Although ILC Dover had conducted a large portion of the R&D on the mask, the production contract had been awarded to Scott Aviation as the low bidder in May 1987. Scott Aviation delivered only 3,358 masks out of a contract target of 300,000, which initially resulted in a stop-work order in 1988, and eventually the termination of the contract "for the convenience of the government" in January 1990. In September 1988, AMCCOM awarded Mine Safety Applications (MSA) and ILC Dover short-term M40 production contracts (120,000 each by September 1989) in an effort to get at least some masks out to the major Army units. Both still faced some technical and production problems, such as difficulties developing the proper tools and molding, which prevented either company from producing masks prior to August 1990.

Scott Aviation's president stated on ABC's *PrimeTime Live* that had the Army stayed with his company, the deployed soldiers might all have superior M40 masks. Brigadier General Dave Nydam, also interviewed on the show, countered that accusation by pointing out that Scott Aviation had failed to meet Army production deadlines and had failed first-article test requirements. The M17-series mask, while initially designed in the 1960s, was improved in 1983 to the M17A2 model and was more than adequate to protect the soldiers against Iraqi chemical agents, especially since all soldiers had repeatedly checked their mask fits before and during the conflict. The public debate caused a flurry of calls from worried spouses to their soldiers in the field, asking if they were sure their protective masks were safe and had been checked. This drop in morale and confidence concerning their masks was not what the soldiers needed at this point.[3]

Since the Gulf War, much has been made of the Manley report, which sites that the M17A2 protective mask had a 26–40 percent failure rate. These numbers arose from a classified Marine Corps's protective mask fit validation study, which people have misinterpreted as a report that identifies the M17A2 as a defective mask. The study actually stated that if an untrained individual attempted to fit an M17-series mask to his or her face, there is that chance that the mask would not fit perfectly. If an individual has an NBC specialist fit him or her, this percentage becomes practically negligible, as hundreds of thousands of military personnel who have ever been inside a CS-chamber will attest. For months soldiers had their unit NBC specialists on hand to check their masks, in addition to the Pine Bluff mask facility, banana oil checks, the PMFVS device, and other tests to verify everyone's fit. No field commander was taking any chances that troops would die unnecessarily. At the time, this validation study was classified because of the chance that Iraq might misread the study as pointing out a vulnerability, and might attempt to exploit the opportunity by initiating chemical warfare.[4]

FINAL PREPARATIONS

The 1st IN DIV had become increasingly concerned over its lack of Foxes, especially after seeing the Marines accept their ten Foxes first in late January. When the first two NBCRS vehicles were ready in January (alone with the USMC allotment of ten), VII Corps NBCC tasked the 1st IN DIV to send its Property Book Officer, the platoon leader and some personnel from the chemical recon platoon to fly to Rhein-Main AFB (the deployment site had moved from Ramstein) to sign for them. While 1st IN DIV had looked forward to receiving the vehicles, the division staff was reluctant to send the chemical recon platoon to travel to Germany to sign for and transport the vehicles back personally. With the 1st IN DIV's critical breaching mission only weeks away, the division did not want to part with half of their NBC recon assets; and they instead requested that logistics channels deliver the Foxes to KKMC. In the interest of time, the VII Corps NBCC sent one of its captains to Kassel to sign for the vehicles in early February.

The 12th Chemical Company crew members traveled to Dhahran on February 11 to accept the two Foxes, only to discover they had not yet arrived. The Foxes had left on the evening of February 13 on a specially chartered C-5A cargo plane, but a Scud scare during the flight caused the plane to turn back to Germany. The plane finally delivered the two Foxes to Saudi Arabia on February 15. Yet there was one problem: due to the shortage of radios caused by wartime requirements, they arrived without vehicle radios and combat vehicle crewman helmets. These vehicles had to stop by the GDLS/PM NBC Fixed Fox Facility to receive final equipment. This allowed the 1st IN DIV to return two borrowed Foxes to the 3rd AR DIV, with a promise to return the other two after the breaching operations on the first day of the ground war. In the early hours of February 19, VII Corps NBCC called to inform 1st IN DIV that the last four Foxes had arrived at KKMC. The 1st IN DIV had its Fox-equipped recon platoon barely a week before the ground offensive started.

Resolving the 1st IN DIV issue still left the last nine Fox vehicles of the sixty-Fuchs loan to go. The 490th Chemical Battalion sent a team to Germany on February 16 to escort the nine vehicles to Dhahran. By February 21, they were ready to return to Saudi Arabia, delivering three vehicles each on the 21st, 24th and 25th, but the Air Force was not ready to deliver. Last-minute theater airlift priorities had prevented their immediate return, although they had been third priority for in-bound logistics (first being Patriot missiles, second being 120 mm tank ammunition).

On the eve of the ground offensive, there were a total of fifty-one operational Fox vehicles in the US forces, not including the one "Nunn" float. VII Corps had twenty-four of the vehicles on-line, while XVIII ABN Corps retained seventeen. The ARCENT Support Command would not have its planned Fox reconnaissance vehicles, but it could still rely on chemical troops in APC recon vehicles. MARCENT had the other ten vehicles, split between their two divisions. The XM21 and biodetection sampling teams increased their vigilance to cover the division marshaling areas. While the greatest concern was focused on the threat of Iraqi chemical strikes against CENTCOM forces in the breach operation, there was equal interest in the possibility of chemical Scud attacks and Iraqi air attacks against the rear area supporting the offensive operations. ARCENT NBCC counted on the inbound nine Fox vehicles to supply the needed capability. Also, the oil wells burning constantly in Kuwait presented new problems to the Marines and VII Corps. In addition to posing health problems because of the hydrogen sulfide fumes, the heavy, oil-laden smoke clogged the M8A1 filter paddles responsible for filtering particulates from the air sampling mechanism. The limited air flow caused increasing numbers of false alarms, until many units simply turned off the detectors rather than constantly checking for chemical agents.

A staffer in CENTCOM headquarters brought up the question of what would happen if the units captured biological munitions. Up to this time, no one had considered what exactly combat units should do with munitions filled with biological agents. Normally, one would call the Explosive Ordnance Disposal (EOD) teams to disarm munitions, but weren't special circumstances present here? While the US had established ways to demil biological munitions at US production sites in the 1970s, there was no mobile capability to do this in Southwest Asia. The Joint Staff began working on procedures to permit a field destruction capability for biological weapons, in the event that CENTCOM might capture armed biological munitions.[5]

With all the divisions in place on February 20, deception operations continued. The mechanized smoke generators of the 68th and 44th Chemical Companies set up a smoke screen to support the 1st CAV DIV Battlefield Deception Teams, who set up loudspeakers and pop-up replicas of M1A1 tanks and M2 Infantry Fighting Vehicles (IFV) around the Wadi al-Batin. Under Operation Knight Strike, Task Force 1-5 of the 1st CAV DIV struck up the Wadi al-Batin in an attempt to convince the Iraqi force that the main attack would follow on that terrain. Division artillery "prepped" the Iraqi side as the engineers moved up to it. Two mechanized smoke generator platoons obscured the engineers as they blasted eight lanes through the berm, allowing the task force to move into the wadi with relatively good cover. This was the first smoke operation conducted on enemy territory since Vietnam. As the smoke generators moved forward with the task force, the American forces came under heavy fire from dug-in Iraqi positions. One smoke generator crew noticed a M163 Vulcan air defense team (4-5th Air Defense Artillery) that had been hit by an Iraqi rocket-propelled grenade. Two chemical soldiers, Specialists John Benavides and James Santos, stopped to render first aid to the wounded. As the probe withdrew, artillery-fired smoke covered the units. The two specialists encountered injured soldiers in a Bradley IFV, and once again stopped to render assistance.[6]

This type of smoke support was just what the Chemical School had intended with its conception of smoke generators on a M113A2 chassis. In contrast, the 1st IN DIV attempted to conduct a fake breach on the same day, a bit west of the 1st CAV DIV attempt, without smoke support. It immediately came under hostile fire and withdrew without breaching the berm. This lack of smoke support would affect the 1st IN DIV's concept of the first day's operations. Because of difficulties in employing smoke during simulated combat operations at the National Training Center, Major General Tom Rhame chose to exclude the two smoke generator companies from the breaching operation. He felt that the breach operation was already difficult enough without smoke; that the Iraqi opposition would not offer stiff resistance; and that the attached US units were not prepared to conduct the operation effectively under obscured conditions. Intelligence reports had noted Iraqi armor units pulling away from the 1st IN DIV sector, leaving the Iraqi infantry units there vulnerable to a hard-hitting combined arms force. The 1st Brigade commander, comfortable in the knowledge that nothing the Iraqis had would penetrate the front armor of an M1A1, suggested that his tanks, outfitted with mine plows, could punch through the minefields before the Iraqis could react. His plan would not require the extensive smoke and engineer support at the onset of the battle.[7]

The 2d Chemical Battalion commander, Lieutenant Colonel Mike Kilgore, worked out an alternative plan with Major Polley, the division chemical officer, that would employ the smoke generators on the east flank of the division. They could obscure the flank of the division as it breached the berms and assist the 2d Brigade's initial attack on the Iraqi recon assets. The 2d ACR and 3rd AR DIV planned to obscure their breaches west of the 1st IN DIV position. They had smoke platoons from the 172d Chemical Company that would drop an obscuring haze over the engineers prior to their blowing lanes through the berm.

In addition to working out the smoke plan, the 2d Chemical Battalion planned two thorough decontamination sites south of the breach and one north of the breach. Engineer support from the 7th Engineer Brigade (ENG BDE) would dig the sump pits necessary to collect the contaminated run-off of the washes. Both of the rear decontamination sites took over a square kilometer of land, with two decontamination platoons ready for action. Logistically, the battalion moved 600 barrels of fog oil up to the line and 20,000 gallons of water to the decon sites.[8] At the other two chemical battalions, similar decontamination preparations were underway. If Saddam was going to try to stop the CENTCOM's offensive, the breach was the most logical place to use chemical agents. Once the offensive moved past the breach, the maneuver forces would rely on their own operational decontamination capabilities to maintain the momentum. The decontamination companies would move behind them and prepare thorough decon sites closer to the battle as the combat units moved forward.

BIOLOGICAL WARFARE SCARES

Just as the units were lining up against the border, a new threat emerged. Reconnaissance elements of the 115th MP Company reported finding groups of dead camels and goats along Main Supply Route Yugo, near Qaryat al Ulya, and on Main Supply Route Cadillac during the week of February 16–21. Along both MSRs the MPs had noted a number of green plastic grain-feed bags, around which the dead animals were clustered. Although the nearby villagers seemed unconcerned, CENTCOM immediately suspected biological agents. On February 23, soldiers noted a large number of dead sheep near Logistics Base Alpha. That same day, the XM2 sampler at Logistics Base Alpha, in the vicinity of Sodowiyat on the Tapline Road, had a positive hit for anthrax on one air sample, while an XM2 sampler at al-Jubayl reported a positive hit on botulinum toxin. The PM10 samplers at Dhahran and Riyadh both reported anthrax samples. Army veterinary and bio-medical sampling teams rushed out to sample all these areas, while the divisions sat poised on the front lines. Subsequent analysis at the forward labs yielded negative reports on all four, but positive confirmation would require laboratory analysis at Fort Detrick and a twenty-four-hour turnaround, more than a day later.

What had happened was a series of unfortunate coincidences. The locals had a practice of isolating sick and weak animals from the herd and killing them with poisoned feed. The animals had died at their owners' hands. There were no reports of mass illnesses nearby in either the military or civilian communities that would indicate a large area biological attack. These alarms, coming so close to the initiation of the ground offensive, could have been either a brilliantly timed stroke by Saddam or a false alarm. There were no immediate ways other than the troops' health and the forward laboratories to tell one way or another. While no one could rely 100 percent on the biodetection teams, they were the only indicators against the one threat capable of stopping the offensive. This brought home the message that a more credible and responsive, real-time biological warfare agent detection system was needed. Meanwhile, the reports compounded fears throughout the leadership on the eve of the ground offensive. The two corps issued orders to increase MOPP status and start taking PB tablets prior to H-hour.

PHASE IV: OFFENSIVE GROUND CAMPAIGN

The Marines had conducted deception operations, artillery raids and cross-border screening operations for several weeks prior to the ground offensive. Over the past few days, their task forces had been successful in penetrating the first obstacle belt and establishing firing positions within Kuwait. Finally, at 0400 hours on February 24, the 1st MARDIV moved from its firing positions within Kuwait into the obstacle belts. The Marines had donned their Mark-IV protective suits and boots (MOPP-2) in order to prepare for the possibility of chemical mines or chemical artillery projectiles. The combat engineers had cleared three of the four lanes, mostly with three-shot line charges followed by M60 tanks with track-width mine plows. At about 0730 hours in lane 3, one mine exploded with a suspiciously low sound. Fearing the worst, the engineers reported a possible chemical mine had gone off.[9] Major General James Myatt immediately ordered the division go to MOPP-4 (full protective posture) until a Fox could confirm the report. Although the Fox vehicle seemed to confirm a mustard agent in the area, the M256A1 kits and M8 paper did not detect vapor or liquid agent traces. A second Fox further upwind detected no agents. The false alarm had cost the Marines only twenty minutes, but that was twenty minutes of lying still, vulnerable in a narrow lane, waiting for the "all clear" to move forward.

During this time the 1st MARDIV's Fox's report of confirmed mustard agent had been intercepted by one of the JSTARS planes and flashed to the Joint Chiefs of Staff. The PM NBC Defense office's secure phone began ringing that Sunday morning, with the Joint Staff questioning LTC D'Andries as to how reliable the report might be. By the PM office's estimate, the MM-1 was a well-engineered piece of equipment, but there were too many variables (environmental interferrents, operator interpretation, level of training, etc.) for them to determine whether or not this was a valid detection. The Foxes used the MM-1 for ground contamination detection only, relying on CAMs on-board and an M8A1 detector for air contamination detection. The PM NBC Defense office advised the Joint Staff to allow the Marines at the site to make the call. By the time this communication had taken place, the 1st MARDIV was back on the move.

The 2d MARDIV crossed its line of departure at 0530 hours, engaging in the same obstacle clearing. It encountered no chemical mines but kept expecting heavy artillery as it struggled through the lanes. The MLRS battery and Marine artillery kept up a constant counterbattery fire to limit any Iraqi artillery fire. A second chemical alarm went off that afternoon, without accompanying explosions or incoming artillery—again a false alarm. The constant smoke from the oil fires kept the skies dark, and it also kept the M8A1 and ICAD chemical agent detectors false-alarming. It would be enough to keep the nervous Marines jumping throughout their push towards Kuwait City. As they pushed toward Al Jaber Air Base outside of Kuwait near midnight, several Marines mistook low-lying artillery smoke for chemical attacks. After masking and checking their M256A1 kits, they noted the negative results and moved on. Iraqi EPWs captured nearby confirmed the lack of any chemical weapons at Al Jaber.[10] Next to the Marines, the Egyptian army had its scares as well. One soldier put on a mask in the breach site. Men behind him took that as a sign of a chemical attack, masked and froze in place, waiting for confirmation. No casualties—again, a false alarm had interrupted the battle's forward momentum.

XVIII ABN Corps had initiated its attack at 0400 hours as the western hook into Iraq. Most of XVIII ABN Corps remained at MOPP-0 (suits nearby, not worn), anticipating little resistance this far west, and counting on speed to avoid enemy targeting. As the French fought elements of the Iraqi 45th Division, no chemical attacks occurred. The 101st ABN DIV got its airborne assault off two hours late due to the weather but encountered no problems establishing Forward Operating Base (FOB) Cobra.

As the reports from MARCENT and XVIII ABN Corps came in to CENTCOM, it appeared that the Iraqis did not intend to retaliate with chemical weapons as had been anticipated. Indeed, the few Iraqi artillery responses seemed to be hitting pre-planned fire zones rather than where the soldiers were actually moving. After conferring with Lieutenant Generals Luck and Franks, General Schwarzkopf made the decision to push the schedule ahead. The 3rd ACR led the 24th IN DIV north at 1400 hours, five hours ahead of schedule due to success on the left flank. Both units anticipated chemical attacks as they crossed the line of departure in MOPP-1 (suits on). As the units moved forward, the chemical attacks did not occur, nor were the chemical munitions stockpiles at the intermediary points as intelligence had warned them they would be.

The VII Corps had the main Army breach operations on the first day of the ground offensive. Initially, the corps MOPP level was MOPP-2 (suit and boots), but Lieutenant General Franks gave latitude to the division commanders as to what levels to set within their own units. The 2d ACR led the way on the left flank at 0538 hours. Its goal was to conduct a movement to contact and fix the Republican Guard, and allow the following divisions to pass through to continue the fight. The 2d ACR assumed MOPP level 1 after crossing into Iraq proper, and it would continue that level until assuming the corps reserve (when it would downgrade to MOPP-0). The two forward cavalry squadrons each had a chemical reconnaissance squad of two Foxes attached, while the third Fox squad remained under the ACR's general control for rear-area operations or to assist the forward squads. The Foxes would mark contaminated areas and find bypasses for the following cavalry regiment, and the 1st AR and 3rd AR DIVs. Initially, smoke operations had been planned to cover the initial breach of the border berm and then to screen the flanks of the ACR. Due to the heavy winds and inclement weather (setting a ten-year record for rainfall in the region), smoke operations were not carried out. VII Corps had attached a decon platoon from the 11th Chemical Company to provide deliberate decon support to the 2d ACR. The initial breach found no chemical mines and no artillery attacks to oppose VII Corps's entry into Iraq.[11] The 1st AR DIV and 3rd AR DIV rolled north behind 2d ACR on their way toward al-Busayyah, at 1400 hours.

1st IN DIV had the same experience as 2d ACR. It had decon platoons of the 181st Chemical Company standing by, two platoons with the engineers and two in the rear area where all the VII Corp supplies would soon run through. After the 7th ENG BDE breached the berm in twenty-four lanes, two combat brigades rolled through to clear and secure the far side. Because there was no resistance or artillery fire at the breach, the division was able to move quickly through the berms into Iraq proper. MG Rhame had successfully gambled on not having smoke support; had there been Iraqi artillery and a counterattack, things might have gone the other way. More importantly, there were no chemical artillery or air attacks. After securing the Iraqi security zone, the 1st IN DIV received orders at 1500 hours to continue exploiting the offensive. Because the British division had not practiced passing through the 1st IN DIV at night, VII Corps decided to hold off on its passage of lines until the next day.

As the end of the first day approached, CENTCOM checked on the suspected anthrax cultures, now twelve hours old. The Theater Army Medical Laboratory found no signs of any anthrax but was waiting the full twenty-four hours to make a solid confirmation. The real damage was rumors flying through ARCENT that biological agents were being used in-theater. British representatives joined up with CENTCOM's NBCC to ask questions about the anthrax alert. Evidently, General Powell had relayed the report of a possible agent attack through Number 10 Downing Street, to the British commander of forces in Saudi Arabia. The story was complicated by the fact that six British soldiers sharing the same tent had come down with flu-like syndromes. CENTCOM NBCC assured them that the report was negative and offered to sample the soldiers' blood to make sure.[12] The absence of Iraqi chemical attacks during the initial breach was still mystifying, but it was gratefully accepted.

Day Two

On G+1 (twenty-four hours after the battle began, February 25), the Marine divisions continued forward. The Tiger Brigade led the 2d MARDIV north toward Kuwait City, while the 1st MARDIV drove toward the Ahmad Al-Jaber Air Base, in fierce fighting. The Marines' M60A3 tank optics relied on ambient light and had difficulty piercing the black oil fire smoke, but the Tiger Brigade's M1 tanks had no such difficulties. Egyptian and Syrian forces drew up behind 2d MARDIV, while the Saudi and Kuwaiti task forces moved up the seacoast. Around 1800 hours, a chemical alert caused the Marines to check with their M256A1 kits, which turned up negative twenty minutes later. While there had been no more reports of chemical mines, radio traffic intercepted from Baghdad to the Iraqi 3rd Corps granting permission to initiate chemical attacks. These attacks never came, in part perhaps to the propaganda warnings that any leader authorizing such attacks would be treated as a war criminal, or perhaps because the coalition attacks were so successful and quick.

To the west, XVIII ABN Corps had completed its wheel. The 3rd Brigade, 101st ABN DIV assumed the flank guard for the 24th IN DIV, northwest of Nasiriyah and just a few miles north of Tallil air base. The 24th IN DIV took operational control of the 3rd ACR and began its drive east toward the two airbases that might still hold chemical weapons. Early that morning it had secured

Objective Grey, where it had expected to find chemical munitions (and once again had found none).

VII Corps continued to attack the Republican Guards. The 2d ACR shifted southeast to make room for 1st AR DIV's advance and began the move east, with 3rd AR DIV trailing. The 1st AR DIV drove to within artillery range of Nasiriyah before pausing for the night. The British 1st AR DIV had passed through 1st IN DIV that afternoon and moved west against the Iraqi forces in the Wadi. 1st IN DIV began to reconsolidate and move up to the 3rd and 1st AR DIVs to begin a concerted strike east. As the two armored divisions moved closer to the Republican Guards, the commanders called for an increase in the MOPP level to MOPP-2 (suit and boots).

As the 1st IN DIV prepared to move out, there was a change of mission from VII Corps. The 2d Chemical Battalion would move with the 42d Field Artillery Brigade and catch up to the 3rd AR DIV. As of 1500 hours, the 2d Chemical Battalion was detached from the 1st IN DIV to join the 3rd AR DIV, the VII Corps main effort. The battalion would support 3rd AR DIV with one smoke generator company and one of the two decon platoons from 323rd Chemical Company. The other smoke generator company and decon platoon would join 1st AR DIV. As the chemical units moved out, the field artillery unit promptly outran them, leaving the 2d Chemical Battalion moving along with the British 1st DIV to catch up to the battle.

The thousands of enemy prisoners of war (EPWs) revealed the Iraqi military's unprepared state. It had been so used to being the stronger side that its defensive equipment was not exactly first-class. Many of the soldiers had thin butyl-rubber fabric overgarments, more a cloak than a protective suit. There was a variety of masks—some Yugoslavian, some Russian, some East German, some US and British, and some an Iraqi knockoff of the M17 masks. Geneva protocols dictate that EPWs are allowed to retain their protective masks as a basic survival measure, but there was concern regarding those prisoners without masks. Had Iraq initiated chemical warfare, would the coalition be expected to provide masks for EPWs, when their own stocks were so low? The laws of war seemed to call for this measure. Fortunately, the issue never presented itself—had chemical warfare occurred, CENTCOM would have been in a real moral quandary. Iraqi soldiers' decon kits and detection kits were equally heterogeneous, coming from Poland, Russia, Czechoslovakia, and other former Warsaw Pact countries. Some of the Iraqi prisoners of war told their captors of markings that would identify the chemical munitions: three red rings denoted nerve agent; three green rings, choking; and three yellow rings, blister. A blue flare was used by the Iraqis to warn of a nearby friendly chemical strike. This intelligence data turned out to be deliberately erroneous—all the chemical munitions found later were unmarked.[13]

Four of the last nine Fox vehicles had arrived that afternoon at KKMC. One Fox went to 3rd ACR, and two Foxes were dedicated as ARCENT ORFs. One would be operated by the 490th Chemical Battalion troops to provide rear-area reconnaissance against any Scud or aircraft attacks against the vulnerable

ARCENT Support Command, with five Foxes on the way. So far, the rear area had remained safe. With the absence of any Iraqi chemical attacks in the breach, most units downgraded their MOPP status to MOPP-1 or 0. As long as the coalition force kept moving tight against the enemy, Iraqi targeting for chemical agents would be difficult.

Day Three

The inhospitable terrain and poor weather on G+2 (February 26) kept progress in the west difficult. The 101st and 82d ABN DIVs consolidated their positions in the Euphrates Valley and far left flank of the army. The 24th IN DIV began its roll down Highway 8 toward Jalibah around 1400 hours and ran into two Iraqi infantry divisions and a Republican Guard division. During a four-hour firefight, the 24th IN DIV destroyed fifty-seven tanks, four artillery battalions and routed the divisions. It stopped south of the two airfields (Tallil and Jalibah).

The Marines circled the outskirts of Kuwait City, fighting off counterattacks as they pushed closer to the city limits. Early that morning, a Fox vehicle reported a lewisite detection. CAMs nearby registered mustard agents, but second readings from the Fox's mass spectrometer and M256A1 kits showed no agent present. Air analysis showed high levels of petroleum products due to the burning oil wells, which may have caused false alarms. The 2d MARDIV and Tiger Brigade circled northwest around the city, while 1st MARDIV attacked and secured the international airport. That night the division had to fight off an Iraqi counterattack to take the airport. With battleship fire support, the division fought back and finally secured the airport at 0300 hours the next morning.

VII Corps had consolidated its "fist," as Lieutenant General Franks called it, and the 1st and 3rd AR DIVs attacked east to engage the armored Republican Guard divisions. The superior optics in the M1A1 tanks cut through the thick black smoke caused by the oil well fires now encountered by VII Corps forces. In the greatest tank battle of the war, 800 American tanks faced off against 300 Iraqi tanks and crushed two Republican Guard divisions. 1st IN DIV attacked south of the armored divisions to consolidate the eastern flank, as the British division continued to attack east toward Kuwait City. This afternoon was the moment of the 2d ACR's now-famous "Battle of 73rd Easting" in its four-hour attack against two Iraqi armored divisions. General Schwarzkopf released 1st CAV DIV to VII Corps, which immediately committed the division forward. The 2d Chemical Battalion, its two smoke generator companies and decon company had just caught up to the action at 1800 hours of the second day. Their third day was spent reorganizing, refueling and resupplying for the final push in the 3rd AR DIV's support command area. By the time the 2d Chemical Battalion caught up to the 3rd AR DIV tactical units on the fourth day, the cease-fire had been announced.

Four more Foxes arrived at KKMC, adding to the 490th's rear area recon capability. One more would arrive early morning of February 27, filling out the rear area recon platoon. This represented the last of the sixty German gift NBCRSs to CENTCOM. Because it was still unclear whether or not Saddam's forces would attack using chemical weapons in a last desperate attack, these Foxes were not too late to be employed.

Day Four

On the fourth day of battle (G+3, February 27), the coalition forces were involved in some brisk engagements with small Iraqi units, but the majority of the enemy force was fleeing towards Basrah. The Marines and Arab forces consolidated their positions around Kuwait City, and the Kuwaiti units officially liberated their capital. Having refueled over the night, the 24th IN DIV occupied the Tallil and Jalibah air fields. Again, while Tallil and Jalibah may have held chemical munitions for the Iraq-Iran war, none were found this day. No chemical munitions were found in the Kuwait Theater of Operations by any US forces. Conjecture was that either the air offensive had prevented Iraqi supply convoys from moving munitions to delivery systems in the forward areas, or that Saddam had never given the authorization to do so.

VII Corps was still engaging enemy armor trying to escape north towards the Euphrates. All five divisions and an ACR were now attacking in synchronization against the Republican Guards. The five Iraqi heavy divisions were broken. Offensive operations were ordered halted at 0800 hours on the fifth day, February 28. This gave just enough time for VII Corps to mount one last morning attack to destroy the remaining Iraqi divisions west of Basrah. As the new defensive positions took hold, CENTCOM began its humanitarian efforts and clean-up operations.

Although this is not a confirmed view, one reason why the coalition forces may not have pushed through and past Basrah was the threat of Iraqi chemical munitions. The Iranians had repeatedly attacked Basrah during their conflict with Iraq, only to be met with stiff defensive positions, massive chemical agent munitions attacks and armored counterattacks. Basrah is the second-largest city in Iraq; its impending fall might have been a tripwire for CB agent munitions releases. Since most of the CENTCOM combat divisions were in and around the Basrah/Kuwait City region, it would have been relatively easy to target US forces, had the coalition divisions pushed the issue.

POST-COMBAT OPERATIONS

One chemical incident occurred immediately after the ground war, on February 28. Private First Class David A. Fisher, a cavalry scout from the 3rd AR DIV, had been exploring enemy bunkers in northern Kuwait for intelligence material and assisting in the demolition of enemy fighting vehicles. During his exploration of one empty bunker, he came into contact with the walls of the interior. Eight hours later, during a radio watch, he experienced blistering and pain along his arms. On March 2, his arms featured more small blisters and reddening. The medics classified him as a possible blister agent casualty and evacuated him to a chemical decon station at C Company, 45th Support Battalion. The doctors identified four blisters about an inch in diameter and confirmed the mustard agent through later analysis of urine and skin samples. Colonel Mike Dunn, commander of the MRICD, personally evaluated and confirmed the results. A Fox from the 3rd AR DIV chemical company arrived, whose detectors confirmed the agent as well. Tech Escort Unit teams evacuated PFC Fisher's ballistic protective vest and coverall sleeve to CRDEC, but the scientists could not detect any agent by that time. Evidently the amount was so small, that it had evaporated.[14]

Because there was no positive information on the marking of chemical munitions, every time CENTCOM units found a weapons cache they treated the site as a potential source of CB agent munitions. In the cases of the larger caches, this called for a Fox vehicle and one or more XM21 RSCAALs to monitor the munitions until it was confirmed safe. Until this time no one had envisioned using the Foxes in this role. While commanders may have thought that the state-of-the-art Fox had the most sophisticated chemical agent detector (the German MM-1 mass spectrometer), it was designed to detect ground contamination, not to operate as a mobile air monitoring system (but its presence made people more confident).[15] The Marines and SOCCENT both called for Fox vehicles to confirm reports of chemical munitions and suspected chemical weapons bunkers in and around Kuwait City, none of which were positive. The Fox vehicles and XM21s were also stationed downwind of munitions demolition sites, with decon units under the 2d Chemical Battalion on stand-by in Kuwait in the event that chemical agent munitions were missed and EOD teams required their assistance.

Two biodetection teams deployed forward to Kuwait City on March 3, collecting eight soil samples in southern Iraq and assisting the FMIB search for chemical munitions within Kuwait. Although no chemical munitions were found, they remained in Kuwait City to assist the FMIB by providing technical information on Iraqi chemical defense equipment. CENTCOM terminated the vaccination program on March 3. The two teams redeployed back to KKMC by March 17, and all teams were back in Fort Lewis by the end of the month.[16]

The corps NBCCs continued to track down reports of possible chemical storage sites throughout the Euphrates River area. Because the demilitarization line ran just south of the river and south of many of the towns and villages, the Army would have to wait for the UN teams to conduct a full inspection of the area. The reserve and active chemical decon companies moved south to support "car wash operations," as the divisions began to load their vehicles on ships and aircraft to redeploy back to Europe and the United States. This mission eventually diminished, as the engineers established nearly 100 wash points in Kuwait City, Dhahran, al-Dammam and al-Jubayl.

As the 1st IN DIV packed its vehicles and equipment for redeployment, it received word from VII Corps that its Foxes had been nominated to stay behind in Saudi Arabia as prepositioned stocks. Given all the difficulties it had seen in obtaining the Foxes, the division bitterly fought the issue, from the chemical company commander all the way to MG Rhame himself. All was to no avail. ARCENT had to select someone's six Foxes, and the 1st IN DIV was at the bottom of the priority list. 3rd ACR also had to turn in its vehicles, as it was not their turn to receive the Foxes by the official fielding schedule. The 1st CAV DIV finally received their Foxes from ARCENT as it was returning to Fort Hood. As the units began to deploy back home, the 11th ACR, whose chemical company had just completed its training at Sonthofen (the last US platoon to do so), arrived to assume the peacekeeping role in Kuwait.

UN INSPECTION TEAMS

The United Nations Security Council passed Resolution 687 on April 3, 1991; it required Iraq to register its NBC weapons and ballistic missiles, and to destroy, render unusable or remove these weapons and all production and research facilities. The resolution further required that Iraq disclose all its holdings and programs, permit on-site inspections, and to permit the destruction of the weapons. In May 1991 the UN set up a special commission (UNSCOM) established by the Secretary General. The UNSCOM teams had a charter to conduct the inspections for weapons of mass destruction throughout Iraq.

The nuclear program exposed by the UNSCOM inspections proved to be much larger than had been previously believed. During the air war, the nuclear site target list had grown from four to eight potential sites; UNSCOM discovered a total of thirty-nine nuclear facilities at nineteen locations across Iraq in its over thirty nuclear inspections. While Iraqi officials had cooperated with the chemical and biological inspections, there was no end of interference with the inspectors for the nuclear sites. Iraqi officials were particularly resistant to granting any access to documents related to the nuclear program. One UNSCOM inspector believed that the Iraqis deliberately gave in on the chemical facilities only in the knowledge that they could rebuild and resupply these production sites quickly. The nuclear weapon production equipment and material were not so easily replaced, and therefore the UNSCOM teams found significantly more resistance.

The inspection teams found no evidence of biological agents in any bunkers, or of manufacturing equipment at any of the suspected locations. Two inspections for biological agents were conducted by the end of 1992. The UNSCOM team that inspected Salman Pak identified research equipment that could have been used either for offensive or defensive programs, with offensive programs as the primary purpose. During the second inspection, the UN teams singled out the single-cell protein facility at al-Hakem as a potential next step in the Iraqi biological warfare program and recommended continued monitoring of the site. Ten suspected biological agent storage sites were inspected. As mentioned earlier, the Iraqi military had used the suspected refrigerated bunkers for conventional munitions and electronic components rather than for storing biological munitions. The Special Commission found no conclusive evidence of an offensive biological warfare program at that time.[17] Later evidence, however, told a different story.

Based on Iraqi declarations through August 1995, the total capability of Iraq's BW program was formidable. It had manufactured 11,800 liters of botulinum toxin, 8,825 liters of anthrax spores, 2,200 liters of aflatoxin and 340 liters of clostridium perfringens toxin (gas gangrene). In 1990 the Iraqi military had tested both anthrax and botulinum toxin in live agent weapon tests. During December 1990 Iraq had deployed 150 filled bombs (100 botulinum toxin, fifty anthrax) and twenty-five Scud missiles with biological agent warheads (thirteen botulinum toxin, ten anthrax, two aflatoxin) to forward storage locations. Three 2,000-liter aerial spray tanks had been stored for the purpose of anthrax dispersement, ready for use in the early months of 1991. In September 1995 Iraq admitted to conducting biological warfare research, development and storage at Al Fallujah, Muthanna, Salman Pak, Al-Kindi and Al Hakam. The Iraqi government had claimed to have destroyed all biological agents and their delivery systems prior to June 1991.

The first inspection of chemical munitions sites was UNSCOM-2, which focused on the primary declared site at the Muthanna facility near Samarra. This inspection, carried out June 9–14, 1991, was not a thorough, detailed investigation but a broad-brush attempt to get an idea of the scope of effort necessary for future inspections. The second chemical inspection was in UNSCOM-9, which took place in August, 1991. The inspection team, consisting of twenty-two people from eleven nations, assembled in Bahrain to prepare for the inspection. On August 15, its members entered Iraq to begin their inspection work. They began with one day at each of the three "precursor" facilities at al-Fallujah, followed by two days at the Muthanna facility, and one day at the al-Taqqadum air base, south of Baghdad. The team was to identify any chemical agents that had been produced, what precursors were used, the industrial site capability, where the munitions and bulk agent were stored, and any other pertinent CBW activities. Muthanna and the three precursor facilities had been elaborately defended, but the overwhelming air superiority of the coalition effectively had destroyed all four sites.

The Muthanna State Establishment facility featured two pilot plants and a destruction site in addition to its manufacturing capabilities. The main complex was quite large, measuring over twenty-five square kilometers. It had been legitimately producing pesticides after the Iran-Iraq ceasefire in 1988; after the war had ended, it was no longer cost-efficient to maintain a chemical warfare production line, and the Iraqis changed the production to pesticides to support the state's agricultural business. It changed back to its original purpose in August 1990 and was producing chemical agents in October and December. These production runs were necessary to replace nerve agent munitions which, due to poor quality, were degrading in effectiveness. In addition to basic chemical munitions R&D, it produced mustard gas, tabun, sarin and nerve agent GF. The plant also filled chemical munitions manufactured at other facilities. It appeared that the initial estimates of poor quality control in the production of nerve agents had been correct. The Iraqis had developed the ability to make 70 percent pure nerve agent at best, with an average standard of 55 percent. The effectiveness of their nerve agent would have significantly degraded if stored over forty-five days.

The largest precursor site, Habbaniyah 2 at al-Maamoun, had produced a wide variety of precursors, including several industrial chemicals (chlorine, hydrochloric acid, caustic soda and sodium hypochlorite) as well as the chemical agent precursors (thionyl chloride, difluoro and dichloro-methyl phosphine oxide, phosphorus trichloride, methyl phosphite). The second plant, Habbaniyah 1 at al-Farouk, formulated pesticides, produced plastic bottles, and stored the precursors. The teams found twelve tons of di-isopropylamine, twenty-five tons of dimethylamine hydrochloride, forty tons of thiodiglycol, and fifty-two tons of 2-chlorobenzaldehyde (the last chemical being a precursor for CS agent). Enough precursors existed to manufacture 500 tons of VX nerve agent. The forty tons of thiodiglycol included a large shipment originating from Baltimore, Maryland, that had been sent through Jordan to Iraq prior to the Kuwaiti invasion (but during the embargo against Iraq).

The last facility, Habbaniyah 3, had no chemicals, as its production had been suspended at the end of 1987. Ironically, it was the most thoroughly bombed of the three sites. At the Al Taqqadum air base the inspection team found 200 mustard bombs, a few of which were leaking. The bombs were not marked, nor were they stored in any special fashion. This was also the case for chemical munitions later found near al-Nasariyah in October 1991. It seems that the Iraqi army had special escort units to accompany movements of chemical weapons from production and filling to the storage areas, and from these storage areas to the delivery systems. This negated the need to mark munitions, since most were made to be employed shortly after production.

The majority of the chemical munitions examined in August were degraded and tactically insignificant. Few of the GB/GF-filled 122 mm rockets were functional, their chemical agents having lost much of their lethality. The "binary" munitions were not truly binary, as the US military had designed its weapon systems. These munitions required an individual to mix the chemicals manually and then rush the weapon to the delivery system. Once made the chemical agent immediately began to degrade, making it essential to use the weapons at that time or not at all. Records showed that the Iraqi Ministry of Defense had ordered 8,320 rockets filled with about fifty tons of binary mix in December 1990. It should be emphasized that although the UNSCOM team found these weapons degraded in August 1991, they were most likely potent and very much a threat to the coalition in the summer and fall months of 1990. For what was found, see Table 7.1.

In addition to what was found, the Iraqis declared that they had destroyed 19,000 122 mm rockets, 800 aerial bombs, and forty-five binary agent-filled al-Hussein missile warheads prior to the inspection. They also revealed 82 mm/120 mm CS-filled mortar shells and CS-filled RPG-7 infantry rockets. Notably absent from this list is any record of chemical-filled land mines.

Table 7.1
Status of Iraqi Chemical Munitions as of August 1991

Munition	Agent Fill	Location
10,780 122 mm rockets	GB/GF "binary"	al Muthanna, Khamisiyah
1100 aerial bombs, 250 pound	Mustard	Various air bases
140 aerial bombs, 500 pound	Mustard	Various air bases
336 aerial bombs, 400 pound	GB/GF "binary"	Various air bases
30 al-Hussein warheads	GB/GF "binary"	Various air bases
12,634 155 mm arty projectiles	Mustard	Half at Nassiriyah, half at Fallujah
280 tons bulk agent	Mustard	al Muthanna

Of the more than 350,000 mines removed since the end of the war, no chemical land mines have been discovered (contrary to Marine Corps's reports). By the end of 1992, UNSCOM had completed fifteen chemical inspections and three biological inspections in Iraq. Technical escort units transported all chemical munitions that were safe to move to al-Muthanna and its chemical destruction facility. All chemical munitions discovered were destroyed by late 1993 by incinerating the mustard agents and hydrolyzing the nerve agents.

Upon returning to Bahrain on August 23, the inspection team made the following conclusions. The Iraqi military command had expected the war to be a sequel of the earlier Iran-Iraq War. Its production sites had been well protected; there had been good communications and unrestricted movement during that war; and the leaders assumed that this would be the case again. The Iraqi leadership had not accounted for the incredible accuracy of allied air attacks and the total loss of airspace control. Its production sites proved to be much more vulnerable than expected. The limited production time had not allowed them to build up a sufficient stockpile prior to the destruction of those facilities in the air campaign. The neutralization of their air force, a prime delivery system, and the destruction of the transportation infrastructure meant that the only real chemical delivery capabilities that Iraq had at the beginning of the ground offensive were artillery and rockets, which were thoroughly targeted.

There were a number of GB/GF-filled warheads for the al-Hussein missiles still available, which could have been used against Israeli or Saudi cities or to harass and delay the supplies and troops at Dammam, Dhahran or KKMC. There was, however, no effective means for Iraq to carry out a protracted CBW campaign against the coalition forces, whatever the desire to do so. Iraqi EPWs stated that the massive artillery suppression had stopped them from even planning a coordinated chemical strike, since they could not hope to mass the amount of chemical munitions on target to be militarily effective. However, their few weapon systems still could have severely disrupted the coalition offensive because of the psychological impact on military leaders and troops. This assumption that the Iraqis could disrupt combat operational tempo and cause massive casualties had kept US forces on edge for six months as they prepared their chemical defense plans.[18]

Figure 7.1
Declared Iraqi CBW Agent Stockpiles

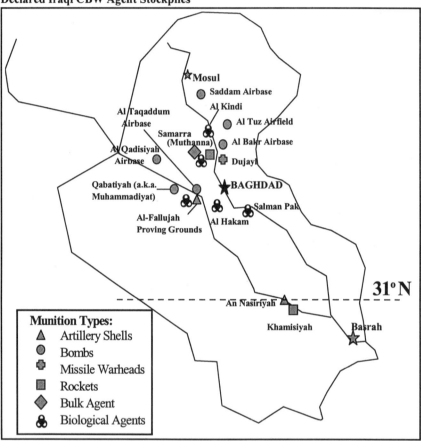

MG McCaffrey offered two insights as to why there was no chemical warfare in a talk to chemical officers at Fort McClellan. First, every time a chemical officer had the opportunity, he or she had shown reporters, congressional delegations and other visitors how prepared their units were to survive and sustain combat operations in a CB-contaminated environment without any substantial effects to their combat strength. Not only did they state that opinion, the soldiers and leaders of the 24th IN DIV believed it. They did not state that it would make life utter misery—but they would be alive. General Powell shared this same confidence, that while the soldiers were threatened by biological agent weapons, and the cities by

Scud chemical warheads, the soldiers could have performed well under chemical warfare conditions. This preparedness may have convinced those in Baghdad that chemical weapons would only anger the Americans, not stop them. This point did not alter Saddam's use of the chemical weapons arsenal as a strategic bluff, one card to force the CENTCOM coalition to spend six months preparing for what they thought would be a grueling and high casualty battle.

Second, McCaffrey remained unconvinced that Saddam would not have ordered the use of CB agent munitions despite the US defense preparations. The Iraqi soldiers had protective masks, overgarments and decon kits ready for something. US national policy still asserted the right to retaliate in kind, despite a commitment by the current administration to demilitarize the chemical arms stockpile. It could be that they did fear the possibility of US retaliation with chemical weapons, or the threat of British, French or Israeli retaliation with nuclear weapons. Steady diplomatic pressure, combined with strong psychological warfare against using CB agent munitions, may have had an effect on the Iraqi field commanders. Iraqi political and military leaders were never quite sure what the coalition nations meant when they talked about retaliation. Later statements from Iraqi commanders stressed their fear that the United States would retaliate with nuclear or chemical weapons. Their forces were not prepared to defend against chemical weapons, and this concern kept CB agent munitions from being used.

Other possible explanations exist. Iraqi forces did not face the situations that had prodded them to use chemical agents against Iran. CENTCOM stopped prior to taking Basrah, as opposed to Iran's attempts to capture one of the major cities in the country. There was no drive against Baghdad to spur last-second desperation tactics. Also, the continually declining quality of nerve agent might have played a part in the decision not to use chemical munitions, especially as the production lines were shut down. There was no capability after January 1991 to replenish the stocks, and it may be that Saddam was reserving his few Scud CB agent-filled warheads, artillery shells and spray tanks for a coalition attack against Baghdad.

The US military had received an unexpected reprieve from a test of its chemical defense capability. Nonetheless, US forces should not have had to build up their readiness so desperately in the last half of 1990. Chemical soldiers met to discuss how these lessons might be captured and what was needed to improve US armed forces' defensive capability for future battles.

CHAPTER 8

After-Action Report

To inquire if and where we made mistakes is not to apologize. War is replete with mistakes because it is full of improvisations. In war we are always doing something for the first time. It would be a miracle if what we improvised under the stress of war should be perfect.

—Vice Admiral Hyman Rickover

In the attempt to identify the lessons learned from a conflict, it must be remembered that every war is unique. The Persian Gulf War had certain unique features, such as six months to deploy and prepare. There was no submarine threat or significant naval surface action. Reinforcements from Germany and the United States did not fear enemy attack en route to Saudi Arabia. Because there was no actual weapons use that stressed the coalition's NBC defense capabilities, it is difficult to identify lessons in that area. Some wonder if the outcome would have been different if Iraq had acquired tactical nuclear weapons earlier, attacked Saudi Arabia in September while only the 82d Airborne Division was in place, possessed a larger arsenal of more sophisticated ballistic missiles, or employed CB weapons in its defense. Not all coalition partners had equal levels of NBC defense preparation. What would have happened if the French or Syrians had refused to advance against Iraqi forces because of large-area CB agent attacks? The result could have been exposed flanks or holes in the coalition lines, potential breach points for counterattacking Iraqis and potential disaster for American forces.

Saddam Hussein had implied that his forces were prepared to use CB weapons to disrupt and defeat the coalition forces. His army had experience in conducting combat operations in an NBC environment, and his armed forces were experienced in delivering these munitions against Iranian soldiers and cities. By 1990 Iraq had the largest CW production capability in the Third World, with a stockpile of thousands of tons of blister and nerve agents. Iraq had developed and weaponized BW agents, to include anthrax bacteria and botulinum toxin. With ballistic missiles capability, aerial bombs, artillery shells, rockets and spray tanks, this threat challenged the coalition in a very sensitive and vulnerable area. This led to the response by American, European and Israeli politicians that their military response to CB warfare would be "absolutely overwhelming and . . . devastating."[1] While some outside the city of Washington chose to interpret this as a nuclear or possibly chemical weapons response, within the Pentagon this policy was never really defined as a nuclear or massive conventional attack against industrial and military targets. We still do not know if these undefined political overtures were a factor in Saddam Hussein's holding back the use of CB agent munitions.

Congress was not long in seeking answers about NBC defense during the Persian Gulf War. It was impossible to hide the lack of military readiness prior to the initiation of Operation Desert Shield. Based on the GAO's assessment, the US military was not ready for NBC warfare on August 8, 1990. Army spokespersons assured Congress that the troops were well trained and well equipped for CB warfare by February 1991 and that Iraq's offensive NBC capability had been significantly blunted, in both verbal and written testimony.[2] While these statements were true and acknowledged, Congress wanted answers on how the Army had allowed the prior low state of readiness to occur in the first place. In August 1991, as Congress developed the fiscal 1992 budget, the House and Senate appropriations committees (HAC and SAC) raised concerns that the NBC defense program was not adequately funded. The House Armed Services Committee (HASC) raised similar concerns in December 1991. The chairman of the Subcommittee on Readiness, Representative Earl Hutto (D-FL), whose congressional district included Eglin Air Force Base (then the site of the Air Force's advanced development work on NBC defense programs), wrote to Secretary Cheney:

> While the Army is the executive agent for chemical defense, the services are instituting a proliferation of research programs to develop their own equipment because the DoD and the Army have not provided adequate oversight and guidance. The failure of the Army to develop and produce the M-40 mask after twenty years is a symbol of the ineffective chemical defense organization within DoD and the need for radical change to the current structure.
>
> Another obvious issue brought out at the [GAO] hearing was the need for additional training that is more effective and realistic.[3]

The HASC comments observed that the Army had been less than proactive in fielding chemical defense equipment prior to August 1990. The committee held the opinion that the Marine Corps's Saratoga suit was superior to the Army's BDO (still a hotly contested issue after the war). The members recommended that the Army improve and reinvigorate the management of both equipment and training programs, especially individual protection and medical antidotes. The committee called on the Army to prepare a report on its efforts to improve NBC defense protection and training.[4]

The Senate Armed Services Committee (SASC) concurred, emphasizing the military's immediate need to develop a BW agent detection capability. It also expressed concern about reports that the Army and Navy were not cooperating in this effort and charged the OATSD(HA) to review the situation and take appropriate actions to control this feuding. The SASC also raised how the Army planned for industry production for NBC defense items, as seen with the late shipments of protective clothing and masks. It directed DoD to take necessary steps to ensure the maintenance and stability of the industrial base, and to submit a report on an approach and implementation plan to sustain the industrial base.

The HAC recommended that additional funds be approved for both medical research and development and for the improvement of protective clothing (but not to be spent on the Army's current BDO). Despite the House's addition of $100 million in the previous year's operations and maintenance budget, most BDOs had not arrived until after hostilities were over. Conversely, the House reduced the budget request for smoke and obscurants programs due to program growth and budget execution issues (and perhaps due to ignorance of the success of smoke operations in the Gulf War).

The SAC singled out the M1 CAM, rather than the Army's protective clothing program, for additional funding. Its concerns focused on the possibility that the current protection equipment might be inadequate to meet existing threats worldwide. This concern included DLA's ability to retain the industrial base for protective gloves in the future. The SAC echoed the SASC's desire that the biological detection program be accelerated to field some capability in this area as soon as possible. The committee was particularly worried about the Air Force's NBC defense readiness, as forward air bases were among the most likely targets of large-area coverage weapons. They instructed the Secretary of the Air Force to report on means of improving the capability of tactical contingency forces to carry out their missions on a contaminated battlefield. This report would include ways to use existing DoD facilities and equipment to improve the realism of Air Force training; determination as to whether or not the Air Force had sufficient manpower and specialists to carry out the NBC defense mission; and the feasibility and desirability of increasing the knowledge of non-NBC defense Air Force members through toxic chemical agent familiarization courses (like the Army's CDTF). The Air Force was tasked to consider collocating its Disaster Preparedness School at Fort McClellan, as Lowery AFB was scheduled to be closed. Last, the SAC called for a report on the status of the four services' NBC defense RDA programs.[5]

THE OFFICIAL DOD RESPONSE

Although the Coalition's CW/BW defense was not truly tested in combat, many elements of an effective CW/BW defense, including a particularly energetic personal protection program, clearly contributed to the overall deterrent and, importantly, to the ability of the Coalition to press ahead with a bold, offensive strategy.

—DoD, *Conduct of the Persian Gulf War*

The DoD *Final Report to Congress on the Conduct of the Persian Gulf War* was released in April 1992. The appendix discussing NBC defense was drafted by the CENTCOM chemical officer, Lieutenant Colonel Silvernail. Accounting for twelve pages of the overall DoD report, Appendix Q (Chemical and Biological Warfare Defense) summarized the highlights and critical issues of DoD's NBC defense preparedness. The appendix acknowledged the initial low readiness of the forces, the extraordinary effort made to correct these weaknesses, and the initial diplomatic and military measures (air strikes against the CW/BW plants) to minimize the chance of CB warfare. It noted the tenuousness of the intelligence assessments of the Iraqi BW threat as opposed to the better-established CW threat. The report discussed the Army chemical force structure, assembled from both the active and reserve components, and training measures undertaken by all services during the conflict.

Because Congress and the services pay more attention to the materiel side of NBC defense than doctrine or organization, Appendix Q emphasized the equipment challenges and successes. The establishment of the JSCC-CDE was seen as a significant part of those successes. The report credited the JSCC-CDE with substantially improving CW/BW readiness of the military. Accomplishments included a rapid increase in defensive readiness, realistic training and good equipment fielding initiatives on the parts of developmental equipment. The report recognized the effort involved in fielding the CAM, XM21 RSCAAL, ANBACIS-II, and XM93 Fox NBCRS vehicles. It asserted while protective masks and clothing may have proved burdensome and initial shortages vexing, soldiers had confidence in their individual protective equipment.

Shortcomings included the availability, durability and suitability of protective clothing in the desert. The report acknowledged the shortages of CAMs and their improper use by untrained soldiers, the XM21's false alarm problems and the shortage of Fox vehicles. Collective protection was clearly inadequate across the board; with the exception of the vehicular CPE gained during the M1A1 tank swapout, there was much room for improvement. Water-based decontamination systems, such as the M12A1s and M17 SANATORs, while adequate for the European theater, were inadequate for desert operations. The report hit on the real logistics nightmare that NBC defense had caused: more than $250 million of worldwide theater reserve chemical defense equipment had been drawn upon to respond to the crisis. The major issues remaining included the need for lightweight protective suits, better integration of collective protection systems, a more adequate biological warfare defense readiness, additional NBCRS vehicles, and a replacement for water-based decontamination systems.[6]

Not identified in the report were some other lessons learned. Protective suits arrived none too soon for the ground war's initiation. The Air Force had canceled its entire collective protection program in the spring of 1990, only to urgently request collective protection systems in September 1990. The Marine Corps's M21 RSCAAL order placed during the conflict arrived well after the conflict. The services' leadership clearly identified the urgent need for these systems during the crisis, but industry could not pivot on a dime for these military-unique applications. This showed the need for careful planning if the services wanted an NBC defense capability in place prior to a conflict.

CHEMICAL CORPS REVIEW

Senior chemical officers met at Fort McClellan in June 1991 to analyze their performance in the Gulf War. The official TRADOC summary on NBC defense during Desert Storm stated:

> Nuclear, biological, and chemical (NBC) *unit infrastructure is sound.* The rapid fielding of NBC reconnaissance equipment is *underway.* The Army fielded 49 modified German Fox vehicles during Operation Desert Storm and 75 additional systems are funded in FY93-94.
>
> The *required* NBC *fixes* are: biological and standoff chemical detection and warning capability; NBC protection clothing to match mission profiles; and lightweight alarm capabilities.
>
> There is a system improvement program that will convert a decontamination company into a reconnaissance company in XVIII ABN Corps in FY93.[7]

If one had to wrap up the Chemical Corps's lessons in one paragraph, that would probably cover the major points. There were, however, other issues to examine, including unit readiness and training, rear area vulnerability, the effectiveness of active defense against NBC weapon systems, command and control of NBC defense units, logistics support, biological agent sampling and response, smoke operations and the need to invigorate the NBC defense sector of the DoD industrial base.

Unit Readiness and Training

Prior to 1981, Army unit readiness and training in the area of NBC defense was inadequate; no one will debate that. By 1990, the Army had successfully integrated individual survival skills into unit training, such as use of decon kits and protective masks. Its chemical defense doctrine was sound and would work. The weakness was training. The Army had not implemented a training strategy to teach units above the platoon level how to conduct large scale operations in an NBC-contaminated environment. The lack of realistic training aids and chemical agent simulants for large-area unit training created this low state of readiness. Unit leaders could not train and evaluate their operations with chemical defense equipment that did not indicate if it was functioning correctly during training. It went against the "train as you will fight" mantra of the Army. In the fall of 1990, the solution to this lack of readiness was to rely heavily on the chemical specialist infrastructure that had been built up in the 1980s. Chemical NCOs and officers developed training programs to reawaken rusty individual skills, then developed small-unit operations such as detector placement and crew decontamination drills.

Concurrent with these efforts, higher-level staffs included NBC-attack scenarios in their war games. Slowly, over the six months of Desert Shield, the US military regained its title as the most highly trained and prepared force in the world. Without a doubt, the integration of chemical soldiers into the combat arms initiated in 1979, from corps down to company level, was the driving force of CENTCOM's defensive readiness.

The majority of the 4,200 chemical soldiers deployed to Southwest Asia had trained in the Chemical Defense Training Facility at Fort McClellan. Many of those chemical soldiers and their leaders stated that their confidence in their equipment and training directly resulted from training in a toxic agent environment. There were scores of non-chemical soldiers in theater who did not trust their masks, protective clothing, or agent detectors to warn and protect them, and they turned to these chemical soldiers for assurance. Chemical soldiers could state confidently that the protective gear, detection and decontamination equipment would work, because they had used the equipment in the presence of actual nerve agents. This was a big plus for the credibility and confidence that commanders had in their chemical soldiers. Major General McCaffrey brought more than 500 of his commanders and their staff to Fort McClellan's CDTF after the war to familiarize them with the toxic agent training; other division commanders did the same.

Reservists had the most difficulty in developing NBC defense skills. NBC defense training in the Reserve Component had been neglected more than in the active duty force. Given the limited time that Reservists actually train as a unit, they generally do not gain expertise in tasks such as setting out agent detectors, running decontamination operations, or operating for long periods of time in protective clothing. Again, the chemical specialist infrastructure within the reserve forces was key to training these soldiers prior to the ground offensive. Without this training, the reservists would have been hard pressed to do more than survive in NBC warfare conditions, let alone support the active units in a fast-moving offensive.

Civilian training was a new facet for the Chemical Corps. For the first time, it had to equip and train government civilians, industry contractors and media personnel in basic NBC defense and survival skills. This had never been planned for or funded. The resulting demands on equipment and trainers had to be met by chemical officers and NCOs at US deployment centers and in-theater, already tasked to get their combat forces prepared. Again, because of the six-month grace period, it was possible to equip and train the civilians to a level at which they might survive a chemical attack. Asking civilians to operate in a contaminated environment might have been asking too much.[8]

These skills are highly perishable, however. Some Desert Storm brigade combat commanders and senior staff members expressed the view after the war that "the threat posed by Iraq was the most formidable and most likely opportunity for weapons of mass destruction to have been used against US forces. Since the use of these weapons did not occur under the most likely set of circumstances, they would never be used and NBC defense training could be significantly reduced or disregarded."[9] Evidence of this exists at today's Combat Training Centers (CTCs). At the JRTC, Fort Polk, light infantry leaders tell their troops to keep their masks in their rucksacks to minimize the load. At Fort Irwin's National Training Center, units show up without adequate chemical defense equipment and with soldiers not trained to operate M8A1 chemical alarms. Training in Germany, brigades send their Fox platoons to reconnoiter ahead of the force alone, making them easy kills. Unit and leader success at the CTCs still does not require proper use of decontamination assets. Many combat arms leaders still do not understand how NBC defense operations "fit" into their perspective of conventional warfare.

Rear Area Vulnerabilities

The most difficult area to protect had been the corps, army and theater rear areas, where the majority of the Army force remained vulnerable. It is hard to say anything positive about NBC defense for the rear areas; rather, it was a disaster waiting to happen (but that, fortunately, did not take place). Poor training of reserve support units and government civilians, who made up a large part of rear support, was the first hindrance. In addition, most chemical agent detectors and decontamination devices were up front with combat units due to shortages of these items. Many combat support units had to rely on radio warnings from higher headquarters and M9 paper taped to the tents and vehicles as initial warnings. The sheer number of base clusters (more than one hundred), spread out over literally thousands of square kilometers, made it very difficult to warn everyone of CB agent attacks and predicted contaminated areas. Difficulties in communicating to rear area units meant long delays between Scud attacks and when the individual base clusters were warned.

Most supplies were kept largely in the open, uncovered and vulnerable to persistent CB agents. There was not enough decontamination support to cover all of the division, army and theater support units in the rear area. Accelerated development of protective covers or protective shelters might have done much to reduce that vulnerability. Corps and division commanders remained acutely aware of these problems as they arrived in the theater, and they placed a high priority on the call-up of reserve chemical decontamination companies. Potential CB contamination of rear-area operations was, and remains, a very vulnerable aspect of the Army field organization.

Another difficulty in rear areas was the mixture of Air Force and Army units which had different alerts, warning systems and procedures. Sirens, MOPP levels and MOPP level designations varied, causing confusion where the two services shared the same base. With the movement of the Air Force's Disaster Preparedness School from Lowery AFB, Colorado, to Fort McClellan in 1994, and of the CBR portion of the Navy's Shipboard Survivability School from New Hampshire to Fort McClellan in 1995, efforts to coordinate doctrine and training among the services can finally take place.

One of the most important tools for determining the threat to rear area units (and others in theater) was the ANBACIS-II software. This computerized CB agent contamination-prediction capability allowed commanders at all levels to pinpoint the areas for consideration for contamination hazard surveys and increased protection. This meant fewer soldiers in protective gear and less overall degradation to the force. Reliance on CONUS-based computers and the inability to communicate directly to divisions remain challenges. ANBACIS-II (or similar concepts) without the need of Cray computer support will be further refined to fit into the Army's maneuver control system. Growing emphasis on battlefield digitization calls for just this kind of capability. Far-term efforts point toward a network of CB agent detectors, resulting in near-real-time situational awareness of CB agent hazards. Improved prediction of contamination hazards will provide much more useful options for military leaders than merely reacting to contamination predictions after the munitions have landed.

"Active Defense" versus Passive Defense

The air campaign was effective in stopping production of CB agent munitions but failed to destroy delivery systems, munition stockpiles or manufacturing equipment that had been moved. NBC agent delivery systems and newly identified production and storage sites continued to demand the highest priority and attention. Despite this intense effort, Air Force and SOCCOM units failed to stop the mobile Scuds, and the majority of Iraq's air force survived as a threat to CENTCOM forces. Prior to the Gulf War, Air Force planners had never envisioned the difficulties of attacking CB production/storage targets. Concerns that CB agents might escape the destructive power of the munitions was a driving factor behind the extensive ANBACIS-II modeling requirements. The Air Force is currently working on several concepts for munitions that penetrate deep, hardened targets such as storage sites, and neutralize CB agents within them, minimizing the chance of large-area contamination.[10] Offensive munitions do not work, however, unless intelligence finds the targets.

US intelligence agencies failed to identify and track the production and proliferation of CB munitions sites and stockpiles in Iraq. It has become increasingly difficult to track and monitor which nations are developing offensive CB weapons programs. Despite the end of the Cold War, there are still 100 analysts dedicated to nuclear weapons proliferation to every one dedicated to CB weapons proliferation. Adding to this misbalance is the near absence of any human intelligence assets in countries that have CB weapons programs.

Legitimate supplies and equipment are commonly used to manufacture CB agents. The advent of a true global economy and the ability to construct front agencies to purchase and move supplies throughout the world market means that nations do not have to buy all their supplies and equipment from one company, or even from one nation. Given this lack of data, intelligence agencies could not significantly identify all CB production and storage sites. Thus, the Air Force could not stop Iraq from using CB agent munitions, as it (and the DoD leadership) claimed air power had at the end of January 1991.

Iraq's Scuds used against Israel and Saudi Arabia could have been armed with chemical warheads. Certainly the capability existed, if not the experience, to attack deep targets effectively in CENTCOM's area of operations. Proliferation of ballistic missile technology across the globe continues today. Advances in ballistic missile development, unpiloted and remotely piloted airframes, special force's operations and protected underground sites will ensure a constant enemy production capability and threat of CB agent employment. More advanced forms of ballistic missile defense, as well as more effective methods of locating and attacking mobile ballistic launchers, will be necessary to protect the force. The Ballistic Missile Defense Office has added the mission of countering ballistic missiles with CB warheads to the future capabilities of a Theater High-Altitude Area Defense.

The Army, as well as the Air Force, attempted to silence the Iraqi CB delivery systems during the battlefield preparation phase of the ground offensive. Each corps drew on additional artillery units above and beyond its normal organizational allotment to counter the Iraqi's long-range artillery and the threat of chemical agent attacks during the breaching operation. In the week prior to the offensive, the corps commanders employed a Soviet-style artillery barrage to knock out systems that might target CENTCOM with CB agent munitions. Without this capability, the ground forces might have been targeted and attacked during the breaching operations by longer-ranged Iraqi artillery firing chemical projectiles. Against an adversary with counterbattery capability, a more mobile enemy force or one with better concealment/deception operations, these massive artillery attacks may not have been feasible.

As later UNSCOM inspections revealed, the majority of CB agent munitions survived the CENTCOM onslaught. Had Saddam seriously wanted to use these munitions, we might have seen the Iraqi CB agent attacks so feared by the two corps commanders. Future commanders will not be able to rely on "active defense" against CB agent storage sites and delivery systems with 100 percent confidence without strategic and operational intelligence on where those sites are located. Even where this information is available, deep underground facilities exist for CB munitions production and storage. These facilities could probably resist nuclear attacks, let alone conventional air attacks. What future commanders can count on is increased reliance on chemical defense equipment and more proactive use of chemical defense units.

Command and Control of Chemical Defense Units

The absence of a chemical brigade to coordinate life support and mission assignments for the chemical battalions and non-divisional companies was keenly felt. Often, non-divisional chemical companies were directly attached to combat divisions instead of to the chemical battalions supporting that corps. In some cases, a company's three platoons were supporting three different divisions. Division and corps NBCCs had to manage the changing cast of these chemical defense units in addition to attending to their own operations planning, logistics and personnel issues. The non-divisional chemical defense units rotated to new assignments with each new operations order, and their rotations were not well managed. Many of the divisions had to coordinate the swaps of chemical defense units between themselves, instead of working through a central point.

The chemical defense companies had to search constantly for their logistics and operations support, receiving it from a new source every time they changed organizations, unlike corps-level units that retain a single higher support source while assigned to various divisions. Three chemical battalions operating under the one chemical brigade would have established the command and control relationship and logistics support that these non-divisional battalions and companies required. Artillery and engineer battalions working in support of divisions already use this concept. In addition, a chemical brigade commander (optimally a brigadier general) would have had direct lines of communication to ARCENT, CENTCOM, and the division and corps commanders in order to assess their needs better and to communicate the non-divisional chemical defense companies' capabilities. This might have enhanced the flow of intelligence information to chemical officers throughout the force structure; that flow was limited due to the intelligence staffs bypassing the lieutenant colonels in CENTCOM and ARCENT. Ideally, future commanders will understand that a sound supporting cast is needed in addition to combat power to ensure survivability in early phases of military operations.

However, this is not necessarily the case. The latest attempts to restructure the Army divisions, under Force XXI, has focused on downsizing the manpower from 18,000 to 15,000. One proposal is to remove divisional chemical companies (about 170 personnel) and move them under a corps chemical brigade. The Fox recon platoon may be moved to the division's cavalry aviation brigade. The corps chemical brigade would also hold the active and reserve decon companies and the theater Biological Integrated Defense System (BIDS) company, without using chemical battalions for "middle management." Whether or not this will reduce a division's ability to train and deploy with its former dedicated chemical companies isn't known yet. What is discouraging is the implication that dedicated chemical companies are not vital enough to consider as part of the division main effort. This plan is not set in stone yet, but it does show once again that combat arms leaders are not taking the time to evaluate exactly how NBC defense operations in the future will play out.

NBC Defense Equipment Logistics

Chemical defense equipment (CDE) logistics had been a struggle throughout the conflict. Through the 1980s, the Chemical School had introduced large amounts of new CDE into the Army. However, combat units were not maintaining adequate quantities for contingency operations, nor were they aware what quantities existed within their own units. As a result, when these units arrived in Saudi Arabia, they had to identify their shortfalls and then order the supplies from the United States. ARCENT NBCC had tried to assist by requiring of the two corps a special report to quantify their status, in an attempt to determine the theater CDE shortfalls. The corps' logistics centers were too busy to implement this process and kept submitting requisitions for more CDE without trying to determine their actual status. This made it next to impossible for ODCSLOG to work up a planning and delivery system to get CDE to the units that needed it most. In addition, there was no policy within FORSCOM for what CDE should accompany deploying individuals, especially those sent through CONUS Processing Centers. These soldiers were told they would receive all their CB defense gear once in theater—which was not true. FORSCOM eventually corrected this problem, but not before thousands of US troops arrived without personal CDE, draining precious theater reserves.

The overall accountability of consumable CDE (protective suits, detector kits, and decon kits) in theater and throughout the armed forces was poor. Stacks of CDE grew in Dhahran and al-Damman, lost among other supplies. Compounding the problem that chemical officers and NCOs were often held responsible for procuring CDE in peacetime, rather than supply sergeants. During Desert Shield, this arrangement of "chemical logistics" in parallel with normal supply continued. Meanwhile, logistics offices were duplicating these efforts in response to their commanders' orders. As an example, one of the chemical soldiers' responsibilities became tracking each individual protective suit, each mask, each agent detector, can of decontaminant, and especially, each piece of new equipment (such as the CAMs and the XM93 NBCRS vehicles) as to when it was available and due in. Had logistics experts been procuring and transferring CDE, they might have been able to avoid the shortages encountered and the difficulties of prioritizing critical NBC defense supplies. The result was an inordinate drain on worldwide theater reserves, a lack of accountability of stocks and poor delivery results.

With the development of the Joint Chemical Defense Equipment Consumption Rates (JCHEMRATES) studies, logistics experts will be able to take back the responsibility. While chemical soldiers will continue to coordinate with their logistics counterparts to maintain a certain asset visibility, logistics experts must take charge and integrate CDE fully with other vital aspects of military logistics. Few other military operations rely so heavily on logistics for success.

Biological Agent Detection and Protection

Failure to eliminate the CB warfare threat through active defense emphasized the need for accurate and timely CB agent sampling and response throughout the theater. There has been a long history of inadequate BW defense preparations, even though the US military suspected that biological weapon technology had spread to over a dozen countries, including Iraq. Military and political leadership had always assumed they could treat biological warfare threats like nuclear warfare threats (that is to say, as a strategic political consideration), and were not prepared for military operational and tactical realities. The military leadership could also count on its individual protection equipment and decontamination systems, designed primarily for chemical agents, to also counter biological agents.

The lack of a real-time automatic biological agent detector, lack of a deployment plan, lack of a tested validation process, and the lack of a vaccination policy all handicapped a full BW defense capability. CENTCOM had to react to post-BW attack symptoms rather than relying on a low-level agent detector system that would permit instituting protective measures. Collecting a biological sample from air samplers or tactical units and transporting to JCMEC and forward labs could take from six hours to two days; transportation back to CONUS labs for verification took another day. This did not match the military's "information age" concept of operations.

Twelve biological detection teams were active for about two months in Southwest Asia, during which time they collected sixty-three environmental samples and 113 biomedical samples, and used over 2,000 biological SMART tickets for air samples.[11] Less than one percent of these gave positive readings at their sampling points, of which all were confirmed as negatives at the labs. The FMIB identified a number of challenges that it had encountered, in after-action reviews. Primary among these was the need to update the Army's 1980s-era doctrine that relied on post-attack indicators to warn of BW attacks. No military unit in the modern force structure had the responsibility for collecting biomedical and environmental samples. Chain-of-custody forms used in transporting samples were difficult to employ, and peacetime Air Force and Army safety regulations on transporting hazardous samples had to be ignored in the interests of time. Procedures for collecting and transporting the samples were equally outmoded, failing to include sampling procedures for the Fox vehicles. Containers used to transport the samples back to CONUS laboratories were adequate, mostly because they were commercial products used in similar biomedical operations. However, soldiers using this equipment were unfamiliar with it, not to mention with the collection, packaging, handling and documentation procedures.

The JCMEC itself did not have sufficient communications or transportation assets to cover a three-corps area. It was forced to rely on tactical units for much of the reporting, transportation and handling of samples. During Desert Shield, unit commanders were able to lend helicopters or HMMWVs to transport samples back to JCMEC; during Desert Storm, however, the tempo of the battle forced unit commanders to deny such transportation assets to the sampling teams in favor of the more urgent requirements of keeping their combat units supplied and moving. This would have limited quick identification of a BW attack, had it occurred, and could have ultimately cost lives.

Another deficiency was the lack of turn-around information from the laboratories in the United States. The Army Tech Escort Unit logged sixty-six missions to CONUS laboratories during the conflict, delivering over 240 samples within one-two days of receipt. The two corps and CENTCOM NBCCs did not receive any immediate feedback from the six or seven sets of chemical samples analyzed at Edgewood or the environmental samples analyzed at Fort Detrick. While this was a result of there being no positive confirmations of CB agents in these samples, the lack of a response unsettled the CENTCOM staff. This made the CENTCOM leadership very reliant on their forward labs for urgent confirmation of any threat. Only sixteen of the 240 samples were analyzed in-theater (they were SMART tickets showing false positives), suggesting that the majority of the samples flown to CONUS were questionable and not based on suspicions of actual CB weapons use but rather for confirmation of negative results.

The lack of biological agent vaccines is an old story by now. While vaccines for both anthrax and botulinum toxin were available to some US and allied forces, the pharmaceutical industry was very reluctant to support the vaccine program. Only two companies of more than ten contacted agreed to produce the vaccines, but not before critical shortages developed that could have doomed CENTCOM. Pharmaceutical companies have stated that the high risk of manufacturing vaccines for biological warfare agents, potential liabilities, high cost, and difficulty obtaining FDA approval made this a no-win situation for them, the result being heavy reliance on government initiatives. The need to rely on investigational new drugs raised concerns in troops, adding to their fears about CB warfare. The majority of US soldiers were not vaccinated, due in part to the escalation to a two-corps mission, industrial surge difficulties and the lack of a DoD policy for producing and distributing the doses. Division commanders felt that not having enough vaccine was worse for the morale and well-being of their soldiers than having no vaccines at all.

After the war, General Powell was furious that the lack of a biodefense strategy had nearly "slashed" CENTCOM's "Achilles' heel." In a classified memorandum to the Army, he blasted the DoD NBC defense program as inefficient and demanded substantial changes to prevent this error in the future. An interim plan dated March 1992 failed to reach joint consensus; the Joint Requirements Oversight Council therefore developed a joint Mission Needs Statement for a new biological defense program. A joint body called the Joint Services Committee for Biological Defense, led by ODCSOPS, outlined a DoD Operational Concept for Biological Defense, which grouped needed improvements into detection (point and stand-off), protection, decontamination and immunization. About a year later, the Office of the Secretary of Defense (OSD) created a special program office, the Joint Program Office for Biological Defense, or JPO-Bio, which would answer directly to OSD rather than to or through the Army. Colonel Gene Fuzy, having led the Army's efforts to develop a biodefense capability, was selected to lead this office, supported by the four services' NBC defense organizations.

Its goals are to develop an interim biological detection point capability by fiscal 1995 and a refined point detection capability by fiscal 2002; develop an interim strategic stand-off biological detection capability by 1997, and field a developed strategic stand-off detection capability by 2004; develop a tactical stand-off biological detection capability by 2005; and develop a biological agent vaccine production plant by 2002. These efforts have thus far been successful. The Army plans to field a biological detection company for Army corps units by 1997. Each company would feature thirty five Biological Integrated Detection Systems, whose HMMWVs resemble mobile laboratories. A contingency platoon of seven vehicles currently exists, capable of biological agent detection in less than twenty-five minutes. As newer technologies emerge, the BIDS will be upgraded until a real-time capability exists. The Navy has developed several Interim Biological Agent Detectors for the fleet. Future plans focus on developing a modular biological agent detector that meets all services' requirements, networked across the theater to alert all units to potential BW attacks.

The JPO-Bio is working with the services to develop new doctrine for using these detectors, in part through computer simulations that show potential employment patterns of biological weapons. The Army's manual FM 3-3, *Contamination Avoidance*, has been radically changed to focus on CB defense and has moved nuclear contamination avoidance to a second manual (FM 3-3-1). It includes a detailed description, based on the Biological Detection Teams' accounts, on how the Army will conduct future biological detection and sampling.

The medical side of JPO-Bio began soliciting industry to bid on the construction of a vaccine production facility and production of vaccines for the four services. To date, no industries have bid or are likely to participate—perhaps because none of the limiting factors of liability, risk, and FDA regulations have changed. The technology exists to develop antidotes and pretreatments for just about any CBW agent in quantities necessary to protect the force (at least for those CBW agents that have an available cure). Because there was such a small annual production requirement for these items (since most of them were stockpiled and not used), there were no industry production lines ready when the military asked for a step-up in production in August 1990. These events may force the Army toward a government-owned, government-operated facility that can run without regard of profit margins and liability suits. This option is being avoided by DoD, given the bend to increase industry participation in the defense sector rather than create more government jobs. Other options continue to be explored, with industry input.

Smoke Generator Operations

There were situations where smoke generator units were allowed to shine, but they were limited in number due to the uncooperative weather and the lack of Iraqi offensive operations. As in the Korean War, many smoke generator units prepared to smoke airfields, logistics areas, and headquarters locations to conceal them from an air threat that never materialized. The KFIA obscuration mission was a definite indication that these missions still have a place on the modern, fast-paced and non-linear battlefield. Also, Iraqi smoke operations definitely hindered the Air Force's attempts to knock out Tuwaitha nuclear facility. Deception operations during the movement to tactical staging areas may have fooled the Iraqi military into looking for an offensive up the middle through Kuwait instead of the actual flanking attack (the Iraqis have not commented yet).

The 1st CAV DIV successfully used smoke to obscure the several Iraqi units waiting in the Wadi al-Batin. When the raiding party ran into heavy fire, it was able to withdraw under cover of the smoke haze—very helpful, considering that this was a day attack in the (relatively) open desert. The greatest disappointment to the Chemical Corps may have occurred when the 1st IN DIV refused the support of two smoke generator companies in its breach operations. First, the use of smoke to obscure river-crossings, obstacle crossings and similar operations is an established and successful operational concept dating back to World War II. Second, two smoke generator companies at one division's beck and call when the normal allocation was one or two platoons represents a staggering amount of resources to discard, presumably after careful consideration of the benefits and risks. In any event, the wind, rain and sandstorm encountered on February 24 would have defeated the weather-dependant smoke operations. Had the weather been better, or had there been some Iraqi response to the offensive, the 1st IN DIV breach may have been very costly in terms of soldiers, resources and the VII Corps schedule.

When the mechanized smoke generator units were tasked to move to the 3rd AR DIV (racing at the head of VII Corps), the chemical companies found that the M113A2 chassis could not keep pace with the more modern armored units' M1A1 Abrams tanks and M2/3 Bradley fighting vehicles. Also, the smoke generator units still rely on 55-gallon drums of fog oil, resupply of which is a very inefficient and time-consuming operation. This indicated a need to either modernize the mechanized smoke vehicles to a Bradley chassis and upgrade its supporting logistics or identify a way to project smoke in front of the combat units in the form of projectiles. Since the Artillery Center and School would rather invest in smart projectiles that kill targets, they probably will not be the proponents of an increased capability in smoke projection. The PM Smoke has developed its latest M58 Wolf mechanized smoke system on an M113A3 APC, with a turbo-charged engine for increased mobility.

Smoke funding remains a low priority, even within the Chemical Corps. Public Law 103-160 created a special OSD funding line for the highly visible agent detectors, protective suits, and non-aqueous decontamination programs. Smoke systems remain an Army-funded budget line, competing against the major defense programs. Many military experts still do not realize the role that smoke operations played in the Gulf War, which impacted negatively on smoke's post-war funding. Yet if one were to ask combat soldiers, they might note that historically smoke generation systems have been the most accepted and successful of the many Chemical Corps' programs. Units training at the CTCs always look for and request smoke support. Further input is needed from the combat arms community on priority of effort before unit proficiency and leader experience in training with smoke is lost.

Given the lack of attention that the few successful smoke operations during the Gulf War have received to date, this attention does not seem likely in the near future, despite great potential in reducing enemy observation and target acquisition. With the evolution of smoke technologies that may soon block both infrared and millimeter wave scanners and target acquisition devices, and the increasing lethality of antitank munitions, the combat arms community can hardly afford to ignore the potential benefits. Perhaps with the increased participation of smoke units at the combat training centers and increased war gaming at the Army Battle Labs and Louisiana Maneuvers, this acknowledgment may yet come.

Industrial Base Issues

Industrial base issues are a hot topic for defense firms and Congress these days. Because of the shrinking requirements of a smaller military, DoD must pick and choose what they consider vital resources and which firms should perform those functions in the future. Most of the attention focuses on the "big boys": the submarine industrial base, the bomber industrial base, the tank production lines. Up to 1990 there had been little attention to the mostly small firms that supported the production of NBC defense equipment for the military. But as the six months of Desert Shield showed, critically weak areas within the NBC defense sector were (and remain) real war-stoppers.

The NBC defense sector of the DoD industrial base was unprepared to make up the extreme shortages in material for which DoD was asking industry to fill by surge production. The only items that the military had in excess were protective gloves and DS-2 decontaminant; everything else was in short supply and required immediate production to support CENTCOM. Only through a frantic, herculean effort by military and government personnel at depots, logistics centers, R&D centers, production bases and industry offices did the minimal necessary equipment get to Southwest Asia. Even given the full effort of these agencies, the NBC defense equipment necessary to survive *and sustain* combat operations did not arrive until mid-January.

This is not to say that the air and ground campaigns were delayed or that chemical defense equipment arriving was a precondition to starting operations; these deadlines, however, increased the urgency behind the NBC defense community. Had Saddam Hussein attacked into Saudi Arabia in August or September 1990, and if his army and air force had used CB munitions in the attack, our forces could have been frozen in place, these operations significantly degraded because of poor logistics planning. The necessary chemical defense equipment, including protective clothing, masks, decontaminant, agent detectors and medical supplies, was not available when it needed to be. This would have resulted in thousands of American and allied casualties and a great public outcry in the United States, which could have resulted in the withdrawal of US forces from the Gulf.

Much of the blame for this lack of readiness goes to the Army for its own reluctance to invest in war reserves of chemical defense equipment. This has resulted in low annual requirements and poor profitability margins, which lead to low bid contracts and less-than-high-quality equipment. There are some poor performers in the NBC defense industrial sector, brought in by the desire to fill contract quotas for small disadvantaged firms or to cater to the low bid, while ignoring high quality standards. These industries will only be weeded out when the overall DoD selection process is improved. Until then, the chemical defense community must work with industry to put plans in place to obtain sufficient quantities of CDE before conflicts erupt. In some cases, these plans for surge productions are being developed.

This issue refers back to the need for careful planning. The overall emphasis in the NBC defense programs remains on research and development, not on their acquisition and sustainment. As a result, the US armed forces have some very fine, sophisticated chemical defense systems—but not in the numbers required to sustain operations. Field commanders and policy makers have no way to measure the benefits of having a certain number of detectors, decontamination systems or collective protection shelters over a long conflict. As noted earlier, there are no modeling and simulation efforts that can demonstrate how effectively US forces can defend against CB agent munitions. If there is no definable "value-added" in terms of equipment and personnel, there is no push to get these defensive capabilities. As a result, there is little planning with industry on how to best meet the necessary equipment quantities prior to and during a conflict.

CB Defense Research and Development Program

Rather deliberately, there have been no official recriminations within DoD by its leadership against the Army's CB defense program. The Presidential Advisory Committee on Gulf War Illnesses has voiced the opinion, echoed by some veterans' groups and others, that the military has not done well in procuring CB agent detection systems (since there remains the question of whether or not low levels of nerve agents or biological agents were actually in the battlefield environment). Others have bemoaned the heavy protective suits, the older technology used for M17 protective masks, and the lack of alternatives to decontaminants that are highly corrosive and reliant on water. These CB defense programs are well researched and developed, but if one does not realize the limits and benefits of using a system, the user blames the developer for its faults rather than its admittedly untested benefits. Imagine a rookie policeman that had never been shot at complaining that his kevlar vest weighed too much to wear, and one immediately sees the parallel with soldiers complaining about chemical defense equipment. While this book did not allow for a proper discussion on how all these CB defense programs came to be, I can address the most ludicrous charge—that chemical agent detectors did not fulfill their designed mission.

Chemical agent detectors such as the M8A1 detector and M256A1 detector kit are designed to give soldiers who are not chemical specialists a device that would maximize time of warning, thus calling for low-level agent detection limits, while being man portable and rugged. As Table 8.1 shows, the suite of existing detectors more than adequately meet the soldiers' requirements of low-level agent detection.

The demand for sensitive detectors means occasional false alarms (mistaking other vapors such as diesel fuel for nerve agents, or false positives); however, chemical agent detectors do not ignore the presence of chemical agents (not alarming to nerve agents, or false negatives). Combat leaders never commented on the false alarm issue, largely because they do not train with detectors and never consider the consequences of false alarms (increased stress, lack of confidence in the equipment, etc.). What they did demand was a "zero-risk" approach to CB warfare, which is not duplicated in any other aspect of military R&D; for example, helmets are not required to deflect all bullets nor are armored vehicles required to stop all munitions from penetration, yet paradoxically, chemical agent alarms are required to detect all concentrations of all known agents.

The current suite of detectors already detects low levels of chemical agents far before they reach incapacitating or lethal quantities. However, this very feature make the detectors prone to confusing chemicals in the environment with chemical agents. If soldiers demanded zero false alarms instead of zero risk, more reliable detectors would emerge but at the price of higher detection limits and less warning time. To demand both zero risk and zero false alarms in rugged, man-portable packages would result in gold-plated detectors costing maybe a hundred thousand dollars each. Given that DoD has not seen fit to order the full necessary quantity of M8A1 alarms in the 1980s, and the future M22 Automatic Chemical Agent Detector/Alarm (ACADA) will not replace the M8A1 alarm on a one-to-one basis (about 40,000 required for the entire force) in the 1990s, what hope is there that DoD would procure these gold-plated ultimate end-state detectors?

There are always compromises made between any current weapon system and its respective gold-plated ultimate objective. In all areas except CBW, DoD determines the cost and benefits of assuming some level of risk in a trade-off between system performance, cost and its effect on military operations. If the Army raised the detection levels slightly to under incapacitating levels and decreased the false alarm rate, the overall cost would not be prohibitive and the operational results would be highly beneficial to the combat arms users. The only way this will happen is if the Army's infantry, armor and artillery leaders (especially the ones that become four star generals and major command leaders) start analyzing the costs and benefits of these options, identify what they really want and what they're willing to compromise on, adequately fund the programs, and work with the Chemical Corps to get these detectors built. Up to now, the chance of that general officer level of commitment does not seem too promising.

Table 8.1
Chemical Agent Detection Equipment Limits

	GB-nerve agent	VX-nerve agent	HD-blister agent	Response Time
Permissive/Airborne Exposure Limit	0.001 mg-min/m^3	0.00001 mg/m^3	0.003 mg/m^3	
Incapacitating Dose	35 mg-min/m^3	25 mg-min/m^3	2000 mg-min/m^3	
Lethal Dose (inhalation) (skin)	70 mg-min/m^3 1700 mg-min/m^3	30 mg-min/m^3 10 mg/70 kg man	49 mg/70 kg man[12] $10,000$ mg-min/m^3	
M8 paper	0.02 ml drops*	0.02 ml drops*	0.02 ml drops*	thirty seconds
M9 paper	0.01 ml drops*	0.01 ml drops*	0.01 ml drops*	twenty seconds
M256A1 detector kit	0.005 mg/m^3	0.02 mg/m^3	2.0 mg/m^3	15-20 minutes
M8A1 detector	0.1 mg/m^3	0.1 mg/m^3	Does not detect	under two minutes
CAM	0.03 mg/m^3	0.01 mg/m^3	0.01 mg/m^3	under one minute
ICAD	0.5 mg/m^3	Does not detect	10.0 mg/m^3	under two minutes
M272 Water test kit	0.02 mg/liter*	0.02 mg/liter*	2.0 mg/liter*	15-20 minutes
M21 RSCAAL	3 mg/m^3	3 mg/m^3	150 mg/m^3	under one minute
MM-1	62 mg/m^3	0.01 ug/liter*	0.001 ug/liter*	under 45 seconds

Note: Asterisk denotes liquid measures; all other measures are gaseous measures.
Source: GulfLINK case narratives and other government sources.

CONGRESS TAKES ACTION

When Congress developed the National Defense Authorization Act for fiscal year 1994, it added a requirement to force certain changes in the DoD NBC defense program. This legislation was named Title XVII—Chemical and Biological Weapons Defense, under Public Law 103-160. The House and Senate committees noted some improvements in the overall DoD program since the end of the Gulf War but remained concerned over the need for a sustained effort to strengthen the program. They also recommended DoD assistance in training US and international Chemical Weapons Convention inspectors and monitoring teams. Last, they encouraged the Secretary of Defense to adopt a verification and inspection regime for the 1972 Biological Weapons Convention. The law included five sections, which included:

- Section 1701: *Conduct of the Chemical and Biological Defense Program.* Improve the joint coordination and oversight of the NBC defense program and ensure a coherent and effective approach to its management. This is to be accomplished through a single office in DoD, a stronger coordinating role by the Army, and a joint coordinated and integrated NBC defense budget for all four services.
- Section 1702: *Consolidation of Chemical and Biological Defense Training Activities.* Moves the Air Force's Disaster Preparedness School would move from Lowery AFB, Colorado, to Anniston, Alabama. This allows the Air Force to use the Chemical Defense Training Facility and increases the likelihood of compatible training of NBC defense specialists.
- Section 1703: *Annual Report of Chemical and Biological Warfare Defense* demands an annual report reporting the overall status of the DoD NBC defense program; it includes readiness issues, such as logistics status of stocks, training and readiness of the armed forces and war game/battle simulations; the status of the DoD NBC defense RDA program, to include future requirements, joint program initiatives, management and coordination improvements and problem areas; and the military's preparations for the Chemical Weapons Convention.
- Section 1704: *Sense of Congress Concerning Federal Emergency Planning for Response to Terrorist Threats.* It recommends an increased effort by the Federal Emergency Management Agency to develop a capability to detect, warn and respond to the potential terrorist use of chemical or biological agents, or natural disasters and emergencies involving industrial chemicals or natural or accidental outbreaks of disease.
- Section 1705: *Agreements to Provide Support to Vaccination Programs of Department of Health and Human Services.* This gives the Secretary of Defense and Secretary of Health and Human Services permission to use excess peacetime biological weapons defense capabilities to support domestic vaccination programs. This ability would allow DoD to retain a surge capability to produce vaccines and antidotes for unusual diseases as the armed forces became involved in a future contingency.

So what was the final word on the CB warfare threat? Modern-day chemical defense doctrine was judged to be good, with the exception of some unique areas such as aircraft decontamination, casualty decontamination and contaminated equipment retrograde procedures. The coalition forces increased their state of CB defense readiness rapidly from very low initially to moderate in six months. The herculean effort moving CB defense equipment, combined with a furious level of training, did improve the overall defense posture to the point that US casualties would have been light instead of the expected thousands. The Fox reconnaissance system, the ANBACIS-II modeling capability, the XM21 RSCAALs and the biodetectors were four vital efforts of the developmental initiatives that could have been completed in the 1980s with a little more funding and a lot more input from the combat arms community. Chemical agent point detectors may have been too sensitive for tactical operations, judging by the number of false alarms. Collective protection systems were inadequate and continue to be a critical issue. Individual protection (masks and clothes) were capable of enabling the individual troops to survive, but comfort and performance issues and the procurement shortages kept everyone's nerves on edge. With the exception of decontamination programs, these materiel fixes are already in the works.[13] We continue to lack are modeling and simulation tools that demonstrate the value of NBC defense equipment in terms of troops and equipment saved.

There is a clear possibility that political sensitivities over Gulf War Syndrome could drive CB defense research and development into developing prohibitively expensive detectors and time and resource-consuming decontaminants. Without credible evidence to support the case that CB agents were in any form responsible for these illnesses, it is hoped that our leadership will not suffer any "knee-jerk" reactions to the loud cries of the ignorant. CB defense equipment is meant to minimize the risk to the troops as they accomplish combat missions; if it interferes with their ability to complete the mission, it will not be used and soldiers will die when CB agents are used. Combat leaders need to ask some hard questions and measure the pros and cons prior to reacting to unfounded allegations.

CENTCOM completed its mission without having its CB defense skills fully challenged. Whether that has made it easier to ignore the need to equip and train against the possibility of CB warfare, or whether the military is now on guard, remains to be seen. What is evident is that without a retaliatory capability, US forces must rely on defensive measures and training more than ever before. Failure to develop these defensive measures might mean that America's sons and daughters will be killed in future combat operations by an opposing force employing chemical weapons, especially given the US military's past track record. If we lose sight of that important point, within the next twenty years the US military will be defeated in battle or suffer catastrophic consequences as a result of CB weapons use. The last thing our leaders should think is that the Persian Gulf War proved that the US military does not need to worry about CB warfare anymore.

CHAPTER 9

Agent Orange Revisited?

I never received, before, during or after hostilities, any report of Iraqi use of chemical weapons, nor the discovery or destruction of Iraqi chemical weapons. I feel sure that had such events knowingly occurred, I would have received reports since this was the highest intelligence priority in my command.
— General (Ret.) H. Norman Schwarzkopf, January 1997

About a year and a half following the end of the war, Persian Gulf veterans began coming forward in increasing numbers with reports of various afflictions. These afflictions were not limited to US active duty soldiers; they appeared in reservists and National Guardsmen, government civilians, and even British and Canadian soldiers. The wide variety of symptoms, appearing in individuals scattered across the theater, appeared to have no rhyme or reason. At first, the lack of an identified source of the problems from the Gulf War caused Veteran's Administration (VA) hospitals to resist treatment of the unknown afflictions until it was positively identified. Regulations governing VA treatment require that the agency refuse disability benefits to veterans with conditions that had not been diagnosed. The main issue was deciphering what illnesses have been caused naturally in the United States, as opposed to illnesses or casualties caused during combat operations in the Gulf, not to mention correctly diagnosing the illnesses.

Cries of betrayal, linking this treatment to that suffered by Agent Orange veterans, quickly got action from military and political leaders, who understood the need to avoid the perception of delaying the treatment of unexplained ailments in groups of returning veterans. Both the House and Senate put forth Persian Gulf Syndrome Compensation Bills, but differences over whether or not the VA had the authority to issue the disability benefits created bureaucratic delays in committees trying to resolve differences between the two bills. Medical agencies from all government agencies began researching the possible causes behind the strange symptoms. This search included over thirty government studies during the next year.

It was not until 1994 that medical research began to yield some concrete theories. Gulf War Syndrome (GWS) veterans had grown in number from a few thousand to several tens of thousands but still totaled less than about 10 percent of the deployed forces. The common symptoms identified at the Tucson VA Medical Center included fatigue, skin rash, muscle and joint pain, headaches, memory loss, shortness of breath, sleep disturbance, diarrhea and coughing. These symptoms varied in intensity from soldier to soldier, and from region to region, with no apparent pattern. Common theories exposed by experts included petroleum exposure, stress reactions, depleted uranium, pesticide exposure, smoke from oil fires, indigenous parasites and bacteria, vaccines and nerve agent antidotes, chemical or biological warfare agents, chronic fatigue syndrome and multiple chemical sensitivity. It might be one of these or a combination of factors that had triggered the symptoms. One rumor made out GWS to be a time-bomb virus developed in Baghdad as a revenge-weapon against the coalition forces.[1]

More than 60,000 veterans have signed on to the Persian Gulf Registry. The majority of these have joined the registry because they believe they may be suffering from GWS. The symptoms described on the registry range even more widely than the early reports: abdominal pain, facial pain, chest pain, blood clots, flushing, night sweats, blurry vision, shaking, vomiting, fatigue, swollen lymph nodes, weight loss/gain, intestinal disorders, sore gums, cough, memory loss, dizziness, inability to concentrate, labored breathing, depression, neurological disorders and leg cramps (among others). In addition, the veterans' families have reported suffering from various symptoms, and some couples have blamed miscarriages and birth defects on GWS. The large range of symptoms, which seem to point to multiple illnesses with overlapping symptoms and causes, are making veterans paranoid about any illness contracted since their return as a possible Gulf War-related disease or agent.[2] The question addressed here is this: are chemical or biological agents, either deliberately used by the Iraqi military or accidentally released by the coalition forces, the source of the Persian Gulf illnesses? And if so, is the government deliberately concealing this knowledge from suffering veterans?

Without a doubt, the second most popular suspect is exposure to chemical warfare agents (the leading contender being the combined effects of PB tablets and insecticides). The possibility that biological agent exposure might be a cause has been dismissed on the basis of existing extensive research on effects of botulin toxin, anthrax, aflatoxin and other biological organisms on the human body. Had soldiers been exposed to these agents, medics would have instantly recognized and diagnosed these cases. In any event, extensive and more comprehensive post-conflict diagnosis would have identified such bacteria and viruses in returning soldiers, and to date no such evidence has turned up. Mustard agent, in a similar fashion, has been researched extensively since 1918 in an effort to understand its effects on the human body. As for nerve agents, there are at least three decades of applied research as background reference material as which to identify or discredit nerve agent exposure as a source of GWS. Yet because the Army had ignored NBC defense training, equipment modernization, and leadership development for decades, many veterans continue to see chemical warfare agents as a likely cause of GWS—because of ignorance, not because of facts.

CHEMICAL AGENT EXPOSURE SCENARIOS

There are three general scenarios that serve as basis for the claims of chemical agent exposure. The first possibility is that Iraqi forces might have employed air or ground-delivered CB agents during the air or ground campaigns. Second, bombed Iraqi CB weapon production sites and storage bunkers might have released plumes of agent to drift towards friendly lines. Last, demolition of Iraqi ammunition bunkers, such as those at Khamisiyah, raise the possibility of accidental release as a result of destroying unmarked Iraqi chemical munitions.

Most scholars agree that the Iraqis did not deliberately use CB agents against coalition forces. Evidence gathered to date includes representations of Iraqi military officials upon debriefing, the UN on-site inspections, US intelligence assets, and recent DoD studies. All support a conclusion that there were no intentional Iraqi chemical weapon attacks, or widespread exposures as a result of any such intentional attacks. Examinations of all the Scud impact areas and the recovered warheads fired at the coalition support this. Numerous division and CENTCOM logs show that all suspected chemical attacks against the coalition turned out to be incorrect reports sent up the chain of command prior to positive confirmation. Fast-moving CENTCOM forces did not find forward-placed chemical munitions at suspected Iraqi locations, while they did capture over 14,000 tons of conventional ammunition. The Iraqi artillery was silenced, the Iraqi air force never returned to the skies, and the few Scud warheads that were CB-capable were kept in reserve.

Even the few Marine Corps claims of Iraqi chemical mines, mostly reports of blister agent detections, panned out as false alarms despite positive readings from eager (though inexperienced) Fox operators. The mass casualties that were expected from such attacks, as evidenced in the Iran-Iraq War, just were not there. Not one incident could compare to the Tokyo subway incident years later, when Japanese commuters were immediately afflicted by nerve agent vapors. While there were numerous reports of a single chemical agent detector false-alarming, there were no multiple positive chemical agent detections from M8A1 alarms in a single site, confirmed by M256A1 kits and XM93 NBCRS vehicles, indicative of a typical chemical weapons attack.[3]

With the reports of Czech nerve and mustard detection in mid-January 1991, many suspected that low levels of chemical agent released from the bombed CB agent production and storage sites might have affected coalition forces. The Pentagon released its assessment that at least two of the seven Czech and French detections were credible (one nerve, one mustard), based on ERDEC's analysis of the Czechs' 1970s Soviet-technology chemical agent detectors and interviews with the French and Czech militaries. In all seven cases, the amounts of agent detected were deemed militarily insignificant (much less than 0.04 milligrams-minutes/cubic meter); there were no signs of agent poisoning in any soldier in that time period; and there was no physical evidence of any enemy-delivered munitions in the area. This led some to believe that the coalition bombings of Iraqi CB production/storage sites could have been the source of the agent.

Yet, of the over thirty suspected CB agent production and storage areas, only eleven actually stored bulk quantities of chemical agents and munitions (according to Iraqi official claims). Of these eleven, only two, Muhammadiyat and Al Muthanna, were seriously damaged by the bombing campaign in February 1991. Approximately 15.2 tons of mustard was damaged at Muhammadiyat, as well as a little less than three metric tons of sarin and cyclosarin mix. At Al Muthanna, stores of approximately 16.8 metric tons of GB/GF mix were apparently damaged. Based on the CIA's worst-case modeling, the farthest chemical agent could travel from these bombings was approximately 300 kilometers; the closest US troops were 400 kilometers away, a difference of 100 kilometers (roughly sixty miles). By these calculations, none of the coalition soldiers could have been exposed to the volatile chemical agents released. This was probably why US forces could not confirm the Czech detections at the same sites, nor did any coalition detector alarm between KKMC and the front lines. In addition, no Iraqi, Saudi or Kuwaiti civilians have been reported as chemical agent casualties. The majority of these targets were far from civilian centers.[4]

The Defense Science Board report released in June 1994 speculated that if chemical agents were released by the bombing campaign, the only possible targets that might have affected coalition forces were the storage bunkers at An Nasiriyah and Tallil. These were the nearest targets, within 150–200 kilometers of friendly forces. To assume that chemical agent exposure would travel such a distance, the bombing would have to release a substantial amount of agent, in excess of sixteen metric tons, beyond the amount consumed in the explosions. The lack of local Arab civilian or animal deaths around those two sites seems to belie that possibility. In any event, DNA modeling of the explosion calculates that a maximum lethal dose would have traveled less than nine kilometers and an incapacitating dose less than ten kilometers. In addition, the rain and wind storms immediately following the An Nasiriyah bombing on January 16 would have dispersed the easily hydrolyzed sarin clouds.[5] To expect that there could be low levels of chemical agent in one spot without high concentrations of chemical agents being detected in another area defies the laws of physics. As a result of these (and other) investigations, the DoD, DNA, Defense Science Board, Army, CIA, and the Presidential Advisory Committee on Gulf War Illnesses all concur that no US service members were exposed to chemical agents or fallout from bombed chemical weapons production/storage facilities. This all leads to the third possibility—post-conflict demolitions of Iraqi munitions depots.

THE DEPOT AT KHAMISIYAH

The Khamisiyah Ammunition Storage Area represents an immense bunker complex near An Nasiriyah spreading out over fifty square kilometers, one of four large bunker areas in southern Iraq storing conventional ammunition of all types. It featured about 100 ammunition bunkers and several other types of storage buildings. Iraqi personnel moved 2,160 unmarked 122 mm nerve agent rockets from the Al-Muthanna CW production/storage facility to a Khamisiyah bunker just before the start of the air campaign. According to Iraqi officials, the rockets started leaking immediately, motivating them to move 1,100 rockets out of the bunker to a pit area two kilometers away, where they were buried. On February 26, elements of the 24th IN DIV overran Khamisiyah. After the conclusion of the ground war, the 82d ABN DIV occupied the sector. To deny the Iraqis the ability to rearm with the thousands of tons of munitions discovered there, ARCENT undertook immediate demolition activities. On March 2, the 937th Engineer Group tasked the 37th Engineer Battalion, with support from one company of the 307th Engineer Battalion and the 60th Ordnance Detachment (Explosives Ordnance Disposal), to destroy the bunkers. Other supporting elements (firefighters, technical intelligence teams, civil affairs detachment) were present for a strength of about 430 soldiers.

By accounts taken by the DoD Investigative Team assisting the Presidential Advisory Committee, chemical specialists in the area were told that the ammunition bunkers were assessed not to be holding chemical weapons, as determined by intelligence assets (as noted, some Iraqi EPWs had claimed that chemical munitions were marked). While it is unclear if the 82d ABN DIV received word from either 24th IN DIV or XVIII ABN Corps about suspected chemical munitions, Lieutenant Colonel Rick Jackson, the 82d ABN DIV's division chemical officer, took no chances. Fox vehicles and unit reconnaissance teams swept through the area looking for evidence of chemical weapons in the bunkers. They found riot control agents, white phosphorus artillery rounds and empty hollow artillery shells that might have contained TNT, but no sign of chemical munitions. Soldiers did find local civilians and animals living inside the many bunkers; they were evacuated prior to demolition operations.

On March 3, the engineers "prepped" two bunkers with demolitions to test their techniques. During this time, the engineer battalion had M8A1 alarms operating on their vehicles. The battalion's chemical NCO dressed in MOPP-4 to check personally some bunkers with M256A1 kits. These results were negative. FMIB teams searched for any chemical, laser-guided or optical-guided weapons, and found one rocket of interest. Everything else looked conventional. The engineers blew up the two bunkers without incident. Alpha Company of the 307th ENG BN was destroying munitions at Jalibah airfield thirty kilometers distant that day, also without incident.

On March 4, the engineer teams rigged thirty-eight bunkers, including bunker number 73. While the ammunition was being prepped for demolition, no one saw any markings denoting chemical munitions, nor was there any evidence of chemical agent leaks. In later interviews, Explosives Ordnance Disposal (EOD) personnel stated that they had been aware that they might encounter chemical munitions in any of the demolition missions, and had actively looked for them. The fact that none were detected did not negate the possibility of chemical munitions. Major General James Johnson, commanding general of the 82d ABN DIV, stated that his forces had received a chemical downwind-hazard message that forced him to relocate units out of the immediate hazard area prior to the demolition. Most of the engineer task force remained north or northwest of the explosion, while the winds blew toward the east or northeast. The three company commanders in the task force all had had M8A1 detectors mounted on their vehicles, and once outside the three-mile safety zone they had ensured that the detectors were functioning.

Less than an hour after detonating thirty-seven of the thirty-eight bunkers at once, the M8A1 alarm in Bravo Company went off, causing a local scramble to increase MOPP levels. Once their M256A1 kits verified the lack of chemical agents, the unit dropped its MOPP status. Medics reported no casualties or signs of health problems related to chemical agent exposure that day. Because of the falling debris reported, troops moved further away from the bunkers.

On March 5, during heavy rains, a bunker (not bunker 73) which had failed to detonate the previous day was destroyed. Present M8A1 alarms did not alarm, and no further operations were conducted on that day due to poor weather conditions. Because of concern over a shortage of demolition explosives and the potential for secondary explosions and munition fly-outs, tests were conducted on March 6 to implode four bunkers. No operations were conducted on the following two days. On March 9, the engineers carried out a reconnaissance of the remaining bunkers to be destroyed the following day. The 37th Engineer Battalion operations officer stated that he practically stumbled over stacks of long-crated munitions in the nearby pit area. The battalion decided to blow these rockets along with the remainder of the bunkers in the area. A 37th Engineer Battalion NCO who set the charges on three stacks of munitions in the pit area recalled that at that time there was not enough explosive material to destroy the munitions completely. Nevertheless, a team set the charges to damage as many as possible.

On March 10, approximately 1600 hours, the 37th ENG BN ignited the fuzes on the explosives, which would detonate the remaining sixty bunkers, most warehouses at Khamisiyah and the munitions stacked in the pit area. The engineer force was about thirty minutes drive from the area, several miles south of Khamisiyah, when the explosion occurred. An EOD NCO from the 60th Ordnance Detachment recalled about six stacks of 122 mm rockets destroyed in the pit. When he returned a few days after the demolition, pictures taken by this EOD NCO showed many intact rockets. Records from the 60th Ordnance Detachment state that 850 122 mm rockets were destroyed that day. No soldiers reported any ill effects at the time of this demolition or at the time of their return when they assessed the results. EOD operations continued in the area throughout March, destroying munitions at Tallil, the An Nasiryah facilities and other munitions discovered in southern Iraq. When the VII Corps assumed control of the area (as the XVIII ABN Corps departed), the 2d ACR was tasked to recon Khamisiyah's bunkers for CB munitions. On March 23, it reported negative results.[6]

In October 1991, the UNSCOM inspection teams visited the Khamisiyah area, where they identified three areas holding chemical weapons. At the time, it was not clear whether the chemical weapons identified had been present during the war or whether, as was suspected at other locations, the Iraqis had moved the munitions between February and October 1991. At the pit area, about one kilometer south of the Khamisiyah storage area, UNSCOM found several hundred, mostly intact, 122 mm rockets containing diluted nerve agent (confirmed through sampling and CAMs). In an open area, about five kilometers west of Khamisiyah, inspectors found approximately 6,000 intact 155 mm artillery rounds containing mustard agent (confirmed by CAMs) covered by a canvas tarp. At a third location featuring 100 bunkers, the team noted remnants of 122 mm rockets but no trace of chemical agents, at a single bunker identified as bunker number 73. The Iraqi officials told the UNSCOM team that coalition troops had destroyed bunker 73 earlier that year. These Iraqi statements were viewed at the time with skepticism, because of the extensive and continuous deception by the Iraqis of UNSCOM in its search for nuclear, biological and chemical weapons information.

In March 1992, when the UNSCOM inspectors returned to Khamisiyah, they reported consolidating and destroying more than 450 122 mm nerve agent-filled rockets found in the pit area (that total includes the original 300 that they had found in October 1991). In addition, they found another 300 intact rockets buried in the pit area; these were sent by UNSCOM to Muthanna's Chemical Destruction Facility. At this time, the focus on investigations was on identifying all the stockpiles of CB agent weapons, not on the possible causes of GWS. As a result, the UNSCOM team and later DIA analysts never considered that agent exposure might have resulted from the destruction of bunker 73.

In the spring of 1995, along with the formation of the Presidential Advisory Committee on Gulf War Veterans' Illnesses, several agencies were tasked by executive order to cooperate in the search for the possible cause of GWS. The CIA changed its focus from identifying weapons stockpiles to identifying possible scenarios of weapons releases. The Department of Defense created a telephone hotline for veterans in May 1995 and initiated its GulfLINK web-page in August 1995. This increased an emphasis on revealing normally sensitive information on topics concerning the coalition's brush with chemical-biological warfare.

In May 1996, UNSCOM revisited the Khamisiyah site as part of its efforts to verify earlier Iraqi declarations. During this inspection, the UNSCOM teams documented the presence of high-density polyethylene-insert burster tubes, fill plugs, and other characteristics of Iraqi chemical munitions. The rockets had been filled with a combination of the agent sarin and cycloserine, or GB/GF, based on analysis of the rockets' contents UNSCOM had found in 1991 in the pit just outside Khamisiyah storage area. Iraqi officials also claimed that fear of coalition bombing had motivated An Nasiriyah depot personnel to move the intact mustard rounds to the open area five kilometers from the Khamisiyah depot, where the rounds were camouflaged with canvas. This information, combined with a recent intelligence review, led to the Pentagon announcement on June 21, 1996, of possible chemical agent exposure to US troops.

On July 9, 1996, the CIA presented its downwind hazard model to the Presidential Advisory Committee. Modeling of the potential hazard caused by the destruction of bunker 73 indicated that an area around the bunker at least two kilometers in all directions and four kilometers downwind could have been contaminated at or above the level for causing acute symptoms (including runny nose, headache, and miosis). An area up to twenty-five kilometers downwind could have been contaminated at the much lower general population dosage limit. This dosage, identified in Army manuals, is for protection of the general population and is a seventy-two-hour exposure at 0.000003 milligrams per cubic meter, or approximately 0.013 milligram minutes per cubic meter (mg-min/m^3). This dosage is substantially below clinical effects, even threshold clinical effects like runny noses and initial twitches. It is lower than the 0.04 mg-min/m^3 limit recommended for civilian workers over eight hours' exposure time, much lower than the incapacitating dose of 2–3 mg-min/m^3, and significantly lower than the 100 mg-min/m^3 necessary to kill an adult human.

The CIA modelers used a number of assumptions to develop this downwind hazard prediction. As a baseline, they used data from a 1966 incident at Dugway Proving Ground that involved the destruction of a bunker filled with 1,850 GB-filled M55 rockets of characteristics similar to the Iraqi rockets found in bunker 73. The US rockets had had a range of about 15–20 kilometers, and the Iraqi rockets a range of 14–18 kilometers. The CIA assumed that 1,060 rockets had been in the bunker, as was indicated by Iraqi officials. They estimated that the rockets would have been filled with eight kilograms of a 2:1 ratio of GB to GF, and assumed it to be 100 percent pure agent. The CIA model predicted 10 percent of the rockets would be ejected from the bunker, half falling randomly within a 200-meter circle, the other half falling within a two-kilometer circle, based on US military test data. All but 2.5 percent of the agent in the bunker would have been degraded by heat from the explosion and other burning debris, again based on past US tests. The winds were light to the northeast and then to the east, based on modeling and analysis of the videotape of destruction activity at Khamisiyah.

The CIA model, however, did not take into account 37 conventional ordnance bunkers detonating simultaneously with bunker 73. The thermal energy created by explosions and fires in the other bunkers, and by solar heating caused by the increased amounts of smoke, would tend to degrade any surviving chemical agent. The heat would force a column of air, dust and debris near the bunker to an altitude of 800 to 1,200 meters. This rapid vertical spreading would tend to lower ground contamination area and actually shorten the footprint of the model. Scientific evidence and the videotapes show that the agent cloud probably rose to the top of the convective boundary layer, which on that day was between 800 and 1,200 meters. The CIA model had used instead a fifteen-meter height for the explosive plume, because that was the worse-case height for a ground contamination pattern. The model also did not account for atmospheric turbulence that would be associated with a hot desert at midday, which would further decrease the footprint (since in hot sunny weather vapors tend to rise straight up rather than hug the ground).

Later analysis of the Iraqi rockets would show that they held closer to six kilograms of nerve agent rather than eight. The CIA model did not take into account any impurities or degradation of products, although UNSCOM evidence showed that Iraqi manufacturing had had severe quality and purity problems. Nor did the model account for rain effects or ground scavaging (agent penetration into the ground), which would have shortened the downwind hazard further. Last, the model had not yet been scientifically validated prior to its presentation to the Presidential Advisory Committee. These issues did not stop DoD or the Committee from making an estimate of troop exposure possibilities.[7]

Upon receiving this information, the Presidential Advisory Committee deemed it advisable that the Pentagon at least inform everyone that might have been exposed to this general populace dosage—just to be sure. This downwind hazard, as mentioned above, was not a 25-kilometer circle from the depot—it was more of a rounded thin triangle four kilometers wide at its origin and extending outward toward the twenty-five-kilometer point, ending at eight kilometers wide (see Figure 9.1). Early estimates of the number of personnel potentially exposed increased from the initial 430 soldiers (the bunker detail) to include the 770 soldiers from the 82d ABN DIV securing the general area. When the Army reviewed this report, it increased the radius to a twenty-five-kilometer distance around the depot, arbitrarily increasing the number of potentially exposed troops from 1,100 to 5,000 troops. This was done without any justification by data, simply as an additional "worst-case" safeguard. In late October, the Pentagon announced that it had doubled its radius to fifty kilometers to include 15–20,000 troops—again entirely without merit, just to demonstrate that it was "aggressively reaching out" to all possible victims.[8] It did not matter if none of the troops actually stayed in the area long enough for what might be termed chronic, long-term exposure.

To summarize, the Pentagon reacted to a worst-case, unvalidated scenario that assumed the agent was 100 percent pure agent instead of its actual lower purity; that increased the agent in the rockets by a third; that did not account for atmospherics which would have driven the agent up into the sky rather than toward troops; and that did not account for the added heat from the other exploding bunkers. Based on this faulty scenario, it arrived at the conclusion that troops over two kilometers upwind of the explosion might have, at the worst case, been exposed to agent levels deemed unsafe for the general populace—if they stayed in the hazard area for over seventy-two hours. Also, despite the lack of any medical evidence that undetectable traces of nerve agent could harm people, despite the most advanced chemical defense equipment in the world and decades of chemical specialist training, the Pentagon accepted a foolish recommendation that there was

Figure 9.1
Locations of Major Commands Relative to Khamisiyah

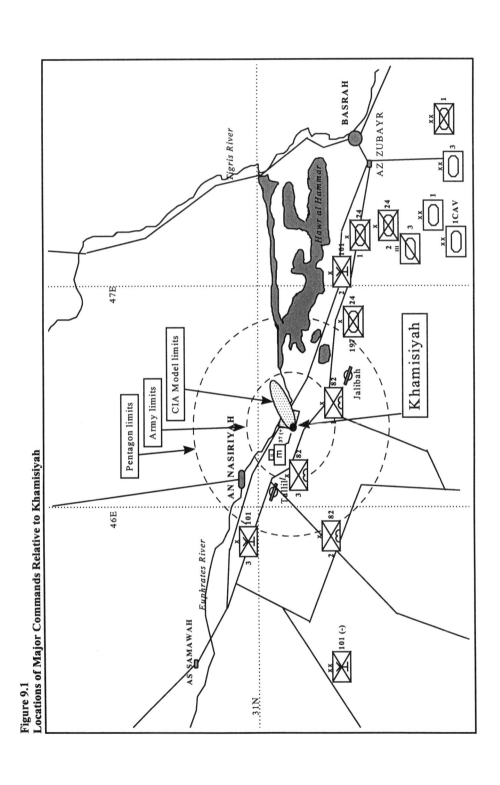

a possible health risk for over 20,000 soldiers that had been in that area during a three-day period (without knowing if anyone had in fact stayed in the area for three days).

Instead of calming fears as it had intended, the Pentagon increased concerns of veterans and their families and fueled suspicions of a cover-up. The exposed-troops estimate, based on a worst-case model, was dramatically increased in fear of political pressures and the publicity over GWS, increasing the group "at risk" from 1,100 troops that didn't even suffer from runny noses to 20,000 that had not been remotely near the site. In an effort to quiet public concerns during an election year over possible nerve agent exposure, the Pentagon ignored its resident experts and made the short-term political effort to gratify the populace and its equally short-fuzed politicians immediately. Instead, it increased fears, raised conspiracy theories, and made its own professionals in the Chemical Corps look foolish, or worse, criminally incompetent.

The media, who up to the summer of 1996 had been skeptical of any claims from the Pentagon regarding CB weapons history in the Gulf War, now enthusiastically accepts the 20,000 number as gospel. Rather than investigating the validity of the CIA model or the Army's reasoning of how it arrived at these numbers, the press sees in this event their having forced DoD to admit failure to disclose this information for years, while others have announced they discovering evidence of the DoD cover-up. Anecdotal stories from sick veterans who did not understand what had affected them, and demands for further investigations into the "cover-up" soon took priority over any search for the truth. Trying to cope with the demands for more information, Dr. Bernard Rostker was appointed as the Special Assistant to the Deputy Secretary of Defense for Gulf War Illnesses with a staff of 110 personnel in early November 1995.

THE "OPEN PIT" ESTIMATE—MORE GUESSES

Because DoD had acknowledged the results of the CIA model, there was a similar demand that the "open pit" demolition be modeled as well. This time, perhaps because of recognized blunders in handling the depot incident, Dr. Rotsker's DoD Gulf War Illness office took a different route. DoD and the CIA planned a series of small-scale demolition tests at Dugway Proving Grounds in May 1997 to replicate the pit explosion, using 122 mm rockets, filled with a chemical simulant called tri-ethyl phosphate, buried in a similarly shaped pit. This simulant chemical has weight and volatility characteristics similar to sarin, but without the lethality. The Gulf War Illness office interviewed the EOD team that had originally set the charges at the Khamisiyah pit to learn how the boxes of rockets had been situated and how it had set the charges. Based upon firsthand descriptions from five soldiers on the EOD team, it estimated the number of rockets in the pit to have been about 1,250, of which less than half had been damaged by the demolition attempts. By placing a series of cards in concentric circles around the pit, the Dugway Proving Ground team was able to blow the boxes in place and record how much simulant escaped the pit, how far it traveled, and how much agent stayed in the soil as opposed to being released. This data was given to computer modelers in the CIA, the Naval Surface Warfare Center, the Defense Special Weapons Agency (the former DNA), and the Naval Research Laboratory.[9]

Other information fed the modelers' efforts. Soot and debris patterns around the site allowed the investigators to identify a south-southeast wind pattern (blowing from approximately 335 degrees). Samples taken by the UNSCOM teams demonstrated a 50 percent purity rather than 100 percent, and the rockets now held a correct six kilogram weight of agent. The Dugway data showed that at the most, 18 percent of the agent in the rockets would have been released into the air, with the rest being consumed by the explosion. Of that 18 percent released agent, one percent vaporized into the air, 1 percent released as liquid droplets, 6 percent evaporated from the soil and 10 percent evaporated from the wooden crates. The modelers also identified a major parameter, the "first noticeable health-effect level," which would include symptoms such as pinpointing of the eye pupils (miosis), runny nose, tightness of the chest and eye pain. The approximate levels of these reactions is 2–25 mg-min/m^3. The second parameter was low-level agent presence of between 0.01296 mg-min/m^3 (the general population limit) and one mg-min/m^3 (below the incapacitating level of sarin).

Based on the cumulative analysis of five different computer models, no troops were exposed to agent levels at or above first noticeable health-effect levels between March 10 and 12, 1991. When the modelers attempted to guess at the downwind hazard from lower levels, they envisioned a plume of agent that extended about five miles south and five miles east of the pit. This may have exposed 19,000 troops, primarily from the 82d ABN DIV, 24th IN DIV, and 101st ABN DIV, to these levels. Based on the surveys returned from 7,415 soldiers in the area (out of 20,000 surveys sent out), 99.5 percent of the soldiers had not noticed any physical affects that could be correlated with sarin exposure. Even given this more credible attempt to model these events, these models can not be validated beyond a reasonable doubt; the US government has stopped open air testing of chemical agents, which means these models are based on data that is over twenty-five years old; there were no chemical agent detections in March 1991 to back up the data; and there were no chemical agent casualties from the war (other than Fisher, whose case was not related to Khamisiyah). Today, depending on the "expert," we hear reports of anywhere from 27,000 to 100,000 troops exposed to low-level nerve agents. Congressional politicians, believing that they are somehow wiser than members of various independent scientific and medical panels, are now calling for the Presidential Advisory Committee to reassess its negative findings on chemical exposure. "It is our belief that more and more scientific evidence suggests that a major cause of . . . illness is the synergistic effect of a wide variety of chemicals to which our soldiers were exposed," Rep. Bernie Sanders (I-VT) wrote in his letter to the Committee; his letter was quickly signed by eighty-five other House members in June 1997.[10]

IF NOT CHEMICAL AGENTS, THEN WHAT?

Perhaps the first area to investigate would include occupational hazards that the soldiers may have encountered during the war. For instance, both CARC and DS-2 have hazardous components that might come into contact with the operators in a normal work environment. Some of these could cause health hazards, and these concerns are outlined in appropriate technical manuals, as well as in training courses. Most occupational hazards resulting from using these materiels seem to have been avoided. Some unforeseen actions were noted, such as using diesel fuel around encampments as a sand suppressant, burning human waste with fuel oil, fuel leaking into shower water, drying sleeping bags in leaded exhaust fumes, etc. It remains unclear if these activities are connected with GWS, but they were not in a great enough number to account for the GWS complaints.

The most obvious natural cause would be infectious diseases endemic to the desert. The Middle East has a long history of unique diseases, dating back hundreds of years. During the conflict, both AFMIC and the Army Institute of Research, Division of Preventive Medicine, performed work on infectious diseases endemic to the Persian Gulf region and outlined ways in which service personnel should attempt to avoid or minimize their exposure to such diseases as leishmaniasis and malaria. These measures included predeployment information and also treatments, such as using permethrin (a pesticide) on bed netting and the area surrounding beds to repel sand flies. Medical labs continue to monitor personnel for these diseases, since variants of leishmaniasis can lie dormant for up to ten years after infection. DoD has since refined guidelines for medical surveillance during deployments.

The Pentagon did not anticipate Saddam's using oil-well fires as a defensive weapon. Accordingly, there was no predeployment information on the effects of exposure to oil-well fires and petrochemicals. DoD did provide guidance after Iraq set fire to over 700 oil wells. Military personnel were advised to avoid the smoke when possible and to practice frequent washing; to use goggles, disposable face masks and scarves; and to alert medical personnel if lung irritation occurred. These oil wells burned for several months. Several organizations sent dozens of doctors, scientists and engineers to research this area, including the Centers for Disease Control (for blood samples) and the Army Environmental Hygiene Agency (for oil in water samples). The blood samples of military personnel in Kuwait showed lower volatile organic compounds than those of oil-well firefighters. The water samples showed similarly high concentrations of organic compounds, some of which could have had potential toxic characteristics. A final report was sent to Congress in December 1996.

Some thought that the depleted uranium warheads of the 120 mm armor-piercing projectile might have poisoned soldiers, as this was the first time that the depleted uranium-tipped munitions had actually been used in a combat zone. The soldiers most concerned should have been the tank crews, who regularly carried large loads of the munitions. DoD studies conducted before deployment had shown that the radiation levels were very faint and did not exceed NRC standards. For those that feared the uranium would pulverize upon impact on an Iraqi target, thus spreading uranium fragments, the Armed Forces Radiobiology Research Institute released three reports after the war. They concluded that any soldiers who might have been exposed to the depleted uranium radiation were unlikely to have been exposed to hazardous levels of radiation exposure. No soldiers have since exhibited signs of uranium poisoning.

Pesticides used by US forces were accompanied with handling and safety instructions. All products were commercially available and had been tested and approved by the FDA. A less known danger was posed by agricultural pesticides used by Saudi and Iraqi governments and businesses in and around the area of operations. Because of arid conditions, the amount of arable land is small, mostly surrounding the major river systems; as a result, there is a strong propensity for heavy use of agricultural fertilizers and pesticides in less productive areas. To date, sampling missions have not revealed excessive use of pesticides, although the British government has revealed concerns that this may be a prime cause.

The most popular suspects of GWS are the prophylactics used to counter the effects of chemical and biological agents. The four accused culprits included the pyridostigmine bromide tablets, the botulinum toxoid, the anthrax vaccine and the diazepam autoinjectors. Of the four, only the PB tablets show definite side effects (headaches, nausea, diarrhea, abdominal cramps and other intestinal problems). Many of these had been noted by the soldiers in the field, and perhaps about a third of the force stopped taking the pills, choosing to rely on just the atropine. Still, at least two-thirds of the force had taken the PB tablets for about three weeks. There should have been more GWS cases than the 10 percent noted if this was the sole culprit. Several studies within the government and among private organizations continue to study PB effects, yet the Department of Defense continues to produce and store it as a nerve agent pretreatment.

What might explain the relatively low number of military personnel affected (less than 10 percent) is synergistic effects of hazardous exposure. Combining two or more hazards together, and adding the high stress of combat might result in symptoms that would not appear were an individual exposed to just one factor. The relatively small number of GWS casualties might also be explained by varying chemical tolerances in each individual exposed. This would certainly answer the question of how so many different symptoms have arisen in this target population. Certainly other multiple-chemical-sensitivity cases match these general symptoms. The question is, what combination of hazards? To date, the focus has shifted to tests suggesting that the combined exposure to PB tablets and the insecticide DEET results in a tenfold increase in the lethality of the insecticide. This has been shown only on cockroaches and has not been confirmed by other sources. Future research is needed on other likely combinations: for instance, petroleum exposure and insecticides, or petroleum exposure and PB tablets.[11]

The Presidential Advisory Committee, in its final report, noted three findings. First, many veterans have illnesses likely to be connected to their service in the

Gulf. Second, there did not appear to be conclusive evidence that any one source—pesticides, chemical-biological warfare agents, vaccines, PB tablets, infectious diseases, depleted uranium, oil-well fires and smoke, or petroleum products—caused the symptoms and illnesses. Third, stress was probably an important contributing factor to the broad range of physical and psychological illnesses being reported. Few veterans wanted to hear that stress, even as a contributing factor, might be partially responsible for their illnesses. Yet a good deal of past medical research on stress-related illnesses does support this view.[12]

REAL MEDICAL EVIDENCE

While the public may never be sure about Khamisiyah, it does not appear that these GWS illnesses have any contagious effects on the soldiers' wives and children, or upon the ability of a woman to give birth. Major General Ron Blanck, commanding general of the Walter Reed Army Medical Center, testified before the Senate on the medical findings of military research into GWS on September 29, 1994. He reported that prior to the war in 1990 the rate of miscarriages at six Army posts had been 380 miscarriages out of 4,762 pregnancies (7.98 percent). In 1991 at those same posts, the rate was 511 miscarriages out of 6,392 pregnancies (7.99 percent). Compared to an average rate of about 15 percent across the US, the military population fared relatively well. Similar medical evidence shows that the Persian Gulf veteran is, by most accounts, just as healthy as the average soldier that did not deploy to the Gulf.[13]

One possible explanation is suggested by Dr. Robert Haley of the University of Texas Southwestern Medical Center in Dallas. Dr. Haley began his research noting that DoD and the VA had not investigated the string of illnesses as one would an epidemic (that is, by the Centers for Disease Control protocols). The lack of a credible methodology, he felt, could be a reason why there was little progress in narrowing down the causes. He and other researchers initially planned to investigate the stress angle, but a colleague pointed out that the symptoms suffered by GWS veterans closely mirrored brain damage and that most signs had been delayed until months or years after the war. This led to a hypothesis that organophosphate compounds might have had a delayed impact on the human body. While all medical personnel recognize the classic immediate effects of organophosphate poisoning, few physicians were aware of any long-term delayed chronic effects.

There was also reason to suspect that pyridiostigmine bromide might be penetrating the blood-brain barrier, which was previously thought not to occur. Studies on hens, exposing them to various combinations of PB and insect repellent, showed that exposure to insect repellent alone would not cause damage. Combining the two, however, caused widespread neurological damage to the hens, supporting the idea that PB can penetrate to the brain. Similar animal studies in Britain tend to support the view that combining the two causes severe damage, but no human or lower primate tests have been conducted to verify this supposition.

Dr. Haley decided to focus on one unit, the 24th Naval Reserve Construction Battalion (SeaBees), living primarily in the southern states. These troops had traveled over a good deal of the theater while performing their mission, and accordingly would have had a higher chance of being exposed to any hazards. Two hundred and forty-nine of the 606 veterans volunteered to participate, of which 175 reported serious health problems related to the war. Investigators tested both the sick and healthy veterans' nervous reactions under various physiological, audiovestibular, psychological and blood tests. The team discovered that it could identify three distinct classes among sixty-three of the ill veterans (about 25 percent of the test group). The first group, composed of twelve individuals, showed some impaired cognition, having problems with memory, reasoning, insomnia and headaches. Group two (twenty-one individuals) had more severe problems with thinking, disorientation, vertigo and balance disturbances. These subjects also had the most difficulty keeping a steady job, being twelve times more likely to be unemployed. The last group (thirty individuals) suffered severe joint and muscle pains, muscle fatigue and tingling of the extremities. CAT scans did not show any damage in any of the test volunteers.

When these groups were further screened to identify what they had been exposed to, certain patterns appeared. Group one symptoms were more prone to appear in those that reported wearing flea collars during the war. Group two troops believed they had been exposed to chemical weapons and had used the PB tablets. The risk of joining the last group increased with the frequency and quantity of using the DoD-issued insect repellent containing DEET combined with the use of PB tablets. In all cases, the illnesses seem to stem from neurological damage caused by chemical exposure. Dr. Haley's explanation is that these veterans may have delayed, chronic neurotoxic syndromes from wartime exposure to combinations of chemicals.[14]

While these studies are remarkable and convincing, there is the possibility that the group two veterans, who feel they were attacked by chemical weapons because they had heard loud bangs and detectors alarming, may have been exposed to a yet unknown hazard. The credibility of these veterans (not their valor) is suspect, since their exposure to chemical weapons cannot be proven or verified by any events during the war. They may have been exposed to nighttime pesticide foggings common during the war or to industrial hazards of Middle Eastern cities. To accept the word of veterans that they were gassed would not be justified without other evidence such as expended Scud CB warheads or bombs found in Saudi Arabia. Even the best modelers supporting DoD cannot confirm that any soldier was exposed to low levels of chemical agents for more than one day. Generally, most medical physicians would catagorize chronic exposure cases as exposure to a low-level hazard over a long period of time (weeks instead of days).

It may be years before we discover the real cause to the Gulf War illnesses. There may be good reasons for veterans to distrust at first the government's attempts to find the truth; the media continues to follow the GWS story, eagerly looking for the "scandals," the "hidden files" that state how the DoD knew the causes all along. I do not think this is the case. There are veterans that have suffered and are suffering from an unknown cause or causes, and they should be treated immediately based on the medical evidence of their aliments, regardless of whether they contracted it in the Gulf or in the United States. However, we must also make a case against false legal and slanderous claims by those without scruples or who refuse to acknowledge the evidence.

There are many Vietnam veterans currently in powerful positions in the military and the government, many advocates of the military in the public, and hundreds of thousands of dedicated military personnel in the Army. There are no parallels between the Agent Orange cases of the 1970s and the GWS cases of the 1990s; society has changed, as has the military culture. After some prodding, DoD has responded favorably by opening up the files and treating the soldiers, and is trying to discover the true causes. Perhaps the military system is trying to help its personnel, despite not knowing the causes ot these illnesses and without subterfuge.

One thing that I have tried to demonstrate is this: there was no deliberate employment of CB weapons by the Iraqis, and there was no large-scale exposure to chemical-biological agents of the coalition forces. Had the military understood the CBW threat and trusted its equipment, perhaps it could have saved millions of dollars in long, expensive studies and avoided unnecessarily panicking thousands of veterans and their families. At the least, this event should increase the desire of the infantry, armor, artillery and other combat branches to get more involved in developing requirements for future chemical defense equipment. If there are valid concerns about the effectiveness of chemical agent detectors and protective ensembles, the users must get involved, rather than turning their backs as they did in 1973. If military leaders bend to political demands for low-level detectors, they should be aware of the impact on tactical operations (i.e., overly sensitive, very expensive detectors that false-alarm and slow down operational tempo). Education about CB warfare combined with further study and war games are the keys to ensure this situation does not occur again. The last thing we should do is shut down or down-scale the Chemical Corps because the military and public does not trust the experts to protect our armed forces.

CHAPTER 10

Conclusion

We must reemphasize the importance of chemical defense to maintaining deterrence and plan to increase the overall level of effort. As the bilateral and multilateral treaties are agreed and implemented, our retaliatory capability will be reduced, and chemical defense will become the key to chemical deterrence.
—Dick Cheney, Secretary of Defense

Professor of history Martin van Creed has written that the rules of war exist to protect the armed forces themselves by defining a common cultural code that differentiates an army from a mob. More importantly, he states that these rules carefully define how armies can and cannot be allowed to kill other combatants and noncombatants. These are in effect a societal rule that draws the line between murder and war. Countries that ignore the rules usually provoke punishment, often through annihilation or later war crime trials. These rules of war once covered the use of crossbows, submarine warfare, strategic bombing and minelaying; today, of course, they still cover CB warfare.[1]

Over the last century, nations have attempted to restrain the use of CB weapons under these special rules, though more from fear of retaliation than from moral distaste. Because of past association with strategic bombing theories developed between the world wars and after World War II, the advent of nuclear weapons, chemical and biological weapons have been put on the same scale as nuclear devices. Contrary to this view, CB warfare has never resulted in thousands or millions of innocent casualties, the nightmare that has driven the international arms control community to such treaties as the Biological Weapons Convention and Chemical Weapons Convention. History has shown that nations continue to develop CB weapons because there are tactical advantages to be gained: when one combines CB weapons use with conventional military tactics against an enemy without a good defense, it dramatically reduces the time needed for victory. In these days of billion-dollar conflicts, that gets attention. Increasing global proliferation of these weapons drives the need for defensive measures despite these special "rules" of war.

The Chemical Corps survived to become part of the Army's twenty-first century military force, not by planned evolution but by world events that constantly demanded that the US military retain an ability to protect itself against CB warfare. In 1972 the Army turned its back on the Chemical Corps because the service's leaders did not see the operational benefits of retaining such combat support. As a result, a decade slipped by without modernizing CB defense equipment; without leaders understanding that CB warfare is a tactical, not strategic consideration; without CB defense specialists staffing combat units and command headquarters; and without the specialized chemical defense companies and biological detection teams supporting combat arms units. While the 1980s featured a great deal of improvement in doctrine development, leadership, education, chemical defense unit build-up and equipment modernization, the GAO report released in May 1991 pointed out the serious deficiencies in the Army prior to Desert Shield. Imagine, if you will, the situation in August 1990 if General Creighton Abrams in 1972 had been successful in relegating the Chemical Corps to a special weapons function under the Ordnance Corps. More importantly, will the four services, having looked into the eyes of the dragon, now forget that the threat of CB warfare ever existed during the Gulf War? Or does the US military leadership now acknowledge the need for continued reform and further efforts? While the Chemical Corps obviously has room for improvement, its efforts are wasted until the three and four-star Army leaders identify these challenges and aggressively support the Chemical Corps in meeting them.

THE NATIONAL POLICY ON NBC WARFARE REQUIRES UPDATING

The US government's policy on NBC warfare has been one of "no first use" only since World War II, as the US Senate had refused to ratify the Geneva Convention in 1925. Because of the potential threat from Germany and Japan, the US military scrambled for eighteen months to develop a retaliatory capability in the form of mustard and phosgene agent-filled munitions. President Franklin D. Roosevelt publicly stated the government's policy that under no circumstances would the United States resort to using CB weapons unless they were first used by the Axis. If used by Germany, Italy or Japan, the US military would retaliate against munition centers, seaports and other military objectives.

After World War II, President Roosevelt's policy remained the unwritten rule for most administrations, although the US government had still not ratified the Geneva Convention. President Richard Nixon publicly reaffirmed the policy of no first use of chemical weapons and abandoned the use of biological warfare agents altogether. The Senate's final ratification of the Geneva Convention in 1975 did not change the US policy of retaliation in kind, using the current stockpile of chemical weapons. The re-initiation of the binary chemical weapons program in 1985, meant to replace the aging unitary chemical munitions, forced the Soviets to return to the negotiations table on the subject. In the 1990 Bush-Gorbachev talks, the US government abandoned the future production and storage of chemical weapons, receiving promises from the Soviet Union that it would do likewise.

Now, as of April 1997, the broader, multilateral Chemical Weapons Convention treaty has come into play. The CWC treaty outlines a verifiable ban on all production, storage and use of chemical weapons and carries over 180 nations' signatories. This represents a great change from the past policy, of maintaining both a strong defensive posture and a viable retaliatory capability, to one of maintaining only defensive measures. The one policy we knew, which worked for over forty-five years—threatening retaliation by chemical munitions if our forces were attacked with chemical weapons—is gone. On the other hand, the CWC treaty affects all countries by, at the least, causing them to go to some effort to shield the size and potential effects of their offensive CB programs. The future threat for US forces will not be a continuous hail of chemical rains. Rather, it will be infrequent and inconsistent use of chemical agents to delay and disrupt combat operations, intended to give the opposing force an advantage at key points in the battle.

The US military is at a dangerous transition. It has given up its retaliatory capability and defensive capabilities remain weak, while the CWC treaty's verification measures have not been tested. If our forces are attacked with CB weapons, the military leadership will have to choose nuclear or massive conventional retaliation. In a recent war game sponsored by the DoD counter-proliferation office, the players explored a combined CBW scenario in the Persian Gulf: after US carriers were attacked by aircraft armed with biological agent spray tanks, and terrorists attacked Dhahran with anthrax bombs, the United States responded by using nuclear weapons against Baghdad.[2] While this ended the war game, it did not represent a satisfactory or realistic conclusion. This game move did not acknowledge that a US president would have to approve the nuclear attack of a country's capitol, let alone address the implications of attacking an Arab capitol in the Middle East. Even considering the consequence of biological agent attack against US forces, would the president be prepared for the consequences of a strategic nuclear strike against civilian and industrial targets? Ordering a smaller tactical nuclear strike against military targets is not an option these days; the DoD yielded up their tactical nuclear weapons years ago.

The more realistic option is the massive conventional response, which is also politically and militarily risky. Experience during World War II, Korea, Vietnam (and, according to many, the Gulf War) shows that massive conventional bombing produces very little political or military payoff for the effort, while increasing pilot and aircraft exposure to increasingly sophisticated air defenses. In any case, to minimize the threat from CB weapons (e.g., strike production facilities, storage sites, delivery systems), you have to find them first. The intelligence job of finding and identifying these targets has gotten more difficult, not less. An increasingly diverse global economy allows countries to order just about anything they want through dummy companies, academic institutions, and public organizations. Taking a page from the superpowers, many countries are investing in deep underground shelters to protect their storage sites and their command, control and communications functions. While the United States can identify most of these facilities, not much short of a nuclear device can get at them.

Military forces cannot predict with 100 percent clairvoyance when or where the CB agent munitions will be used, even with extensive intelligence assets. This means that US forces would need to retain a strict defensive posture against CB agent use at all times in a theater, increasing logistics demands and decreasing morale. Meanwhile, the enemy needs only a minimal investment in defensive equipment since it controls the time and location of chemical weapons release, thus minimizing effects on its forces. This lopsided arrangement actually increases the possibility that an enemy force would use CB agent munitions, since its chemical weapons will eliminate the US military's high-technology edge. Army studies prove that chemical warfare results in a drop in overall preparedness and effectiveness, anywhere from 25 to 100 percent, depending on the scenario and the troops' level of training. Adversaries using CW munitions will multiply their combat power by degrading the performance of opposing troops that lack defensive equipment or training. Given that current force structure decisions are putting smaller US forces against larger opponents, losing the high-technology advantage will result in being overwhelmed on the battlefield. If we are trying to minimize US casualties, this should not be an acceptable course of action.

Can the US military survive and sustain its forces on the future NBC battlefield through strictly defensive methods? In theory, yes—but it would call for careful planning, expensive stockpiling and extensive training. It requires an aggressive development program that provides state-of-the-art defensive equipment. It requires continued reliance on chemical defense units that can decontaminate military equipment and large areas of terrain (such as ports and airfields), while keeping pace with mobile forces. That means maintaining active and reserve units that are ready, well trained and have worked with combat units, integrating CB defense into combat operations. It calls for an increased focus on how combat arms units can minimize the impact of persistent CB agents. By integrating chemical defense training with their mission-oriented combat training, soldiers could learn to fight on contaminated battlefields, making CB warfare irrelevant. This would enable them to retain most of their intended lethality, which today can be seriously degraded, as seen in the CANE tests.[3]

Last, and perhaps as important, we need to reexamine our investment in human intelligence sources. The US government needs to remain alert to new and changing dangers such as terrorist use of CB agents and emerging Third World threats. Yet our government has made little attempt to shift its vision in this respect from the Cold War to the "New World Order." There are less than fifty CB intelligence analysts in the entire federal government, as compared to nearly ten times that number dedicated to nuclear weapons intelligence. As seen with the intensive research conducted for the Khamisiyah incident, there are few analysts that understand and can validate CB weapons effects. More are needed to track and verify offensive CB weapons programs in countries like Libya, North Korea, Iran and Iraq. Unless this imbalance is corrected, US forces will again have no idea what their opponents have in the way of CB weapons, where the weapons are located, or how to attack them.

The US military must reexamine its policy concerning enemy use of CB weapons, and find a solution that is practical and feasible. Because we are not facing a massive use of CB agents, we can no longer justify a righteous massive retaliation. If massive force is no longer a credible deterrent, US forces in the future will be as fear-stricken as they were when the Scuds filled the skies in January 1991—unless they have full faith in their defensive capabilities.

THE DOD NBC DEFENSE RDA PROGRAM IS STILL RECOVERING

Several material areas sorely required attention during the Gulf War. The most evident was the need for improved airlift and sealift capabilities. While C-17 cargo planes, heavy trucks and merchant marine ships will never be as sexy or alluring as F-22 fighter aircraft, Abrams tanks and Seawolf submarines, there certainly was a strong case made when the military had to rely on commercial aircraft and ships older than the generals and admirals in order to get to the theater of operations. Of course, NBC defense equipment was another area of concern. Despite the Gulf War (or because of the lack of CB warfare during this conflict), CB defense equipment continues to struggle on as a small, relatively insignificant portion of the Pentagon's acquisition funds (less than one-fifth of 1 percent).

NBC defense equipment has always been criticized by both the military troops that use the equipment and the chemical specialists that train with it. Protective suits are too hot; protective masks are too restrictive; collective protection shelters are not adequate; decontamination apparatuses use too much water; CB agent detectors false-alarm too often; and medical antidotes can not be trusted. All these complaints came too late for the troops in Operation Desert Storm. These concerns were primarily a result of the combat arms sitting by the sidelines, allowing the Chemical Corps to determine what the combat troops were going to use. The Chemical Corps did deliver detectors that detected chemical agents, protective ensembles that would have saved lives, and decontaminants did work very well. The *BUT* part is that the combat arms units did not understand that getting CB defense equipment that works is only half the equation; there remains such matters as false alarms due to overly-sensitive detectors, hot burdensome suits, corrosive decontaminants. If the combat arms incorporated CB warfare considerations into their war gaming, they might see the benefits and challenges of CB defense equipment, and they might get more involved. This active involvement will become more and more important as the military gives up its chemical munitions and relies solely on defensive equipment.

As a result of Public Law 103-160, there is an increased emphasis on better management of the NBC defense program. With the evolution of the one-star command CRDEC into the two-star command US Army Chemical and Biological Defense Command (CBDCOM) in October 1993, the Army is attempting to put much of its NBC defense program authority under one major subordinate command. The commanding general of CBDCOM also "wears the hat" of Deputy Chief of Staff for Chemical Matters, Army Materiel Command. CBDCOM is charged to manage all NBC defense programs for the Army and to work with the other services to manage better the DoD NBC defense program. CBDCOM will manage chemical stockpile sites, to include Rocky Mountain Arsenal and several programs at Dugway Proving Ground, Pine Bluff Arsenal and other locations. This is not to suggest that the Army has gone full circle, back to the single consolidated NBC defense program it had prior to 1962; CBDCOM still has no direct cont over medical NBC defense programs or the chemical demilitarization prog But it does have a great deal of authority to request funds, conduct stud procure NBC defense equipment.

Public Law 103-160 also meant reorganization for the entire   ,C defense community. The four services have formed a Joint Service   ation Group (JSIG) for joint doctrine and training issues and a Joint Service Material Group (JSMG) for joint material issues, both chaired by the Army, and both including all services as equal partners. The JSIG resides at Fort McClellan, with the Chemical School's commandant as its chair. Its sister organization, the JSMG, is chaired by the commanding general of CBDCOM at Aberdeen Proving Ground. These groups officially started their functions in January 1995, both overseen by a DoD Joint NBC Defense Board, which in turn is overseen by the Assistant to the Secretary of Defense (Atomic Energy) (Chemical-Biological Matters) (or ATSD(AE)(CBM)). The Joint NBC Defense Board is a high-level, general-officer panel (including civilian acquisition members and officers from all services) designed to oversee the DoD NBC defense program and to sort out interservice conflicts. The new joint groups may be more effective than their predecessors, primarily since they make recommendations on the annual NBC defense budgets through a joint consolidated Program Operations Memorandum strategy. As the Golden Rule states, those who have the gold make the rules.

The other services still do not trust the Army to control the DoD NBC defense program entirely. The four services still have difficulties agreeing on basic doctrine, or on roles and missions for the future. The other services continue to fight tooth and nail to retain exclusive control over their own destinies in the NBC defense program areas. Each service had its own offices, programs and "rice bowls," specifically for NBC defense ever since DoD gave them leeway to initiate their own NBC defense programs in 1960, programs that became further entrenched when the Chemical Corps was down-scaled in 1972. These two joint groups have the budget authority and congressional language to make the tough decisions necessary to reform the DoD NBC defense program, but this does not guarantee any quick or near-term improvements. Existing bureaucracies always fight change, and it will be some time before we see results.

One key to developing better NBC defense equipment may lie in using computer models and simulations to understand CB agent effects on military troops, units and equipment during combat. The Army's "Battle Lab" program at six TRADOC schools uses advanced models, simulations and war gaming tools to test new concepts of warfighting and to determine future program requirements. The Dismounted Battle Space Battle Lab at Fort Benning initially had the responsibility for "weapons of mass destruction," with NRDEC as its partner, but it focused almost exclusively on individual protection efforts. Other labs, such as the Mounted Battle Space Battle Lab at Fort Knox, the Depth and Simultaneous Attack Battle Lab at Fort Sill, and the Early Entry Lethality and Survivability Battle Lab at Fort Monroe, have smaller, but not insignificant, roles for NBC warfare aspects. The Engineer School and Center initiated its Maneuver Support Battle Lab, which has taken over the champion role of working "weapons of mass destruction" issues, working with the Chemical Corps as it moves to Fort Leonard-Wood. It will be up to these Battle Labs to revisit the issue of NBC warfare on the modern battlefield. To date, there are no proven models of how CB agents affect troops and equipment, and therefore, there is no way to show senior leadership the benefits (or detriments) of fighting with a certain type of CB defense equipment. This is vital to assess the "value-added" of these programs. If warfighters, NBC defense subject-matter experts, and industry cannot gain a mutual understanding of NBC warfare, there will be no acceptance or understanding of modern CB defense equipment.

CB AGENTS AND DOMESTIC TERRORISM

Terrorist organizations have taken an interest in CB weapons since at least 1972. Prospects for CB terrorism have increased with the international spread of dual-use technologies, increased access to published sources on producing, storing and handing CB agents, and the relative ease in acquiring or producing CB agents. US intelligence sources have noted Moslem terrorist organizations conducting chemical defense training at their camps. Simple biological agents such as botulinum toxin can be developed with a moderate amount of education and equipment. They are inexpensive to procure and culture, easy to hide, require far less material than chemical weapons and are very easy to employ in an indiscriminate target-rich area such as a city. Most biological organisms, however, are more difficult to develop, store and disperse safely than chemical agents, lending to a pattern of terrorist groups external to the United States using chemical agents rather than biological agents.[4] This could change, given today's global accessibility of technical and scientific resources.

Chemical and biological agents are inexpensive, easily understood, easily controlled, and easily dispersed under a single terrorist's control. As the world's nations have not condemned the use of chemical agent weapon use in Yemen, Afghanistan, Laos, Iraq, etc., terrorists may feel that they can safely use CB agents rather than resort to nuclear devices. Some past examples of CB terrorism include:

- In 1974, Muharem Kerbegovic was arrested in Los Angeles after mailing toxic material to a Justice of the Supreme Court and threatening to kill the president with nerve gas;
- In 1980, the Paris police raided a Baader-Meinhof safehouse and discovered a culture of clostridinium botulinum (used to make botulin toxin) in a home laboratory;
- In 1984, the Rajneesh cult in Oregon was accused of using salmonella to contaminate salad bars in local restaurants in an attempt to influence local elections;
- In 1991, German authorities thwarted a neo-Nazi plot to pump hydrogen cyanide into a synagogue;[5]
- In 1992, the FBI arrested two members of the Patriots Council in Minnesota for possession of less than one gram of ricin, under the Biological Weapons Anti-Terrorism Act of 1989; and [6]
- In 1996, a former Aryan Nation member was arrested for mail-ordering three vials of bubonic plague to his home by giving a false lab code number to the American Type Tissue Collection.[7]

The use of sarin in the Tokyo subway system on March 20, 1995, illustrates how easy it is to employ chemical agents in an open society, and how much media attention a small, previously barely noticed group can receive as a result. Between 7:00 and 8:30 in the morning of March 20, several individuals left at least four containers wrapped in newspaper, disguised as lunch boxes, on various trains of three subway lines. Some were placed on hat racks, others on or under the seats. These containers were punctured, allowing its contents to evaporate. Shortly afterward, people riding the three lines began coughing and complaining of headaches, diminishing vision, and nausea, classical nerve agent poisoning signs. Some collapsed to the floor, and as the trains halted at the next stop passengers rushed out, screaming for help and collapsing on the ground.

By 8:15, police were receiving emergency calls from sixteen subway stations. Tokyo's Metropolitan Police Department dispatched 11,000 police and rescue workers to assist the affected passengers. One assistant station manager, Kazumasa Takahashi, went aboard one train to remove a plastic bag holding a leaking container. He died soon afterward, along with seven others. In all, twelve individuals died, another fifty-four were in critical condition, and more than 5,000 were treated for related symptoms.[8] By 8:45, service on all three subway lines was stopped, with twenty-six stations closed. About three hours after the first attack, the authorities realized they were dealing with a nerve agent. They moved into full response mode, sending police, firefighters and medical response teams into the subways.

The police targeted the Aum Shinrikyo, or Supreme Truth, a Buddhist sect that recruited dissatisfied college-educated citizens, as the probable perpetrators. Several of their members were arrested in Japan, and the police seized bulk precursor chemicals, including phosphorus trichloride, sodium fluoride, and isopropyl alcohol. In the sect's buildings police discovered behind false walls industrial equipment for preparing bulk chemical mixes. As their leader, Shoko Asahara, explained a few days later, these are chemicals that can be used for commercial purposes. They also are the prime ingredients for sarin; in fact, the Chemical Weapons Convention specifically names phosphorus trichloride as one of the dual-use chemicals on its "schedule 3" list.

The panic and concern over the next few months was largely due to the fact that the Japanese police had been completely unprepared to react to this new form of terrorism. Perhaps more frightening was the failure of intelligence agencies or police to predict this attack. There were a number of related cases that stretched back nearly two years, beginning with a case on July 2, 1993, when over 100 residents in Tokyo's Koto district complained of noxious white fumes rising from buildings owned by the sect. One year later, on June 21, 1994, seven people died and more than 200 were sickened by sarin fumes in the nearby town of Matsumoto. It was later discovered that Aum Shinrikyo cultists had used a truck-mounted agricultural generator to target three judges in an apartment building (they were ruling on a local real estate issue involving cult members). On September 1, more than 230 people in seven towns in the state of Nara (in western Japan) suffered from rashes and eye irritation from unknown fumes. On December 1994, material by-products of sarin were discovered in Kamikuishiki; January 4, 1995—the Aum Shinrikyo filed a complaint accusing a company president of spreading sarin into its facilities in Kamikuishiki; March 5— eleven people were taken to a hospital after nineteen individuals inhaled noxious fumes in a train car in Yokohama (a test case?). On March 15, police discovered three attache cases containing an unknown (but nontoxic) gas. Each case held small motorized fans, a vent and a battery. Despite all this evidence, the March 20 episode came as a surprise to the Tokyo emergency responders.

Experts still wonder why more subway riders did not die, considering the high lethality of the nerve agent. One theory rests on these possible speculations. First, the sarin mix was not pure. Later analysis showed that the chemicals were only 30 percent sarin by composition and were therefore not as lethal as they could have been. This design may have been deliberate, contrived to permit the couriers time to flee. Second, the delivery system was crude. Accounts told of the suspected couriers rupturing the one-quart containers immediately before departing the trains, allowing natural seepage to initiate the fumes. Not the most efficient process; a portable fan next to the package would have spread more quickly the fumes throughout the cars. Third, sarin is what is known as a semi-persistent chemical agent—it has about the same consistency as water, taking up to hours to evaporate completely. This would explain why the only individuals who died were the ones traveling in the same cars as the containers, like the assistant station manager who picked up the package to remove it from the train. Last, the trains may have had a positive-pressure ventilation, using fans to circulate air out of the trains and into the subway tubes. This precaution is a normal engineering method to keep gasses or smells in the subway tubes from intruding into the individual cars; the District of Columbia Metro, for instance, has this feature. In all, the Japanese citizens were very fortunate that most survived the physical effects of this deadly agent.

Another subway in Yokohama was attacked a few weeks later on April 19, sending nearly 600 Japanese sent to the hospital for treatment of what was suspected to be exposure to phosgene gas. While this agent is not immediately lethal, it can kill as the gas hydrolyses within the victim's lungs over a period of one to two days. Many people do not realize that this World War I chemical warfare agent is also a legitimate industrial chemical, used in the textiles and clothing industry as well as plastics manufacturing. As such, bulk quantities of the chemical travel across the country every day in tankers on rail cars and trucks; there is no need for illicit manufacturing, since it can be purchased (or stolen). If someone had wanted to manufacture phosgene, it is a very simple chemical compound to synthesize in the laboratory. A third suspected gas attack at a grocery store two days later caused twenty-five people to seek treatment. Because the attack occurred outdoors, the lethal chemical agents may not have had their full potency. On May 6, the police defused a binary device that would have again released hydrogen cyanide into a Tokyo subway station.

The Aum Shinrikyo may have been coming after American citizens as well. A task force composed of representatives of the FBI, Los Angeles police, the Federal Emergency Management Agency (FEMA), Environmental Protection Agency, Public Health Service, Centers for Disease Control, and CBDCOM's Technical Escort Unit traveled to Los Angeles airport on April 13 to intercept two Japanese men associated with the cult. These men had in their possession written instructions on how to make sarin, and a videotape that indicated an intended attack against Disneyland. Authorities at Disneyland had received a tip that a possible terrorist incident was going to take place over Easter weekend, when their attendance was expected to be higher than average. Although details are still vague, it appears that the terrorist group was planning to release sarin within one of the many theaters or exhibition halls at Disneyland. Because of quick reactions based on the tip, these men were apprehended, and America's version of Tokyo's experience was averted—for now.[9]

Since March 1995, federal agencies have banded together under a program titled "Domestic Preparedness," to prevent and respond to acts of CB terrorism conducted within the United States. The FBI leads what is termed "crisis management" (what to do prior to a CB terrorist incident), while FEMA leads "consequence management" (what happens after the event occurs). Forces were in place at the Atlanta Olympics and the 1996 national political conventions, with a mission to prepare for any sign of CB terrorism. While it was an interim agreement among federal government agencies to cooperate prior to 1996, the Domestic Preparedness program has since been codified by executive order and public law and is under way. This program had just been started when it had its first acid test. Preplanning for large events can be accomplished, but the following case showed the real dangers.

In Washington, DC, on the evening of April 24, 1997, someone left a smelly manila envelope in the mail room of the B'nai Brith offices. Two employees opened the envelope; it contained a petri dish filled with an unknown, red, jelly-like substance and markings that suggested it held anthrax. The police took immediate steps to cordon off square blocks around DuPont Circle, an area that included the Australian Embassy and several traffic commuter routes. Firefighters were called in, as well as the FBI and CBDCOM's Technical Escort Unit. They evacuated the dish, as inside the building, 108 people were quarantined for nearly eight hours as medical technicians at the Bethesda Naval Medical Center analyzed the compound. Meanwhile, the two employees declared they were feeling sick. They, along with twelve firefighters, were decontaminated with a chlorine solution.

As things turned out, there was no anthrax in the petri dish. While FBI and city officials praised the firefighters' quick reaction, it was a major overreaction to a minor threat. First, airborne anthrax is the typical biological warfare agent used, due to its much higher lethality than percutaneous anthrax. Since the sample was in a liquid-gelatinous substance, there was no chance of its escaping into the atmosphere. A two hundred-meter safety radius would have been as good as several square blocks; had this actually been anthrax, there would have been very little threat to the surrounding area outside the building itself. Second, any biological agent needs time to incubate in a human host prior to causing signs of sickness. Certainly any symptoms felt by the two employees and the firefighters had to be psychosomatic. Exposed personnel could have been treated with vaccines prior to any real dangers to their health. The point here is that, left to their own resources, emergency responders will over-react to CB agents and make the wrong decisions unless they learn more about this area.

The Washington case was a free trial-run for federal counterterrorism forces and city emergency response forces. It pointed out several challenges: the need for CB defense equipment for local responders, the need for an expert source of information around the clock, and the need to train and educate local emergency responders in how to identify and manage the incident. Trained federal forces will be hard pressed to respond to unplanned emergency events in less than eight to twelve hours. This puts the burden on police, firefighters, emergency medical services, and 911 operators to know how to deal with the threat. It may be that this specialized training and equipment is the best local responders can do is to keep from becoming casualties themselves. If we expect that all the major metropolitan areas require this kind of expertise, a major investment of funds, equipment and time will be required, of which time is probably the most critical.

While the FBI and FEMA have traditionally led counterterrorism and disaster preparedness missions, the expertise on CB agents is in the Department of Defense. This has led to the development of an interagency federal task force and several programs for federal support to metropolitan emergency responders. An ambitious training program has targeted 120 major cities in the US, training their emergency responders to identify and respond correctly to CB agent terrorism. It will take some years, but this interagency task force envisions a certain degree of expertise at the local and state levels that will at least ensure that firefighters, police and emergency medical technicians are not killed rushing into a CB terrorist incident. But it should be understood by all that this will not guarantee against a similar Tokyo subway incident in the US—all it does is minimize the ensuing chaos and the casualties among responding professionals. As in any terrorist bombing incident, few things can minimize the number of civilian casualties other than interdicting the terrorist group iteself prior to the event.

There are a number of additional cases, some still classified, where terrorist use of CB agents in the United States has been only narrowly averted. One reason why terrorists have not adopted these weapons more readily in these already unstable times may be the argument of cost versus availability. The "bang for the buck" comparison shows that CB agents kill their victims much more cheaply per casualty than bullets or explosives do. Bullets and explosives, on the other hand, are far more available on the open market than CB agents, and they are still effective attention-getters. As long as a terrorist group can achieve its goals with conventional weapons, it will probably do so.

These days, terrorist incidents compete with drive-by shootings, mass suicides, uprisings, and international incidents for front-page news. One day soon, exploding a van under the World Trade Center resulting in six deaths may not receive much attention. Worse yet, could the next federal building be attacked with CB agents instead of a fertilizer-based explosive? Or will terrorists attack key industrial sites to reproduce the next Bhopal, *Exxon Valdez*, or Chernobyl catastrophe? Is the United States ready to combat domestic terrorism in the form of CB agent attacks? As one of the most open nations in the world, our society is very vulnerable. One fact remains: in the midst of news stories recounting the falling yen, a major earthquake, and North Korean demands for nuclear reactors, worldwide publicity catapulted the name Aum Shinrikyo, the Supreme Truth, to the homes of billions across the globe within one week. That alone should prompt concerns that others will seek to imitate its efforts.

THERE IS A FUTURE FOR THE CHEMICAL CORPS

Future threats are not diminishing in number or volume, despite the successful completion and signing of the Chemical Weapons Convention in 1993. In every corner of the world, particularly in historical and regional conflict areas, proliferation of CB warfare programs continues. Many countries begin with production of industrial chemicals, move into first-generation (World War I) chemical agents, rapidly progress into development of second-generation chemical agents (World War II and later), and last, biological agent production. While the CWC will continue to put pressure on these countries, the extreme liquidity of the global economy, and the increasing sophistication of other nations' arms programs will make it increasingly difficult for the United States and its allies to control this proliferation. We can be assured that the next major conflict will include the use of CB agent munitions, in an attempt to resolve a conflict before its high price can take its toll and before major powers can get involved.

The US military's future is undergoing its own evolvement, as seen with the Quadrennial Defense Review (QDR) and its successors. With a diminished manpower and budget, a decreasing involvement overseas, and an increasing reluctance on the part of the American public to suffer any casualties in an overseas conflict, the military is searching for a new, defined role. The QDR's language concerning weapons of mass destruction, asymmetric threats and the threat of ballistic missiles shows that DoD understands the danger exists. Military leaders just have not figured out exactly how they want to combat them. The lack of CB warfare during the Gulf War has caused more questions and theories than would have been the case if the Iraqi military had used these agents. Some emphasis focuses on a "21st Century Land Warrior" program combining protective clothing, mask and integrated CB agent detectors into the troops' combat ensembles. Others insist on more proactive measures, such as Theater High Altitude Air Defense systems and planes with high-powered lasers designed to defeat CB agent warheads on ballistic missiles. The main weakness is a continued search for a technological "fix" for a problem, a search that ignores the need for integrated NBC defense training and trained chemical specialists in future combat forces. The military still needs to test these concepts, using validated computer models that mimic the physical and physiological effects of NBC agents on troops and units, to understand the costs and benefits of these approaches.

Despite their close brush in 1991 with CB warfare, the four services did not immediately acknowledge the need to reform their roles and responsibilities in the DoD NBC defense program. Although the Gulf War division and corps commanders are in high positions throughout the Army today, their near experience with CB weapons use has not trickled down to the new generation of commanders. Despite the worry prior to the conflict over these weapons, some still feel that conventional firepower alone is more than adequate to deal with the threat of CB warfare. This attitude may have explained the many attempts to shut down Fort McClellan since the Gulf War.

In January 1991, the Army leadership recommended shutting down Fort McClellan and moving the Chemical School, claiming that the Army had no special need for toxic agent training such as at the CDTF. Based on the experiences of Gulf War soldiers, the Chemical School convinced the Base Realignment Committee (BRAC) otherwise. In 1993, the Army proposed moving the Chemical School to Fort Leonard-Wood, Missouri, and keeping the CDTF open; it would fly trainees to Alabama for the specialized training. Again, the Chemical School successfully argued that the CDTF and the School should not be separated, due to the need to integrate up-to-date doctrine, training and equipment into the CDTF. In the 1995 recommendations to the BRAC, the Pentagon recommended the closures of both Fort McClellan and Dugway Proving Ground. The Army's argument to move the schools (both Military Police and Chemical) was based on a new plan to develop an Army Maneuver Support Command, tieing in the

Engineer Center and School with the two other schools to develop an integrated combat support concept. This time, the Army agreed to build a new CDTF at Leonard-Wood in addition to the move. The 1995 BRAC, on a very close (5–4) vote (with two Missouri politicians tipping the results), agreed to this plan.

Chemical officers remain concerned over the potential loss of the Chemical Defense Training Facility. The CDTF will remain active at Fort McClellan until one is constructed at Fort Leonard-Wood—at least, as plans now stand. The CDTF has a very successful record of preparing soldiers, both chemical specialists and non-chemical personnel, for the all too real threat of a toxic environment. Tens of thousands of American soldiers have passed through the training, as well as hundreds of British, German, Canadian and other foreign military personnel. This was accomplished while maintaining a perfect record of no training days lost to maintenance or chemical agent accidents. Major General McCaffrey stated: "Then and now, they [soldiers and leaders] wholeheartedly value the opportunity to train with actual agents, real detectors/alarms and real decontaminants. The presence of CDTF-trained soldiers in every company of the Division directly improves our combat readiness. These soldiers have great confidence that their equipment works. Your training program is right on target."[10]

While moving the Chemical School to Fort Leonard-Wood will not stop the Army's NBC defense program, it will disrupt the infrastructure and momentum of CB defense doctrine and training. Also, this plan assumes that there will be no delays in building a new CDTF in Missouri. The last CDTF was a five-year undertaking before the state of Alabama and the EPA approved its operations. Can we assume that Missouri will be more cooperative? If Fort Leonard-Wood cannot build a comparable CDTF by the time the Chemical School will move at the turn of the century, there will be a measurable drop in preparedness.

The attempted closure of Dugway Proving Ground is an even more serious issue. The loss of Dugway Proving Ground would eliminate the one place in the United States where extensive CB agent testing can still be accomplished. Without accurate testing of detection, protection and decontamination equipment with actual CB agents, how will the military be assured of good defensive equipment? As armored vehicles undergo live-fire tests, so must NBC defensive equipment undergo toxic agent tests. The argument for closing Dugway Proving Ground may have centered on the fact that since Congress drastically restricts open-air agent tests, the over 850,000 acres of desert are too expensive to maintain. Since testing with CB agents is all conducted indoors, the argument could be made to relocate the valuable test facilities elsewhere, although the cost would be high. The 1995 BRAC did feel that Dugway Proving Ground's unique testing facilities and proving ground was vital enough to spare, and did not approve its inclusion on the closure list. Some type of ability to perform this testing is necessary. The Army has not yet presented an effective argument as to who would assume the responsibility for this testing, and it may not have calculated the total cost of moving the test laboratories to other sites and shutting down the post.

I will not suggest any "plots" or "conspiracies" to disband the Chemical Corps (although there does seem to be a historical pattern). A cynic would point out that as long as the Infantry Ranger School trained its students at Dugway Proving Ground, there were few recommendations to close the base (the Rangers left Dugway in 1992). Rather, I will point out that these actions take place without careful thought as to potential consequences. Yes, the Chemical School can still operate at another post. Yes, the testing facilities at Dugway Proving Ground could be replicated elsewhere. But no one has put any thought into minimizing the impact of these moves. Who will maintain the reforms in doctrine and training? Who will continue developing the NBC defense equipment requirements? Who will pick up the mission of testing military equipment to measure its ability to meet the rigors of an NBC-contaminated environment? How much time and money will it cost the military to regain these capabilities? As seen with the DoD's attempts to model the Khamisiyah explosion at Dugway, there is still a role for this expertise. It comes back to the need to maintain that high level of defense in a post-Cold War era, in a political environment that denies to the United States armed forces the use of retaliatory chemical weapons.

The Engineer Corps at Fort Leonard-Wood has a vision of a future combat support relationship. If there is one silver lining in the Chemical Corps move to the future Maneuver Support Command, it is that the Chemical Corps might emulate the successful "teaming" that engineers have developed with the combat arms branches. The cooperation seen between the Chemical and Engineer Corps in constructing deliberate decontamination sites in Southwest Asia suggests that there is room for both to grow together within that command. There is little question that the Chemical Corps could learn something from the Engineer Corps's ability to work closely with, and in support of, combat branches. There are two concerns foremost in the minds of chemical officers. History shows the many times that the US Army has attempted to nest the Chemical Corps within another branch (or eliminate it altogether). The Engineer Corps should be cautioned against ignoring or submerging the potential role of a strong and vital Chemical Corps. The Chemical Corps's mission as a joint service leader, mandated by Congress, as well as its status of an international leader in NBC defense, mandates that it retain its autonomy to a degree. The US military cannot afford the Engineer Corps to assume the Chemical Corps mission within its own. What the Chemical Corps needs is a strong partner, not new management.

The Persian Gulf War should convince most that there is a strong need in this area for a force of full-time professionals. The military was clearly unprepared for CB warfare in 1990, and remains uncomfortable with the concept of CB warfare even today. The Army needs to study the future trends of warfare, analyze potential avenues for future investment and determine how to prepare for conflicts that will include NBC weapons employment. More importantly, the Army needs the Chemical Corps to develop doctrine and to recommend chemical organizations that fits the future Force XXI concept, and to develop leadership skills to ensure the entire military force has the capability to survive and sustain combat operations in an NBC-contaminated environment. To do this, the Chemical Corps must become a true partner with its sister branches of the Army, as well as its counterparts in the other services. In the past, the Chemical Corps has retained a technical specialty; for the future, it must become an integral part of the combat arms teams. The Chemical Corps must understand the combat arms' doctrine and leadership demands, and it must communicate its potential to the combat arms into terms their leaders understand in order to achieve these goals.

IN CLOSING . . .

Future US administrations must decide how the Department of Defense should respond to enemy use of CB munitions. The CWC exists, but treaties have never stopped nations from researching and developing more advanced CB agent munitions. Treaties have rarely stopped those same countries from employing CB agent munitions. Faced with the fact that the US military still has problems facing World War I and World War II-vintage chemical munitions, other countries do not have far to go to produce an effective weapon that will disrupt military operations. Arms control experts and politicians who rail against CB warfare research are living in the past. Their transition to the present must come in the realization that while they can strive to limit future warfare, they will never totally eliminate it. Countries find CB agent munitions just too tempting, too easy to develop, too easy to hide, and too easy to deny having used, to pass up. When the military experts, politicians and arms control experts come to consensus on how best to integrate the trend of chemical warfare into future warfare policy, we can be assured that the United States has a sound national policy and a strong defensive capability in this area. Until then, our forces will remain dangerously vulnerable to CB weapons.

The underlying reason why politicians, the military, and the public have feared, and continue to fear, CB warfare so much is sheer ignorance about its nature. Either they completely underestimate its effects by ignoring the possibility of CB warfare during plans and exercises, or they completely overestimate the CB agents killing ability on the battlefield and in the eight stockpile sites. Chemical and biological weapons have never been on the same scale of destruction as nuclear weapons, yet many seem determined to treat them all the same way. At the least, chemical weapons have as much, and as little, potential killing power as any number of conventional bombs, artillery shells, and rockets in use today. Any weapon system is as safe or as deadly as the military force that uses them. As long as the media remains bent on sensationalistic journalism, and as long as novelists such as Tom Clancy and Hollywood screen writers make out CB weapons to be the doomsday devices *du jour*, we may never learn about the true threat of CB warfare to our own forces. Without understanding the tactical nature of these weapon systems, the military and government politicians remain unprepared to plan defensive strategies and will make the wrong decisions. This ignorance will continue until military leaders and politicians make an effort truly to understand the implications of CB warfare in modern combat operations.

We can no longer afford for this divisive battle of arms control experts versus the Chemical Corps versus the combat arms community. If there is a future vision for the Chemical Corps, it is to ensure that combat forces can maintain their full mission capability in future wars despite the threat of a CB agent-contaminated battlefield. This calls for both highly trained and motivated chemical officers supporting the combat arms, modern CB defense equipment and most importantly, trained and educated military leadership. As General Creighton Abrams once told Colonel Gerald Watson in 1972, it is the infantry and armor combat leaders—not its technical branches—that must decide how to fight and survive on the modern battlefield. The military may not like training for CB warfare, but the Chemical Corps's capabilities and CB defense equipment remain the sole "insurance policy" that maintains the United States military's ability to defend itself against the use of CB munitions. Until the Chemical Corps specialists are seen as true supporters of the combat soldier, and until the combat arms community comes to grips with the true scope and nature of CB warfare, the potential for future Desert Shield/Storm panics remains.

Chemical Defense Units Serving in Southwest Asia (Shield and Storm Task Organizations)

Task Organization of Chemical Defense Units on 5 November 1990

ARCENT HQ	**Support Cmd (ARCENT rear)**

63rd Chem Det (JA)   ·   51st Chem Det (JB)

490th Chem Bn
    318th Chem Co (Decon)
    371st Chem Co (Decon) (due in 18 Nov)
    413th Chem Co (Decon) (due in 18 Nov)

22th Army Support Group
    433rd Chem Det (JB)

593rd Army Support Group
    907th Chem Det (JB)

XVIII ABN Corps

Corps HQ
    1st Chem Det (JA)

3rd Armored Cavalry Regiment
    89th Chem Co (ACR)

82d Airborne Division
    21st Chem Co (Smoke/Decon)

24th Infantry Division
    91st Chem Co (Hvy Div)
    5th recon plt, 69th Chem Co
    197th Chem Det (Decon)

1st Cavalry Division
    68th Chem Co (Hvy Div)
    5th recon plt, 22nd Chem Co
    44th Chem Co (Hvy Div) (-)

101st Airborne Division
    63rd Chem Co (Smoke/Decon)
    7th recon plt, 92d Chem Co
    761st Chem Co(Smoke/Decon)

Corps Artillery
    101st Chem Co (-)(Decon)

1st Corps Support Command
    82d Chem Det (JA)
    1 decon plt, 101st Chem Co

2d Chem Bn
    5th recon plt, 25th Chem Co
    (due 16 Nov)
    59th Chem Co (Smoke/Decon)
    181st Chem Co (Decon)
    327th Chem Co (Decon)

Note: the symbol (-) designates a company that has detached a section(s) of itself to fall under the operational control of another military unit(s).

Task Organization of Chemical Defense Units on 24 February 1991

ARCENT HQ

63rd Chem Det (JA)

513th Miltary Intelligence Brigade
    9th Chem Co (-) (under FMIB)

1st Cavalry Division*
    68th Chem Co (Hvy Div)
    44th Chem Co (Hvy Div) (-)
        (1 smoke, 1 decon plt)

(* - really theater reserve....)

Support Cmd (ARCENT rear)

51st Chem Det (JB)

490th Chem Bn
    318th Chem Co (Decon)
    371st Chem Co (Decon)
    413th Chem Co (Decon)

22th Army Support Group
    433rd Chem Det (JB)

593rd Army Support Group
    907th Chem Det (JB)

XVIII Airborne Corps

Corps HQ
    1st Chem Det (JA)

3rd Armored Cavalry Rgmt
    89th Chem Co (ACR)
    1 decon plt, 340th Chem Co

24th Infantry Division
    91st Chem Co (Hvy Div)
    5th recon plt, 25th Chem Co
    197th Chem Det (Decon)
    327th Chem Co (Decon)
    1 decon plt, 101st Chem Co

82d Airborne Division
    21st Chem Co (Smoke/Decon)
    7th recon plt, 92d Chem Co
    340th Chem Co (Decon)(-)

101st Airborne Division
    63rd Chem Co (Smoke/Decon)
    761st Chem Co(Smoke/Decon)

Corps Artillery
    101st Chem Co (Decon) (-)

1st Corps Support Command
    82d Chem Det (JA)
    1 decon plt, 101st Chem Co

457th Chem Bn
    59th Chem Co (Smoke/Decon)
    327th Chem Co (Decon)
        (opcon to 24th IN DIV)
    340th Chem Co (Decon)(-)
        (opcon to 82d ABN DIV)

VII Corps

Corps HQ
    496th Chem Det (JA)

1st Infantry Division
    12th Chem Co (Hvy Div) (-)
    1 decon plt, 44th Chem Co
    2 decon plts, 181st Chem Co (-)
    2d Chem Bn
        46th Chem Co (Mech Smoke)
        84th Chem Co (Mech Smoke)
        323rd Chem Co (Decon) (-)
            (2 two decon plts)

2d Armored Cavalry Regiment
    87th Chem Co (ACR)
    1 decon plt, 11th Chem Co (-)
    172nd Chem Co (Mech Smoke) (-)

Tiger Brigade, 2d Armored Division
    (attached to MARCENT)
    1 decon plt, 44th Chem Co

1st Armored Division
    69th Chem Co (Hvy Div)

3rd Armored Division
    22d Chem Co (Hvy Div)
    2 decon plts, 323rd Chem Co
    1 smoke plt, 172nd Chem Co

11th Combat Aviation Brigade
    11th Chem Co (Decon) (-)

7th Engineer Brigade
    181st Chem Co (Decon) (-)
        (2 decon plts)

2d Corps Support Command
    242d Chem Det (JB)
        51st Chem Co (Decon)

(After the breach):

3rd Armored Division
    22d Chem Co (Hvy Div)
    1 smoke plt, 172d Chem Co
    2d Chem Bn*
        46th Chem Co (Mech Smoke)
        84th Chem Co (Mech Smoke)
        323rd Chem Co (Decon)

1st Infantry Division
    12th Chem Co (Hvy Div) (-)
    1 decon plt, 44th Chem Co
    181st Chem Co (Decon) (-)
        (2 decon plts)

*Note: The 2d Chemical Battalion had orders to detach one mechanized smoke company and two decon platoons to 1st Armored Division after its M113s caught up to the faster armored units. With the ground offensive closing so rapidly, this action never took place.

APPENDIX B

XVIII ABN Corps G-3-NBC Significant Events: 24 January–18 March 1991

Date/Time Group	Significant Event

JANUARY

240450	NRDEC saying once overgarments are put on body the "clock" starts and doesn't stop. ARCENT challenging message. Issue remains unresolved. Continue with current Corps guidance [repacking unused chemical overgarments].[1]
241137	ANBACIS-II team [from DNA] arrived in country.
241315	Received CECOM msg on BA3517's, 9000 waiting shipment, 3415 for Corps also 300 of 6000 power cables for Corps. Total of 70,000 BA3517's scheduled for Feb.
250900	XM21 fielding; 9th Chem Co(-) (CPT Greg Reasons) will deploy within next several days with unknown quantity of XM21.
251430	ANBACIS-II team arrived. Provided Corps 3 STU-III's and 3 secure fax. Discussed concept of operations.
252100	CRDEC will push 100 M40 protective masks into theater for hard-to-fit personnel. CPT John Murphy is POC [Pine Bluff Arsenal's Mask Maintenance Facility].
270947	ARCENT notified Corps that 100K BDO due in 7 Feb, 100K NLT 15 Feb, 395K from USAREUR and 200K are being shipped from ROK [Republic of Korea] date TBD.
271310	13000 barrels of fog oil at KKMC, 4500 to be pushed to Logbase CHARLIE.[2]
272150	COSCOM to receive first delivery of plastic on 30 Jan, first priority is ASP's, thereafter to Logbase BRAVO (1300-500/day), 21 steam cleaners located contract still working.
281200	Corps Main CP relinquishes command and control to Rear CP, begins movement forward to Rahfa.
291620	Arrived at Rahfa began final set up for resuming command and control

292050	Quality control shelf life extension for Nerve Agent Antidote [Kit], lot #TU8100/TU7056 expires 7/92.
301120	340th CM CO en route from SPOD [Sea Point of Debarkation] to KKMC, ETA 31 Jan 91. 457th CML BN moved to Logbase CHARLIE (MTO55045).
311642	340th CM CO closed at Logbase CHARLIE.

FEBRUARY

012220	6th NBCRS vehicle will be available for 3d ACR on 20 Feb 91 at earliest. Plt for 24th ID(M) (request for waiver) is not receiving ARCENT support.
021837	CPT Murphy arrived with 65 M40, 40 XS M17 protective masks and 16 cases of banana oil. Fitting team will be at Logbase CHARLIE 5-6 Feb and Rahfa 7 Feb.
022120	Push packages of masks, filters and battery cables arrived in theater along with 2 pallets of BA3517.
041215	CNN announces neurotoxins affecting civilian populace near destroyed biological production facility, requested confirmation from G-2.
041840	FONECON with NRDEC ref BDO: any overgarment with woodland pattern is a true BDO in terms of protection (24 hours and 22 days) and wear life regardless of packaging.
050700	Hard-to-fit team begins fitting at Logbase CHARLIE. M25's [masks] available for 3d ACR pick up. 2000 ampules of banana oil available for distribution to units.
052000	6th LT AR DIV had another decon platoon arrive from French NBC school.
061345	67,000 doses of CANA have arrived for Corps, corps surgeon is working distribution plan for units. Follow-on distribution to meet 1/soldier and 5/CLS/medic expected soon.
070937	82d ABN DIV to release 4 NBCRS vehicles to French 6th LT AR DIV on G-7.

071700	Hard-to-fit fitting team sized 103 personnel and provided 14 M40 protective masks during 5-7 Feb 91.
080600	Three man bio sampling team to arrive at Logbase CHARLIE o/a 10 Feb 91.
091810	10,000 5 gallon pails of DS2 located at SPOD. 5000 drums being pushed to KKMC.
081230	RCA employment authority continues to be retained by CINCCENT. Political sensitivity and Iraqi's interpretation of RCA use as the initiation of chemical warfare limits employment to defensive modes IAW Executive Order 11850. Queried units, no requirements identified.
100845	ARCENT verifies 141 East German shower/decon vehicles inbound primarily for SUPCOM use with no planned redistribution of M17 LDS. Asked ARCENT to relook M17 distribution.
101125	M17 LDS due in o/a 15 Feb (*Almedia Lykes*) and 24 Feb (*Raleigh Bay*). 22 of 60 due in by ALOC [Air Logistics Operating Center] have been located and earmarked for 1st CAV DIV.
101300	Plastic sheeting for contamination avoidance is on hold based on ARCENT ACSLOG decision on current threat.
111422	FRAGO 28, tasks 6th LT AR DIV (FR) to establish decon sites and provide decon support between the LD [line of departure] and observe while on MSR TEXAS and vic OBJ WHITE/Logbase OSCAR prior to initiation of COSCOM movement.
120710	Three man bio sampling team arrived at KKMC. Supported by Corps but not attached had them link up with 457th CML BN. Unit to return at unspecified future time.
120815	CPT Chinowski, AMCCOM, said 400 CAMs are supposedly inbound. Corps to possibly receive 200+.
141235	Two SCUDs launched toward Hafr Al Batin (KKMC). First time weapons fired toward forward deployed troops [as opposed to Israeli/Saudi cities]. No chem.

151730	Corps to receive 34 East German shower/decon systems.
160720	FRAGO 34, 59th CM CO to provide one platoon to support Corps deception operations from 18 Feb to G+6.
161733	82d places Fox platoon OPCON [operational control] 6th LT AR DIV (FR).
170822	Three NBCRS vehicles scheduled to depart Germany 21, 24, and 25 Feb. Fills 3d ACR 6th vehicle requirement.
172250	Italian RPV used by Iraq are capable of delivering chemical munitions. However, no evidence if Iraq will be able to use it in this manner.
182130	Hazardous waste disposal; ARCENT wants units to package wastes and leave it in place, secured if possible and report location for local contractor can pick up and disposal.
190300	Corps receiving 8 chemical officers (captains) for Operation DESERT STORM. Assigned them to fill and plus up units based on missions.
190827	Request for waiver, CENTCOM requirement for school trained crews for vehicles was approved for 24th ID(M).
190830	Corps to receive 139 [M17 SANATOR] LDS, projected arrival dates: (12) 20 Feb, (45) 21 Feb, (82) 30 Mar.
190900	89th CM CO commander relieved. CPT Volk assumed command.[3]
211730	SCUD launched towards KKMC was intercepted.
222130	FRAGO 48 established Corps minimum MOPP level as zero [VII Corps was MOPP one]. Commanders have flexibility to upgrade based on threat in their sector. NAPP consumption will begin NLT G-Day, H-4 hours. Evaluate NAPP consumption G+3.
222140	Nine NBCRS vehicles at Rhein Main awaiting transport. 1st shipment of 3 vehicles (2 -Egyptian, 1 - 3d ACR) due o/a 26 Feb 91.

| 230800 | Siren test conducted, system deemed inadequate. |
| | |

230800   Siren test conducted, system deemed inadequate.

231500   COSCOM received 7 East German shower/decon systems at 406th (rear). Corps will receive 18 vice 34. Next 7 due in 24 Feb, other 4 unknown.

240001   Corps consumption of NAPP began as per FRAGO 48.

240400   G-Day, ground offensive begins.

240750   Received NBC-1, vic MARCENT area. Confirmed as a bogus report.

240930   24th MMC picked up five M12 engines (4 - 24th INF DIV (M), 1 - 457th CM BN).

241310   Reports of high readings of anthrax in dead animals; this region of the world has a naturally high background reading for anthrax. Samples have been taken and retrograded [to Ft. Detrick] for evaluation.

251555   7 NBCRS vehicles with 490th CML BN. 1st COSCOM is to sign for. Transport and release 1 NBCRS to 3d ACR. Remaining 6 vehicles will be held by 1st COSCOM as ORF.

260325   ARCENT reports no M256A1 detection kits at NICP. Units should save expired kits. Expired kits retain sensitivity but may give false positive for nerve agent.

271745   CPT Murphy, USASG, is able to send mask fitting teams to unit locations if necessary.

281500   ARCENT has 121 M17 LDS in country at this time. Distribution table is being worked.

MARCH

012200   Worldwide Chemical Conference is scheduled for 18-20 Apr 91 at Ft. McClellan, AL.

021045   FRAGO 82, reevaluation of NBC threat warning system reduces NBC THREATCON AMBER to GREEN.

030425	VII Corps reports a soldier with possible CX and Lewisite contamination. Trooper [PFC Fisher] was wearing a NOMEX suit in 3d AD sector. Burning sensation reported on upper arm, blisters on arm ¼ to ½ inch in size with surrounding area being puffy w/redness. NBCRS checked clothing, positive reading for CX (phosgene oxime) and lewisite. Reverified by 2d NBCRS.
030840	Follow-up report received from VII Corps, COL Thornton. Two agents thought to be involved (Lewisite (L) and sesqui mustard (HQ) which is 5x persistent than HD). Soldier showed small traces of L on flack vest. HD found on sleeve of uniform. Soldier received burns while clearing bunkers 2 days ago. No other soldiers in team reported similar symptoms. Army chem medical defense expert (Dr. (COL) Dunn) will examine soldier.
031840	VII Corps reported Dr. Dunn verified blisters as being chemically related. Fox returned to bunker complex and received low positive reading for blister agent. Waiting on confirmation from tape reading.
041920	Forwarded Fox NBCRS performance input to ARCENT.
050930	Units notified to input attached CML units on MSC TPFDD for redeployment.
051115	ARCENT stated zero bar reading on CAM ensures decon complete for redeployment.
071416	ARCENT's guidance on disposition of captured chemical/biological munitions is the same as that of CINCCENT.
071636	ARCENT provided XVIII ABN Corps with three slots for WWCC X. COL Barbeau allocated one slot per division.
081010	ARCENT stated shipment and distribution of CAM have been stopped by DA.
090645	CPT Martindale (corps surgeon) provided verbal guidance on turn in of medical chemical defense items.

091030	ARCENT states DA decision on distribution of Fox NBCRS is hindered by Egyptian requests for the Fox. CINCCENT said no to Egyptian request.
091200	457th CML BN tasked to assist 3d ACR in final washdown of equipment at the SPOE [Sea Point of Embarkation].
091600	2/340th closed at AO CACTUS w/3d ACR.
100020	CPT Miller and SFC Weber departed Dhahran enroute to Ft. Bragg on MSN #A17319.
101735	82d requested procedures for civilian w/chemical burns. CPT Martindale (corps surgeon) indicated division surgeons know the procedures. Civilian will not be brought back, urine and blood samples will be collected.
112105	Received CRDEC reply on M40/M42 mask fielding msg. DA DCSOPS would determine who/when mask will be fielded. Rigging procedures for M40 mask for airborne operations have been established, pending doctrinal approval.
122210	COL Sanderson (USACMLS) stated color coded THREATCON is being incorporated in new coordinating draft FM 3-3.
131645	ARCENT provided heads up on redistribution of Fox NBCRS w/a copy of DA msg. 1st CAV DIV will receive 1 plt (6 from 25th CML CO, 1 from 82d ABN DIV).
141330	3d ACR confirmed receipt of the 6th Fox vehicle.
142200	HQDA (MAJ Wolz) stated DA guidance was to issue all in-theater CDE up to MTOE authorized level.
151452	Coordinate with 82d ABN DIV and 24th IN DIV (M) to effect the transfer of 1 Fox from 82d to 24th on 17 Mar 91 NLT 1300C at vic TAA VICTORY.
160935	Received 24th IN DIV (M) POC for Fox transfer. Provided info to 82d ABN DIV.

161315   457th CML BN provided situation update on washdown operation at port of Jubayl. BN received 15 new steam cleaners. Washing a tank took 6-8 hours using M17 LDS, 3-4 hours using M12 PDDA.

161500   3d ACR indicated BG Scholes stated 3d ACR didn't have to transport the Fox's and that other transportation will be arranged.

161615   Coordinated w/457th CML BN for drivers to move 3d ACR Fox's to KKMC.

171600   Coordinated w/3d ACR and 1st CAV DIV to effect Fox transfer. 1st CAV DIV is to send a PBO rep to Jubayl to sign for 6 Fox's from 3d ACR PBO. 457th CML BN personnel will drive the vehicles to Fox Maintenance Facility (GDSC) in Dhahran upon completion of transfer.

172000   LTC Jackson indicated Fox transfer between 82d ABN DIV and 24th IN DIV (M) was completed.

180715   CPT Turner coordinated w/ARCENT on status of TPFDD.

180745   CPT Turner provided corrections on TPFDD to CAC for changes.

181400   24th IN DIV (M) indicated 3 Fox's are at GDSC for services. 3 more Fox's will go to GDSC on 19 Mar 91. The 7th Fox will have services done NLT 25 Mar 91.

18200   1st CAV DIV will sign for 6 Fox's from 3d ACR on 20 Mar 91. They will go direct w/3d ACR and 457th CML BN.

APPENDIX C

Glossary

Battle Dress Overgarment:	Two-piece protective suit (jacket and trousers) made from charcoal-impregnated foam with a nylon/cotton outer layer sporting a woodland or desert camouflage pattern. Weighs about 4 pounds, resists a 10 gm/cm^2 liquid challenge for 24 hours, shelf life of 22 days when opened, extendable to 30 days.
Blister Agents:	CW agents that affects the eyes, lungs and irritates the skin, causing the formation of large blisters especially in moist warm parts of body. Includes mustard gas and lewisite. Non-lethal persistent agents, used for harrassment and terrain denial.
Blood Agents:	First generation CW agent, interferes with body's ability to transport oxygen in the blood stream. Includes hydrogen cyanide and cyanogen chloride. Lethal nonpersistent agent, must be employed in large quantities for effective results.
Automatic Chemical Agent Alarm, M8A1:	Designed to continuously sample the air to detect nerve agent vapors at 0.1 mg/m^3 or more. Can be remoted up to 450 yards from alarm. Detector uses an alpha emitter radiation source to ionize and identify CW agents. Detector and battery weigh about 16 pounds. Field issue about two per company.
Chemical Agent Monitor, M1:	Hand-held manually operated monitor employed to confirm presence or absence of either mustard or nerve agent vapors (one at a time) on personnel or equipment. Detector uses an alpha emitter radiation source to ionize and identify CW agents. Weighs about 5 pounds.
Convulsant Antidote for Nerve Agents:	Disposable autoinjection device holding ten milligrams of diazepam. Designed to reduce brain injuries caused by convulsions brought about by nerve agent poisoning.
Chemical Detection Kit, M256A1:	Sampling kit used to identify the presence or absence CW agent vapors, particularly to confirm M8A1 alarm and ability to unmask. Uses wet chemistry and colormetric changes to alert individual to presense of agents. Each squad carries one kit of 12 samplers.

Chemical Protective Overgarment:	Predecessor to BDO, uses same charcoal-impregnated foam with an OD green outer layer. Good for 6 hours after exposure to liquid chemical warfare agents. Estimated shelf life of 14 days after opening
Choking Agents:	First generation CW agents that irritate the respiratory system causing the formation of water in the lungs, resulting in death from lack of oxygen. Includes phosgene and chlorine. Lethal nonpersistent agent.
Collective Protection Equipment:	Series of large protective filters, air circulation devices, and protective entrances that can be added to vehicles, vans and shelters to create a safe operating environment.
Collective Protection Shelter, M51:	First mobile NBC shelter designed for the Army; double-walled, air-inflatable, and self-supporting with an airlock for entry and exit. Requires 5-ton truck for transportation (5400 lbs). Primarily used by medical units.
CP Equipment, Simplified, M20:	Lightweight mobile shelter that converts existing structures into protected command and control centers. Plastic liner expands to fit the dimensions of the room and can be attached to other liners.
CP Equipment, Simplified, M28:	Plastic liner, large protective filter and entrance used to transform 64 foot long medical TEMPER tents into protected shelters. Included a special airlock to decon contaminated stretcher casualties prior to treatment.
Decontamination Kit, Personnel, M258A1:	Kit contains three sets of two foil-packaged decon wipes in an alcohol base. Each soldier has at least one kit, used for immediate decon of face, small areas of skin and individual equipment. Slightly corrosive in nature.
Decontamination Kit, Skin, M291:	Replacement for M258A1, contains three sets of two resin-impregnated cloths. Again used for immediate decon of face, hands, small areas of skin.
Decontaminating Solution #2:	Extremely corrosive decontaminant, consists of 70% diethylenetriamine, 28% ethylene glycol monomethyl ether, 2% sodium hydroxide.
Decontamination Apparatus, M11:	Nitrogen-charged pressurized container resembling a fire extinguisher, holds 1 1/3 quarts of DS-2. Used by crews

to decontaminate selected areas on vehicles or crew-served weapons.

Decontamination Apparatus, Portable, M13:

Manually operated pump, brushes and disposable container holding 14 liters of DS-2, replacing the M11. Mounted on vehicles, used by crews to decontaminate their vehicles or crew-served weapons.

Decontamination Apparatus, Power Driven, M12A1:

Truck-mounted system composed of a water tank, water heater, pump unit and shower assembly. Uses a STB-slurry mix to thoroughly decontaminate large vehicles. Also provides personnel with hot water showers and can double as fire-fighting equipment.

Decontamination System, Lightweight, M17:

American-adapted Norwegian pump, heater and 3000-gallon water bladder provides high pressure hot water for operational decontamination of vehicles. Intended fielding is one per battalion.

Decontamination Procedures:

Three basic levels: immediate decon used for life-saving measures (decon kits); operational decon to remove gross agent contamination from vehicles and equipment (M11/M13/M17 decon apps) or personnel (MOPP suit exchanges); and thorough decon for elimination of all agent contamination (equipment and personnel decon).

Detection Procedures:

Detection procedures can be split into manual and automatic. Manual measures (M8/M9/M256/CAM) used to identify agents and confirm presence or absence of liquid/gaseous chemical agent. Automatic measures (M8A1/ICAD/RSCAAL) used to provide continuous monitoring and early warning of low levels of gases. Recon measures identify clean areas.

Detector Paper, M8:

Book of 25 sheets impregnated with a chemical dye that changes color (red, green, yellow) if dipped in liquid nerve or blister agent. Does not detect vapors. Issued one book per soldier.

Detector Paper, M9:

30-foot long roll of two-inch wide dye-impregnated paper that acted as a litmus test for liquid chemical agents. Adhesive backing allows attachment to vehicles, around arms or legs, or on an antenna. Turns red when exposed to nerve or blister agents. Issued one roll per squad.

Individual Chemical Agent Detector:	Pocket-sized detector weighing less than a pound, designed to be clipped onto individual soldiers. Uses wet chemistry to detect nerve, blister, blood and choking agents with disposable sensor cell (14-day life).
Mission Oriented Protective Posture:	Flexible system of wearing protective suits, mask, boots and gloves in response to expected threat. Allows individuals to quickly increase protective posture if under chemical attack. MOPP 1 is wearing the suit only. MOPP 4 is wearing suit, mask, boots and gloves.
Mustard "Gas":	H or HD. Not really a gas since it has the consistency of motor oil, smells like garlic. Non-lethal persistent chemical agent, can last days to weeks in temperate climate, but only hours to days in the desert.
Nerve Agents:	Second generation CW agents that interfere with the body's nervous system by disrupting the acetylcholinesterase process. Includes GA, GB, GF (non/semi-persistent), VX and VR-55 (persistent).
Mark 1 Nerve Agent Antidote Kit (NAAK):	Composed of two disposable autoinjectors. One holds 2 mg atropine and 220 mg obidoxime chloride solution. The other holds 600 mg of pralidoxime chloride (also known as 2-pam chloride). Each soldier carries three kits.
Nonpersistent Agent:	Chemical agents that vaporize quickly and present an immediate hazard. These agents generally last minutes to hours and do not require decon procedures. Nonpersistent agents should be expected along the front lines against units in contact with the attacking echelon.
Persistent Agent:	Chemical agents that vaporize very slowly for a considerable period after delivery. These agents generally last hours to days and require thorough decon procedures. Persistent agents impede the use of critical terrain, channelize the attacking force, or contaminate materiel.
Protection Procedures:	Individual protection refers to the protective suit, mask, boots and gloves. Because of heat burden and lessened combat efficiency, leaders must manage work schedules, implement immediate decon and use manual chem kits to reduce protective levels as soon as possible. Collective protection refers to the use of large filters and protective

areas that permit individuals to operate freely without protective suits while in a contaminated area. Can be in vehicles, vans, shelters, airplanes, ships, etc.

Protective Mask, CB, M17A2:
Originally designed in 1959, the M17A2 was improved and fielded to Army units in 1983. Noted for the built-in pear-shaped filters and extensively used by police and military units world-wide.

Protective Mask, CB, M24/25A1 :
M24 aviator mask and M25A1 tanker mask, originally fielded in December 1962 and May 1963, respectively. Features a single face lens, a microphone for plugging into comm systems, and a filter canister at the end of a hose. Hose permits crewmen to plug into the vehicle/aircraft filter system.

Protective Mask, Apache, M43:
Special mask for Apache helicopter because of the need for compatibility with the AH-64 Integrated Helmet and Display Sighting System (IHADSS) and the Optical Relay Tube (ORT). This highly engineered, close-fitting mask, designed in 1983, features a powered fan-filtration system.

Protective Suit, Mark IV:
Two-piece protective suit (jacket and trousers), uses a charcoal-impregnated cloth inner layer and a flame-resistant nylon outer layer. Features a smock on jacket and suspenders on trousers. Weighs about two pounds, resists about 3-4 gm/cm^2 liquid challenge for 24 hours.

Protective Suit, Saratoga:
Two-piece protective suit (jacket and trousers), uses carbon spheres sprayed on a fabric layer, an inner polyethylene knit liner and outer treated cotton shell. Launderable, weighs about 3 pounds, meets 10 gm/cm^2 challenge.

Pyridostigmine Bromide Tablets:
Also known as Nerve Agent Pretreatment Pyridostigmine (NAPP) Tablet Set. Comes in a sheet of 21 tablets, each dose 30-mg. If chemical exposure is expected, individual takes one per eight hours prior to (not after) exposure. Procured by NATO and other Middle East and Far East countries.

Reconnaissance System, NBC, XM93:	Six-wheeled light armored vehicle, manned by four individuals, weighs 18 tons combat loaded, max speed 65 mph. Holds a CAM, M8A1 alarm, AN/VDR-2 radiac, MM-1 mobile mass spectrometer, vehicle orientation system, sample jars and NBC warning markers. Collective protection allows crew to perform recon on the move in contaminated areas.
Remote Sensing Chemical Agent Alarm, XM21:	Tripod-mounted passive infrared detector, senses chemical agent clouds up to five kms distant. Weighs nearly 50 pounds, cannot detect on-the-move and cannot identify the chemical agent type. Used for recon and area surveillance.
Riot Control Agents:	Also known as tear gas, includes agents CS and CN. Non-lethal chemical agents used to cause flow of tears and irritation of skin. Currently used only for prisoner control, riots, POW rescue attempts, etc.
Sarin:	GB. Non-persistent nerve agent, primary agent of choice for US military up to 1990. Colorless, odorless liquid, turns into vapor at room temp, causes death in 1-2 minutes through skin, 15 minutes through respiratory system.
Soman:	GD. Semi-persistent nerve agent, primary agent of choice for Soviet Union. Colorless liquid, slight fruity odor, three times as toxic as tabun, turns to vapor but can be thickened to increase persistency.
Super Tropical Bleach:	Dry bleach powder, contains 30% chlorine, added to water for chemical or biological decon of canvas and vehicles. Also used dry on ground for large area decontamination and for decontaminating boots in personnel decon line.
Tabun:	GA. First nerve agent discovered, semi-persistent, colorless liquid turns into vapor at room temp. Not employed often due to less than lethal properties as compared to other nerve agents, but easier to manufacture.

VX: Third generation CW agent, colorless and odorless liquid,
                       created just after World War II. Low volatility
                       (persistent) and extremely lethal on skin contact.

Water Testing   Lightweight portable chemistry kit, uses a number of
Kit, M272A1:   tablets and bottles to test and identify agents in raw and
                       treated water. Can detect cyanide, mustard, lewisite, and
                       all nerve agents. Used by chemical specialists, medical
                       units and quartermaster units.

Notes

CHAPTER 1: INCIDENTS IN THE GULF

1. Combat leaders often forget of the combat support role played by chemical soldiers in Vietnam, including the aircraft-mounted M3 concealed personnel detectors ("people-sniffers"), the flame support missions and Ranch Hand operations. Also forgotten were the smoke, flame and chemical mortar operations of the Korean era. All these operations put chemical soldiers in the line of fire next to their combat arms brethren.

2. Field manuals released include FM 3-3, Contamination Avoidance, dated May 1987, FM 3-4, Protection, dated October 1985, FM 3-5, Decontamination, dated June 1985, FM 3-6, Field Behavior of NBC Agents, dated November 1986, FM 3-50, Deliberate Smoke Operations, dated October 1984, FM 3-100, NBC Operations, dated September 1985, FM 3-101, Chemical Staff and Units, dated April 1987.

3. The 71st Chemical Company was the first smoke/decon unit. Other dual units activated prior to 1986 were actually decontamination units refitted as dual-purpose (Smoke/Decon).

4. Colonel Mike Ahern, personal letter to author, April 10, 1995.

5. Lieutenant Colonel (Ret.) Mike D'Andries, interview with author, Edgewood, MD, February 1996.

6. Colonel Rick Read, interview with author, Edgewood, MD, July 1996.

7. Association of the United States Army [hereafter AUSA], *Personal Perspectives on the Gulf War* (Arlington, VA: Institute of Land Warfare [ILW], 1993), p. 21.

8. Specialist Frank Clark, e-mail message to author, March 17, 1995.

9. Lieutenant Colonel Stephen Franke, e-mail message to author, June 8, 1995.

10. AUSA, *Personal Perspectives*, p. 75.

11. AUSA, *Personal Perspectives*, pp. 86–87.

12. Captain Shirley DeGroot, e-mail message to author, August 28, 1995.

13. Colonel (Ret.) Bob Thornton, interview with author, Anniston, AL, May 22, 1995.

14. Captain Nick Swayne, e-mail messages to author, March 21 and 23, 1995.

CHAPTER 2: DEPLOYMENT TO THE DESERT

1. The West German government has always been sensitive to the issue of CBW, and even more so to suggestions of tactical nuclear warfare. During the Cold War, the US Army did not conduct decontamination exercises in the public view, and its troops often did not to go to full MOPP (protective suit, mask, gloves and boots) in order not to panic the German citizens (who might interpret this action as the prelude to an actual war). The US military did train their units on NBC defense within European training areas, and frequently war gamed possible NBC warfare scenarios in command post exercises.

2. Michael Gordon and General Bernard Trainor (Ret.), *The Generals' War* (Boston: Little, Brown, 1995), pp. 43–45.

3. Brigadier General Robert Scales, Jr., *Certain Victory: The US Army in the Gulf War* (Washington, DC: Brassey's, 1994), pp. 43–44.

4. Thomas B. Allen, *War Games* (New York: Berkley Books, 1989), pp. 290–1, 301–2.

5. Unitary chemical munitions (projectiles, mines, rockets and bombs) were the older munitions that were prefilled with one pure chemical agent. These were often dangerous and costly to store and to transport due to the potential for leaks. Binary chemical munitions meant that two chemical precursors (two chemicals that, once mixed, would form a chemical warfare agent) would be stored and transported separately and loaded into a projectile, missile or bomb immediately prior to firing. The two chemicals would mix during flight and disperse as its intended chemical warfare agent.

6. US News & World Report, *Triumph without Victory: The Unreported History of the Persian Gulf War* (New York: Times Books, 1992), pp. 68–69; and GEN (Ret.) Norman Schwarzkopf, *It Doesn't Take a Hero* (New York: Bantam Books, 1992), pp. 301–2.

7. *Triumph without Victory*, pp. 116–18.

8. Ibid., p. 118.

9. On 23 August, Captain Paul Schiele and three chemical officers from CRDEC joined the forward-deployed Chemical Division. Between late August and mid-September, three CONUS-based chemical officers arrived to constitute the CENTCOM Chemical Division (Rear).

10. Notes from Colonel Ray Barbeau's brief to the Worldwide Chemical Conference, August 1991. The shortage of decontamination assets was in part due to the "roundout brigade" status of the 24th IN DIV and 1st CAV DIV. As both divisions had two active duty combat brigades and one National Guard brigade, so also their chemical decon companies had two active platoons and one reserve platoon. This was partially offset by the 197th's Separate Infantry Brigade chemical decon detachment and the Tiger Brigade's portion of the 44th Chemical Company. More serious was the concern that the dual-purpose smoke/decon companies did not have water haulers needed to maintain a decon technique that relied heavily on thousands of gallons of water. They were purposely kept "light" to aid in a quick deployment and still afford a limited smoke/decon capability. Last, the M17 LDS SANATORs had only begun production in the previous year, and priority had them going to Europe rather than to the XVIII ABN Corps (as was the case for the CAMs as well).

11. According to "official" accounts, ODCSOPS planners cut as many "superfluous" units as they could in an effort to rush combat units to the theater. A reserve chemical brigade headquarters with no assigned permanent battalions fell into that category. The Army decided the chemical battalions could get the necessary administrative and logistical

support through the corps support commands instead of the chemical brigade. Another version is more scandalous. Because the chemical brigade was headed by a one-star Army Reserve chemical general officer (or senior colonel), the Reserve general could pull rank and advise the Corps commander directly instead of their Corps chemical officer providing that role (not that there were any indications of that happening). Therefore, XVIII ABN Corps decided they did not want the brigade, even though this decision directly contradicted standing deployment plans and proper organizational command and control philosophy.

12. This augmented staffing was also due to a need to operate around the clock in the Army Operations Center as well as to continue normal Army Staff business.

13. The dual-purpose chemical companies (smoke/decon) organic to the 82d ABN, 101st ABN and 10th IN DIVs have no chemical reconnaissance units. These APC-equipped units are found only in heavy (mechanized) divisions and heavy corps chemical defense units. The corps's 101st Chemical Company also had no reconnaissance assets.

14. Early discussions at HQ DA focused on whether US forces in Germany would and could participate as part of the coalition forces, thus using their reconnaissance platoons in the theater of support.

15. Defense Intelligence Agency, *Chemical and Biological Warfare in the Kuwait Theater of Operations; Iraq's Capability and Posturing*, (Washington, DC: August 1990). This and related DIA assessments can be found in unclassified form on the DoD World Wide Web GulfLINK site.

16. Rick Atkinson, *Crusade: The Untold Story of the Persian Gulf War* (New York: Houghton, 1993), pp. 85–87.

17. August is the traditional vacation month in Bavaria. Most of the ABC-SeS, as well as Bavaria, had departed the week previously for thirty to forty-five days vacation all across Europe. The ABC-SeS personnel were 90 percent absent on holiday that Sunday night.

18. The PM NBC Defense office purchased five German Fuchs vehicles in July 1988 under the Nunn-Lugar legislation authorizing DoD to acquire allied military equipment for test and evaluation; they have since been known as the "Nunn" NBCRS vehicles. When the production contract was protested, Congress ordered a competition between TRW/General Motor's Light Armored Vehicle (LAV) and General Dynamics Land Systems/Thyssen-Henschel's Fuchs vehicle. The German Fuchs won the competition, leading to a contract award to in March 1990. Since it would take years to develop the full capacity NBCRS, the Army decided to procure forty-eight vehicles as an interim measure (enough for forces in Europe and the Chemical School). The initial XM93s would be "Americanized" German Fuchs, first system to be delivered in 1992. These Fuchs would be "Americanized" in Germany by building them to US specifications, including US Army radios, NBC defense equipment (CAM, AN/VDR-2 radiac, and M8A1 chemical agent alarm), a US 7.62-mm machine gun, US smoke grenade launchers and an air conditioning system. A second contract award (awarded the same day) would pay for the development of the full-capacity Fox with remote detection, a meteorological sensor, digital communications, provide organic maintenance and reduce the crew from four to three. The second contract also provided for the purchase of ten prototype objective systems, the XM93E1. After successful development, a second production contract would fill the full Army force requirements as the M93A1 NBCRS.

19. Daniel E. Spector, *US Army Chemical School Annual Command History*, 1990 and 1991 (Fort McClellan, AL: US Army Chemical Center and School [hereafter USACMLS]); and Lieutenant Colonel Michael D'Andries, Major Jeffrey Bothen, and Thomas Huczek, "The NBCRS Project Office and Operation Desert Storm" (Aberdeen Proving Ground, MD:

Historical Records, 1992). The vehicles at Fort McClellan were modified at Anniston Army Depot. The modifications included a chip changeout in the mass spectrometer's computer so its display would "speak English" instead of "sprechen Deutsche." The air conditioning system was not standard in German systems, since under that nation's constitution, they could not deploy outside of their country.

20. Since the American NBCRS Fox program was in R&D, the purchase request came from the Army R&D side of the Pentagon, rather than from DLA or other sources. Once the German government offered the Foxes as a gift, they returned the $106 million dollars. The PM NBC Defense office would use a little over $20 million dollars of that to support the "Americanization" and deployment of the Foxes to Southwest Asia. The remaining $85 million was returned to the Army.

21. Brigadier General Orton had talked prior to the deployment to Major General McCaffrey, who agreed to accept the two initial vehicles. McCaffrey perhaps appreciated the gesture the most since he, more than other division commanders, had been concerned for years about NBC operations. The USACMLS soldiers that deployed to the Gulf with the two "Nunn" vehicles trained two crews of the 91st Chemical Company; they returned to Fort McClellan by the end of September.

22. The Chemical School made a firm decision not to mount .50 caliber machine guns on the Fuchs (and later, M93A1 Foxes). Part of their rationale was that the School did not want its recon units aggressively engaging the enemy. Their job was recon, and if they had heavy machine guns, someone might be tempted to use them in roles other than what had been intended.

23. Major Jeffery Adams, "Chemical Corps in the Attack—allied troops react to Desert Shield and Desert Storm," *Army Chemical Review*, January 1992, pp. 25–28. The majority of the support for US personnel in training came from the German Army. This included all the Fuchs instruction, teaching materials, use of Fuchs vehicles, gasoline and oil for the vehicles, billets, mess, laundry, etc. Estimates of the cost to Germany ran approximately $127 per soldier per day for the two weeks of training. All other administrative support, such as mail delivery, coordination with units, and other services, came from USAREUR and VII Corps. By the end of August, over 100 US soldiers had trained on the Fuchs at Sonthofen; by March 1991, a total of 278 US, seventy-four British, and thirty-four Israeli soldiers had trained there. The British received eleven Fox vehicles, while the Israelis received eight.

24. Lieutenant Colonel Walt Polley, e-mail to author, July 2, 1995, and notes from Lieutenant Colonel Tony Funderberg. In recognition of Major Polley's support to the German armed forces during this time, the German Ministry of Defense awarded him the Cross of Honor in Silver.

25. There is a longer story to the issue of no fielded biological detectors, but essentially the US Army had none because (1) the real concern from combat fighters was on chemical warfare, a real and credible threat with demonstrated results on the battlefield (in over fifty years of battles), while true sustained biological warfare was still an untested theory; (2) the US bio warfare program had shown that weaponization was very difficult and impractical for battlefield use (but good for deterrence), and so the same problems should hold true to the enemy (again lessening the chance an enemy would really use BW weapons); and (3) designing a rugged, relatively inexpensive and dependable biological agent detector prior to 1990 was too hard. No one was pushing to build a detector and vaccine stockpiles were not a medical priority. As one senior government civilian later commented, "Nobody cared about biological detectors before the Gulf War."

26. The "people-sniffer" was the M3 Concealed Personnel, Aircraft Mounted Detector, type-classified in December 1970. Mounted on helicopters flying over enemy terrain (ideally, enemy field latrines), it identified large urine concentrations. It did not discriminate between "friendly" and "enemy" urine or even that of animal herds, but the detector did work well.

27. Chemical Systems Laboratory had developed a prototype field automatic biological agent detector by 1977. The biological detection and warning system (BDWS) was a two-piece system, consisting of an aerosol sampler (XM2) and an automatic protein-sensing detector (XM19). The technical approach used chemical luminescence to detect possible biological agents in a liquid sample, requiring approximately forty-five minutes per sample to process and identify biological agents. Operational tests demonstrated a poor reliability, a very limited detection capability to detect more than a few known biological warfare agents, and a high false-alarm rate. The system had to be hauled in a trailer due to its size, weight and power requirements (110 volt, 60 Hertz generators) and required high maintenance. Although there were no fielded biological agent detectors at the time, the Chemical School decided to terminate the program in May 1983 rather than let a faulty system enter the field.

28. Major Robert Buchanan, "Preparing Coalition Forces for the Chemical Threat," *Army Chemical Review*, January 1992, pp. 13–16.

29. ODCSOPS had been fully engaged in equipment fielding issues with ODCSLOG, in addition to supporting unit deployments, and in educating and advising Army and other service leadership.

30. Because of the expected fielding of the M40/M42 protective masks in 1988, the Army had stopped M17 field mask and M25A1 tanker mask production in 1986 and 1988, respectively. The M24 aviator mask was due to be replaced by the M43 aviator protective mask, type classified "limited production-urgent," with a first-unit issue date of July 1987. Contractor production issues had stalled all mask production until 1990.

31. The Communications and Electronics Command (CECOM) developed 300 and 450-foot length power cables for the M8A1 alarm to reduce the requirement for BA3517 batteries. CECOM defended the battery's performance, stating in one message that the BA3517 had excellent high-temperature performance characteristics. The battery was designed to perform without degradation at temperatures up to 160 degrees Fahrenheit, and was capable of delivering an average of approximately 60 percent of its energy when exposed to temperatures of 190 degrees Fahrenheit for periods of up to seventy hours. It could be that the battery poor performance was due more to long storage in unit supply rooms (indicative of the lack of peacetime unit NBC defense training).

32. As a point of accuracy, ODCSOPS asked XVIII ABN Corps to put in the request for protective sheets. With a wartime "field request" on the record, the Army could break through the usual R&D red tape that slowed up development programs.

CHAPTER 3: BUILDING UP THE DEFENSE

1. The British military, understandably proud of its distinguished history of chemical defense readiness, claimed it had the best-equipped force in the Gulf. Certainly its protective suits, masks and chemical agent monitors were in high demand in the Gulf. The British ability to support the coalition with these items was largely due to the fact that it was supporting a military force 10 percent the size of the American presence (not including the civilians in theater) and therefore they were not straining their domestic manufacturing or

sustainment facilities, by any means. The Saratoga is a two-piece German protective overgarment using von Blucher carbon spheres instead of the messy carbon foam of the BDOs. Similar to the Mark-IVS, the Saratoga weighed less than the BDO but cost twice as much. It is launderable without losing effectiveness, which stretches out its useability (as long as it is not contaminated).

2. GAO, *ODS: DOD Met Needs for Chemical Suits and Masks, But Longer Term Actions Needed* (Washington, DC: GAO, April 1992), p. 16. Between August 1990 and February 1991, Pine Bluff would inspect over 93,500 masks, of which 50–70 percent were repairable. This helped ease the mask shortage; however, the average cost of repairing each mask ($120) nearly equaled the cost of a new M40 mask ($125). The majority of the M24/25 masks retired had damaged lenses that could not be replaced or repaired. The one-piece lens of the M24/25 protective masks was chemically bonded onto the faceblank, like that of the MCU-2/P (and XM30 mask program). As a result, when these lenses cracked, they could not be simply replaced with a new lens. The chemically bonded older lens would not cleanly separate from the faceblank. The only solution was to scrap the masks. This was no problem for the soon-to-be retired M24/25s, but a pertinent issue for the new MCU-2/Ps.

3. Kimberly Porter and Herbert LePore, *Legacy in the Sand: The United States Army Armament, Munitions, and Chemical Command in Operations Desert Shield and Desert Storm* (Rock Island, IL: HQ AMCCOM, 1992), p. 214. HQ AMCCOM would eventually send a total of 314,585 M17 series protective masks, 27,585 M25A1 tank protective masks and 3,962 M24 aviator protective masks to the Gulf (including Pine Bluff's efforts).

4. US Army Chemical and Biological Defense Agency (CBDA), *Report to the Senate Appropriations Committee: US Military Chemical-Biological Protection Equipment* [hereafter called the SAC Report] (Aberdeen Proving Ground: CBDA, 1992), pp. 22–3. Also, John Roos, "Allies Filled Some Big Voids in US Chem Defense Preparedness," *Armed Forces Journal*, October 1991, p. 17.

5. Colonel Richard Read, Aberdeen Proving Ground, MD, interview with author, April 1996.

6. Notes from Colonel (Ret.) Barbeau. All of the first four platoons would become six-vehicle platoons. They would operate in pairs, usually one Fox team per combat brigade in a division. Often the plan was to attach one team to each of the two lead brigades and let the third team recon in the division rear. Initially, the plan was to field thirty NBCRS vehicles to the 24th IN DIV, 101st ABN DIV, 3rd ACR, and 2d Chemical Battalion, allowing for six corps maintenance floats. The two "Nunn" vehicles were to be taken out of theater and refurbished at Kassel. This plan was changed after "Desert Dragon III," as XVIII ABN Corps kept the one USAREUR platoon with the 1st CAV DIV, retained the two "Nunn" vehicles and planned to equip 3rd ACR's chemical recon platoon with five Fuchs (they only had five chemical recon squads). Retaining the two "Nunn" vehicles ensured three maintenance floats for ARCENT.

7. The issue was twofold: dusty mustard, a "dry" aerosol agent, would not show itself on M8 and M9 paper, and the dry aerosol could blow into carelessly sealed protective gear. The only way to detect the agent was through the CAMs, M18A2 detector kits, M256A1 kits, M272 kits or the MM-1 mass spectrometer, which all required manual operation. Increased care in wear of MOPP gear could prevent much of the agent from penetrating. This information was relayed back to the CENTCOM forces.

8. The Mark-IV used a woven-fiber technology that wicked liquid contamination away from the skin, rather than the BDO's carbon-impregnated-foam suits with liquid protection

fabric. While the Mark-IV was lighter and reduced heat stress in temperate climates, it was also less durable and offered less protection than the BDO. NRDEC tests later showed that the level of heat burden on soldiers wearing *anything* in addition to the normal combat uniform would rise very quickly in the desert. The heat burden difference between wearing a light, plastic raingear cover, the Mark-IV, or the Army BDO was negligible in the desert, which meant that wearing the Army BDO was the best protective solution. As noted, soldiers perceived lighter uniforms to be less burdensome, even when they had been scientifically shown to be no different.

9. USACMLS, *Historical Review*, 1991 (Fort McClellan, AL). The Marine Corps would order 100 M21 RSCAALs from Brunswick Corporation in January, none of which arrived prior to the end of hostilities.

10. Both the XM19 point detector and the XM2 aerosol sampler measured 22 inches wide by 31 inches high by 16 inches deep. The XM19 weighed 145 pounds, and the XM2 weighed 140 pounds. Both units operated on 110 volts, 60 Hertz power. The XM19's false alarm rate had never been resolved.

11. The Army had a forward laboratory at KKMC, the Air Force had a lab in Dhahran, and the Navy had a laboratory (with a slightly larger staff) at the al-Jubayl port. The biodetection team would use whatever lab was closest to the initial detection. In either event, the process of culturing enough organism to make a definite call would take hours—hours that the commanders would spend wondering how quickly these biological agents were spreading through the ranks.

12. Captain Shirley DeGroot, interview with author, 1995, and Lieutenant Colonel Mark Wagner, e-mail to author, 1994.

13. Colonel Raymond Barbeau and Captain Pratya Siriwat, "Lessons from the Gulf—NBC Warning and Reporting," *Army Chemical Review*, July 1991, pp. 2–5.

14. USAMRICD, *Annual Historical Report for 1990*, p. vi.

15. What had really happened was even more depressing. Hundreds of yards of protective plastic covers had been manufactured, paid for and sent to the Gulf. Once there, some enterprising logistics office redirected the covers to be cut up and used for turret sun screens for an unnamed Army division. The need for umbrellas against the hot sun were obviously more critical than protecting rear area supplies against CB agent contamination.

16. "Army puts rush on cream to block mustard gas," *The Army Times*, February 4, 1991; and USAMRICD, *Annual Historical Report for 1990*, p. v. Problems in final production and product quality would result in the canceling of the MultiShield® product in January 1991. One of the two government versions did make it to the Gulf, but its use was discontinued shortly after arrival: it caused skin rashes.

17. Gordon and Trainor, *The Generals' War*, pp. 77–80; and Department of Defense [DoD], *Conduct of the Persian Gulf War: Final Report to Congress* (Washington, DC: April 1992), p. 122.

18. Gordon and Trainor, *The Generals' War*, pp. 124–27; and Schwarzkopf, *It Doesn't Take a Hero*, p. 356.

19. DoD, *Conduct of the Persian Gulf War*, pp. 85–86; Schwarzkopf, *It Doesn't Take a Hero*, pp. 359–60; Gordon and Trainor, *The Generals' War*, pp. 135–36.

20. Lieutenant Colonel Mike Brown, interview with author, 1995; and Major Barry Hooks, memorandum for commander, 226th Army Support Group, subject: Command Report Operation Desert Shield, dated 16 February 1991.

21. Lieutenant Colonel (Ret.) Mike D'Andries, interviews with author, 1995.

22. Only five vehicles of the second batch of thirty would be produced in December 1990, due to the planned Christmas holiday for the German workers and the lack of a declared war. Holidays are a sacred institution for German union workers, and after all, Germany had no forces in the Gulf.

CHAPTER 4: MOVE TO THE OFFENSE

1. Colonel (Ret.) Bob Thornton, *Bundeswehr* Chemical Corps Conference, May 1992.

2. The Marines made a deal to give the Army 1,419 M8A1 detectors (of their inventory of approximately 5,500 units) in exchange for the Army's assuming some of the Fox "Americanization" costs. While it might seem an odd decision to give up chemical agent detector systems, the Marines had settled on the Individual Chemical Agent Detector to replace/augment the M8A1 alarms. The Army needed all the M8A1 detectors it could get to make up for the shortage of chemical alarms (which was increasing as chemical alarms broke down in Saudi Arabia).

3. This equipment would arrive from Germany by mid-November 1991. It was set up by Bruker Instruments, the US subsidiary of the German manufacturer, and was operational by November 27, 1991.

4. 11th ACR trained at Sonthofen in March and deployed on June 8, 1991, in support of Operation Provide Comfort. They used Foxes from prepositioned theater stocks.

5. Major General (Ret.) Watson interview. MG Watson had referred to Colonel Jan Van Prooyen, then the USAREUR chemical officer, as a potential candidate for that role. Deploying the 415th Chemical Brigade even as late as December may have been a second consideration.

6. Major General (Ret.) Watson interview. This hazard prediction model is detailed in ATP-45 (a NATO document); it was used as a manual method by the Air Force and Army. It was extremely simplistic and "safe-sided," but easy to learn and use.

7. D'Andries, Bothen, and Huczek, "The NBCRS Project Office," pp. 3–7. The Fixed Fox Facility would remain in Dhahran until December 1991, when the task force pulled out of Kuwait.

8. Julian Robinson, Chemical Warfare Chronology Bulletin [hereafter CWCB] No. 11, March 1991, p. 5.

9. Lieutenant Colonel (Ret.) W. "Tony" Funderberg, *History of the 69th Chemical Company*, unpublished manuscript, 1995.

10. The high-speed wipe-out resulted in injuries to all four members of the crew (the most serious being a broken leg). This accident nearly caused the withdrawal of all Fox vehicles from Saudi Arabia for safety concerns because the crew claimed the vehicle ran out of control. It was later determined that the accident had been caused more by operator error than by any defect in the highly tested and quality-engineered German military vehicle.

11. Information provided in summaries from Project DO-49 program fact sheets. A DIA assessment of a hypothetical attack using the generators and anthrax follows:

Subject: HYPOTHETICAL BIOLOGICAL WARFARE ATTACK WITH ANTHRAX: Assumptions and Conditions:

1. East to Northeast wind at ten miles per hour with neutral to moderately stable conditions.

- East to Northeast winds occur approximately 20–25 percent of the time (i.e. 6–7 days/month).
- Neutral to moderately stable conditions occur approximately 75 percent of the time.

The most probable time for these conditions to occur is from 1500–2000.

2.   The Saudi coast would be attacked along a 100-mile (160-km) line by several boats with aerosol generators about two miles off the coast.

- four boats traveling at 25 mph could disseminate the anthrax in one hour; obviously less time if more boats or faster speeds.
- a minimum of 200 gallons (total) of liquid anthrax (500 billion spores per milliliter) would be disseminated.
- the type of aerosol generators acquired by the Iraqis can disseminate over 700 hundred gallons of agent per hour. This is more than enough capacity.

Anticipated Results:

- coastal facilities would be heavily contaminated within 15–30 minutes with high casualties.
- the western edge of the major oil field is 50–100 miles (100–150 kms) from the coast thereby requiring 5–10 hours for the forward edge of the anthrax cloud to encompass the field with a wind speed of 10 mph. It's possible for proper meteorological conditions to be maintained for this period. Casualties would be lower than at the coast due to agent dilution. Contamination of the major oil fields would effectively shut down Saudi oil production.
- Riyadh is approximately 175 miles from the coast and would require 17–18 hours for the aerosol cloud to reach it. It is possible; but unlikely, that meteorological conditions would hold for that period. Casualties would be even lower if Riyadh were reached—again due to agent dilution.

Potential Problems for the Iraqis:

1.   Unfavorable weather conditions could result in dissipation of the aerosol cloud shortly after reaching the coast, thereby limiting its effect. The BW attack would be detected with the first casualties.
2.   An unexpected shift in the wind could blow the agent cloud toward and into Kuwait, out to sea and into Iran, or into Qatar.

CONCLUSION: Although the Iraqis are technically capable of a coastal attack, it is unlikely they would risk the adverse political and military consequences if the attack were conducted but went wrong. The Iraqis would have to be quite desperate or willing to gamble for very high stakes to conduct such an attack.

12. For the record, these issues do not reflect any inadequacies on the parts of the Chemical Corps or the fine testers at Dugway Proving Ground. Rather, these practical issues had never surfaced in the minds of the medical community (concerned with contaminated casualties), the armor and artillery community (contaminated major systems), and the

logistics community (hazardous chemical defense materials). Without acceptance and urging from the rest of the Army, there could be no successful resolution of these issues.

13. Colonel Gene Fuzy, interview with author, June 20, 1995.

14. Porter and LePore, *Legacy in the Sand*, pp. 93, 110–11.

15. Robinson, CWCB No. 11, p. 7. Cuba and Yemen voted against the measure, with China abstaining.

16. This DNA modeling is a combination of weapons-effects, target-response modeling and simulation, and hazard prediction and assessment capability. The latter, called HPAC, has a series of tools, one of which is designed to characterize a hazardous material source from a strike on a facility where CB weapons are produced or stored. This data is correlated with weather and terrain data to result in a time-phased source-model release. Potential effects due to the source at ground zero can be added to define hazardous areas. This package is not available on a portable system; thus the Army's continued efforts on ANBACIS—to develop an NBC hazard modeling and decision aid for maneuver commanders that does not require super-computers.

17. Gordon and Trainor, *The Generals' War*, pp. 191–92; Atkinson, *Crusade*, p. 89; Lee Feinstein, "Iraqi Nuclear, Chemical and Biological Facilities Attacked", *Arms Control Today*, March 1991, pp. 19–20.

18. Lieutenant Colonel (Ret.) Merryman adds:

"My reluctance to introduce equipment into theater that had not been type-classified was not restricted to the biological detectors, but included the XM21. The reasons are simple:

1) If these systems could not do the job they were intended to do (identify CB events within a specified time, with a minimum of false positives, with acceptable downtime, and maintenance capability in theater), the systems would do more harm than good. Planners and operators would make wrong decisions based on false information.

2) Poor performance by these developmental systems would result in negative opinions by the intended [end] users and would seriously impact the equipment developers' ability to receive additional funding to complete development [of these chemical defense systems].

3) the spill-over from a non-functioning developmental NBC system (coupled with the vaccine shortage, change in MOPP gear wartime policy, etc.) could cause soldiers to doubt the serviceability of their chemical defense equipment."

19. On a side note, Major Newing was called into the Army Crisis Action Center to explain what the Tech Escort Unit was doing in theater (implying that CENTCOM was planning to move US chemical weapons). When he explained that they were moving environmental samples back to the US, a collective sigh of relief flooded the room. Evidently, other action officers had just gotten done briefing Operation Steel Box, the removal of US chemical weapons from Germany to Johnston Island, which Tech Escort was also supporting in November-December.

20. FMIB brief, "Desert Storm," at CRDEC Chem-Bio Sampling Program Outbrief, 29 May 1991. As the AMCCOM lessons learned publication showed (*Legacy in the Sand*, p. 144), just about everyone was taking liberties with the hazardous-material regulations in the race to get personnel and materiel into the theater. At no time, however, was potential biohazard material in any danger of being released. The TEU personnel took extra precautions to seal and maintain safe cargo containers for all environmental and biomedical samples. They used available commercial equipment for biohazard transport and adapted it to military policies and practices.

CHAPTER 5: TENSIONS RISE IN THE GULF

1. General de la Billiere, *Storm Command: A Personal Account of the Gulf War* (London: Motivate Publishing, 1992), p. 133.

2. Edward Spiers, *Chemical and Biological Weapons: A Study of Proliferation* (New York: St. Martin's Press, 1994), pp. 110–12.

3. The Army Acquisition Executive made the deliberate decision to only procure 60 percent of the necessary M8A1 detectors, since the next-generation chemical agent point detector (the XM22 ACADA) was planned to enter the field by 1989. But the XM22 was delayed several years, leaving a shortage of M8A1 detectors in the active and reserve military units. Prior to the ground war, ARCENT released a distribution plan that would field 415 ICADs to VII Corps, forty to 1st CAV DIV, 365 to XVIII ABN Corps, and 180 to units in echelons above corps (in that order). Because the war ended so quickly, the ICADs were not fielded. The ICAD program was later abandoned by the Army due to the false-alarm rate and high detection threshold of the detector. In late 1997, the Marine Corps had identified a desire to abandon the ICAD as their primary chemical agent detector as well.

4. While testing the PMFVS on soldiers' masks, the Air Force and Marine Corps noted several issues. First, the skill of the NBC NCO who measured and fitted the mask played an important role in its performance. A soldier might not receive the correct size mask or might try to adjust it himself, leading to potential leaks. Second, the MCU-2/Ps and M40s were measurably better than the M17-series and M24/25 masks. This is not to say that the M17-series was faulty; it usually meant it would take more time and more skill to properly fit a soldier with an M17 than with an M40, which sealed much more quickly and easily for untrained individuals.

5. The previous VII Corps chemical officer had been transferred to Geneva, Switzerland, for the Chemical Weapons Convention talks. Colonel Thornton had been the 82d ABN DIV chemical officer prior to April 1990, and so had good experience in both the XVIII ABN Corps operating procedures and VII Corps.

6. Colonel Thornton's notes. The chemical units had to haul roughly 12,000–20,000 drums of fog oil to the COSCOM logistics base from KKMC in January and February. While this would usually be delegated to logistics units, the XVIII ABN Corps was beginning its move west, which meant priorities for moving ammunition, food, and water.

7. CWCB No. 11, March 1991, pp. 5–6.

8. Spiers, *Chemical and Biological Weapons*, p. 120.

9. DoD, *Conduct of the Persian Gulf War*, p. Q-4.

10. Colonel Fuzy interview, and notes from Colonel Silvernail and Colonel Newing. There had been additional concerns about the laser stand-off system's eye-safety measures, its reliability and about how to integrate and use the data gathered. The stand-off system could not identify the type of agent, only that there was a large increase in biological organisms in an area. The doctrine and procedures to use the aerial stand-off systems had not been fully developed, and the Air Force really did not want an AWACS committed to the untested program when it could be helping to kill Iraqi airplanes. This unease with both the doctrinal employment of the system and the reliability and safety of the equipment led most people content that the system had never reached the Gulf.

11. Captain Thomas F. Manley, *Marine Corps NBC Defense in Southwest Asia* [hereafter called the Manley Report] (Quantico, VA: Marine Corps Research Center, July 1991), p. 40.

12. Major General Watson interview; and project report on ANBACIS, written by Colonel Joseph Phillip, Lieutenant Colonel Ben Moberley and Captain David DeVries (Washington, DC: Defense Nuclear Agency, 10 July 1991).

13. Senate Committee on Veterans' Affairs, *Is Military Research Hazardous to Veterans' Health? Lessons Spanning Half a Century* [hereafter called the Rockefeller Report] (Washington, D.C.: GPO, December 1994), pp. 27–28; and Atkinson, *Crusade*, p. 90.

14. The 490th Chemical Battalion had a number of reserve officers who worked at the Chemical School, including its executive officer and assistant S-3. Since it had several Foxes at the School prior to the war, it was no great difficulty to train four crews "on the job" to aid in their mission of protecting the large rear area.

15. The 59th Chemical Company was probably the most active chemical company, serving under all three chemical battalions throughout the war. This constant "musical chairs" reflected the need for a chemical brigade to support the constantly changing administration, operations and logistics of non-divisional chemical defense units. As a secondary note, the reader may observe the frequent use of the 59th Chemical Company. This may be because as one of the two non-divisional active duty smoke/decon units, this unit was not necessarily detailed to support divisional training or contingency operations for any one unit (the 761st, once assigned to the 101st ABN DIV, remained committed there). As a result, it remained very active in broad support roles throughout the theater. This is not to denigrate the fine efforts of the divisional chemical companies, without whom their combat brigades would have had no effective unit training, decon support or smoke support near logistics areas, helipads and airfields.

CHAPTER 6: OPERATION DESERT STORM BEGINS

1. Spiers, *Chemical and Biological Weapons*, p. 113; and CWCB No. 11, Nov 1990 through February 1991, p. 10.

2. Gordon and Trainor, *The Generals' War*, pp. 197, 494.

3. DoD, *Conduct of the Persian Gulf War*, pp. 125–28.

4. Feinstein, "Iraqi . . . Facilities Attacked;" and Bill Gertz and Paul Bedard, "General: Damage in Iraq severe," *Washington Times*, January 21, 1991.

5. James E. Perry, "Allied Forces Are Preparing For Prospect of Chemical and Biological Warfare," *Wall Street Journal*, January 31, 1991.

6. Feinstein, "Iraqi . . . Facilities Attacked"

7. Spiers, *Chemical and Biological Weapons*, pp. 114–15.

8. Gordon and Trainor, *The Generals' War*, pp. 181–82, 457–58.

9. Ibid., p. 256.

10. Ibid., pp. 182–83.

11. Gordon and Trainor, *The Generals' War*, pp. 326, 503; Peter Honey and Karen Hosler, "U.S. insists that Iraqi baby formula plant made biological weapons," *The Baltimore Sun*, January 24, 1991; Al Kamen, "Accounts Differ on Role of Bombed Iraqi Factory," *Washington Post*, February 8, 1991.

12. Gordon and Trainor, *The Generals' War*, p. 183; Feinstein, "Iraqi . . . Facilities Attacked."

13. William Booth, "Gas Masks, Antidote Cause Three Deaths and Illness in Israel," *Washington Post*, January 19, 1995; Internet e-mail conversation on January 18, 1991. In Riyadh, Saudi citizens bought up all the multiband portable radios on the market to monitor

the police bands, listening for reports of "burnt almond or burnt pistachio" smells at the impact sites. After a Patriot interception, a very fine liquid mist sometimes settled onto the homes and cars downwind of the detonation. This corrosive mist, probably nitric acid, ate through Mercedes and Rolls Royce painted exteriors but did not affect non-metallic surfaces.

14. Gordon and Trainor, *The Generals' War*, pp. 230–33; Scales, *Certain Victory*, p. 183.

15. Atkinson, *Crusade*, p. 278; and Reuters, "Anti-chemical missile sought," *Early Bird Wire News Highlights*, January 24, 1991.

16. Scales, *Certain Victory*, pp. 184–86; and Gordon and Trainor, *The Generals' War*, pp. 238–47. While published sources state the inability to confirm destroyed launchers, special forces operating in theater maintain they did destroy a number of SCUDs.

17. Gordon and Trainor, *The Generals' War*, p. 327; Atkinson, *Crusade*, pp. 223–24.

18. About January 12, the Joint Staff had forwarded a memorandum for decision for General Powell's signature, to be forwarded through Secretary Cheney to President Bush, subject: Authority to Use Riot Control Agents. It outlined that CENTCOM had requested to use riot control agents for strictly defensive measures, such as: (1) controlling rioting POWs in areas under direct and distinct US military control; (2) situations where civilians were used to mask or screen attacks and civilian casualties could be reduced or avoided; (3) for US rescue missions in remote and isolated areas (such as recovering downed pilots); (4) rear echelon areas outside of immediate zones of conflict to protect convoys from civil disturbances or terrorists; and (5) on US bases, posts, embassy grounds and installations for protection and security purposes. Approval was granted on January 16, effective January 24, 1991.

19. Robinson, CWCB No. 12, p. 9.

20. This comment (about the CB agent originating from bombed Iraqi facilities) originated from an ARCENT intelligence officer, who had no corroborating evidence. His comment was immediately discounted by ARCENT NBCC, for obvious reasons sited.

21. David Rocks, "US accepts Czech report of chemical traces in gulf," *Baltimore Sun*, June 1991, p. 3A. This rather minor event became a full-fledged event after the war, when the Czech team's instruments were examined at Edgewood for their reliability. The Pentagon issued a statement that accepted the Czech instrument results as reliable, although they maintained that at no time were any large chemical agent events detected anywhere in the theater.

22. CENTCOM NBCC logs and Chemical School historical notes. Major Mathis and Captain Naser of the Chemical School trained the division, corps and army staffs in theater. The training took three weeks, allowing for some war gaming to fine-tune the system. In early January, the two officers were "kidnaped" into the ARCENT NBCC, only to return to the Chemical School (under great pressure from CONUS) immediately prior to the ground offensive. They were replaced with three other chemical officers to supplement ARCENT NBCC.

23. The British 1st AR DIV chemical officers had begun visiting the 1st IN DIV NBCC in an effort to ensure smooth coordination and support for NBC defense, given the passage-of-lines operation (where the British 1st AR DIV units would pass through the 1st IN DIV's stationary lines) and concerns that the Iraqis would respond to the breach with chemical weapons. They were particularly interested in the M1059 mechanized smoke generators, which would conceal the 7th ENG BDE's personnel from Iraqi observation during the breach.

24. As a side note, Major Buchanan (USACMLS) was at Khafji at the time, conducting an CB defense MTT to the Saudi Arabian National Guard on that occasion.

25. Colonel Thornton's notes. He carried the message in his notebook for four months, just in case it would be needed. After the war, the Dugway Proving Ground scientists completed the studies and recommended procedures to decontaminate casualties and transport the remains back to the United States. The Quartermaster School took the study results for inclusion in doctrine.

CHAPTER 7: "... AND THEN WE ARE GOING TO KILL IT"

1. 24th Infantry Division Attack Plan, OPLAN 91-3 Fire Support annex, reads, "Corps targeting priority throughout all phases of the operation is to destroy confirmed IRAQI chemical weapons storage and delivery assets. The intent of Corps deep operations is to neutralize fire support systems that can range the Corps penetration points and fire from positions in depth."

2. Colonel Bob Thornton, memorandum to the USA Chemical School, 30 March 1991.

3. The M40 and M17-series protective masks have very similar protective qualities. The M40's advantages include increased fields of vision, better voice communication ability, NATO-compatible filter canisters, a quicker seal (not necessarily better), and a more comfortable fit. Both protect against all ranges of CB agents at all levels expected on the battlefield.

4. Manley Report, p. 39.

5. Guidance finally came through on February 27: authorization to destroy small quantities of biological munitions using field methods was granted. Bulk quantities of biological agent munitions were to be secured and not destroyed, due to the possibility of international repercussions from finding and disposing of the munitions.

6. Staff Sergeant David Muniak, personal letters to the Chemical School Historical Office, dated 14 April 1991, 7 March 1993. The two soldiers were awarded the Army Commendation Medal for Valor.

7. The 1st IN DIV had two brigades and the 3rd BDE, 2d AR DIV (Forward) attached. The attached brigade and its unfamiliarity with division SOPs increased the concerns that the entire division was not prepared to execute a movement through the minefields and obstructions under smoke obscuration.

8. The 2d Chemical Battalion had planned to allocate 20,000 barrels of fog oil from Saudi sources. The barrels were misplaced at either Log Base Alpha or Charlie and were not recovered prior to the start of the ground war. This left the 2d Chemical Battalion with the fog oil supplies the two smoke generator companies had brought with them into the theater—enough for limited, but not protracted, smoke operations.

9. Since chemical munitions are filled with liquids instead of explosives, they require only a small burster to release the agent. Hence, a low, muffled explosion may be an indication of a chemical attack. In this case, it was not. Fears of the soldiers and their imaginations may have led them to report chemical munition explosions, since no actual chemical casualties resulted and no chemical mines were ever recovered after the war.

10. GulfLINK narrative, "Chemical weapons presence at Al Jaber Air Base judged 'unlikely'," 15 October 1997. Interviews with Marines noted five alerts where they checked with M256A1 kits between 2000 hours February 24 and 0200 hours February 25, although these incidents were not logged in any unit logs.

11. Captain Gerald Simmons, "Desert Storm NBC Operations—NBC training, planning for the 2d ACR," *Army Chemical Review*, January 1992, pp. 30–32.

12. Blood samples were sent to the 996th Medical Laboratory. In the early hours of February 26, lab tests returned with negative results for anthrax cultures.

13. 1st Infantry Division NBCC log, 26 February 1991. The information on the chemical markings turned out to be bogus. Most chemical munitions were unmarked and escorted by special troops to keep the ammunition segregated from other conventional munitions. This false information, however, kept the US forces looking anxiously for markings at all overrun Iraqi ammunition dumps.

14. Information Paper, "Chemical Agent Exposure—Operation Desert Storm," Gulf War Veterans homepage on the World Wide Web; Office of the Under Secretary of Defense for Acquisition and Technology, *Report of the Defense Science Board Task Force on Persian Gulf War Health Effects*, June 1994, pp. 36–37; and lab analysis at CRDEC as told to author at FMIB after-action report meeting.

15. Recall that the MM-1 mass spectrometer was not an automatic vapor detector but rather a ground contamination detector. It could detect high levels of vapor in the air, but could not heat up its probe high enough to conduct low level analysis. Therefore, it could not give better advance warning than the M8A1 detectors the units already had, but it could analyze any liquid samples submitted to its probe.

16. The 9th Chemical Company was deactivated in February 1994.

17. House of Representatives Committee on Armed Services, *Countering the Chemical and Biological Weapons Threat in the Post-Soviet World* [hereafter the Browder report] (Washington, D.C.: GPO, February 1993), p. 20.

18. Mr. Bill Dee, interview by author, October 1993. Mr. Dee was one of the main representatives of the US portion of the UNSCOM-9 team. His briefs, assembled after the war, were invaluable evidence of how the chemical weapons inspection teams operated at the blasted Iraqi sites.

CHAPTER 8: AFTER-ACTION REPORT

1. Quote by Secretary of Defense Dick Cheney, December 23, 1990; DoD, *Conduct of the Persian Gulf War*, Appendix Q, p. Q-2.

2. US Army Focal Point for CW/NBC Defense Research, Development and Acquisition [RDA], "Report to the House Armed Services Committee: US Army Program to Improve Chemical Warfare Protection and Training" (Aberdeen Proving Ground: US Army Chemical and Biological Defense Agency [CBDA], 31 March 1992). The Army report stated that "the overall summary [of XVIII ABN and VII Corps soldier comments] showed that CDE to include masks, overgarments, boots, gloves, alarms, overpressure systems, and NBCRS was mission capable." The second point of the report was that *at the time of the ground offensive*, CENTCOM forces were trained and equipped to meet the Iraqi threat.

3. The Honorable Earl Hutto, memorandum from HASC to OSD, December 18, 1991.

4. US Army Focal Point for CW/NBC Defense RDA, "Report to the HASC: US Army Program to Improve Chemical Warfare Protection and Training."

5. US Army Focal Point for CW/NBC Defense RDA, "Report to the Senate Appropriations Committee: US Joint Nuclear, Biological, and Chemical Defense Equipment" (Aberdeen Proving Ground: US Army CBDA, 30 July 1992). Its comments on NBC defense equipment included the anecdotal heat stress issues, physiological degradation,

compatibility problems and shortages of spare parts. The report stressed that the US technology was not inferior to currently available technology and was not obsolete in comparison to other allied countries and adversaries. Rather, it pointed out that any reduction in protective-clothing heat stress could be expected to be accompanied by a decrease in protection. As the report read, the overwhelming majority of soldiers had complete confidence in their equipment and there was no real danger to soldiers at any time resulting from faulty or insufficient quantities of chemical defense equipment.

6. DoD, *Conduct of the Persian Gulf War*, Appendix Q.

7. HQ TRADOC, "Desert Storm Conference Report," Fort Monroe, VA, March 3, 1992 (italics original). The count of forty-nine fielded systems does not include the two "Nunn" vehicles initially given to 24th IN DIV (which were *not* modified in Kassel), and does not include the ten Marine systems—only systems fielded to the Army. It also does not include the one vehicle that was shipped back to Kassel in November 1990 with a broken axle.

8. Third-country nationals included the truck drivers, laundry and mess personnel, security forces, etc., from countries both within and outside the Middle East (some as far away as the Phillippines) hired to facilitate rear area needs. At one point, truck drivers went on strike until German masks were purchased for them.

9. Colonel Silvernail, letter to the author.

10. Frank Oliveri, "Pentagon Planners Work to Penetrate Problem Targets," *Defense News*, October 9–15, 1995, p. 14.

11. Outbrief from the Operations Officer, FMIB, June 1991. The biomedical samples were blood samples drawn from Iraqi EPWs. The environmental samples included fifty-six air/materiel samples from the XM2s and seven samples collected by Fox crews.

12. Note on mustard gas—mustard gas is a non-lethal agent, does not kill but can be fatal if ingested.

13. Decontamination programs continue to be underfunded and undervalued. The Air Force and Navy have since acknowledged that persistent chemical agents could shut down their air bases and ports. A noncorrosive decontaminant that does not rely on water continues to elude the military, and the lack threatens to shut down a military force that is increasingly reliant on electronics. Despite these statements, the services still do not seem to have a concept of what they want for future decon capabilities, nor do they attach much priority (or funding) to this area.

CHAPTER 9: AGENT ORANGE REVISITED?

1. Senate Committee on Armed Services, *Department of Defense Response to the Persian Gulf Illness* (Washington, DC: GPO, SH 103-867, September 29, 1994).

2. Michael Fumento, "What Gulf War Syndrome?" *The American Spectator*, May 1995, pp. 28–30.

3. In 1993, at the request of the Office of the US Army Chief of Staff, a panel of chemical defense experts (including participants from the United States Army Chemical School, the Chemical and Biological Defense Command, and other U.S. Army and industry mass spectrometry experts) was convened to review the surviving Fox tapes. The tapes were incomplete and the panel was unable to perform a comprehensive evaluation. Its findings were published in a memo to ODCSOPS: "Based on this evaluation, we cannot confirm any of the reported chemical warfare agent detections from the information supplied, nor can we deny with 100 percent certainty, that chemical warfare agents was detected by the MM-1.

We firmly believe that all the reported detections are false alarms caused by interference from air contaminations, from air contaminated by oil well fires and burning vehicles." The Presidential Advisory Committee has identified only nine positive M256A1 kit and less than a dozen MM-1 detections throughout the entire conflict. These two detectors, far more sensitive than the M8A1 detector, belie the claim of hundreds or thousands of false alarms. Transcripts, Public Meeting, Presidential Advisory Committee on Gulf War Veterans' Illnesses, September 9, 1996, Washington, DC.

4. Ibid.

5. *Report of the Defense Science Board Task Force on Persian Gulf War Health Effects*, June 1994, p. 40–43. Incidentally, the Tallil air force base bunkers were not bombed until February, making them unlikely sources for the Czech and French detections.

6. These details of American military operations at Khamisiyah during March 1991 were gathered from the DoD Persian Gulf Task Force's case narrative for Khamisiyah. This document is available on its Internet site.

7. CIA modeling described in transcripts of Public Meeting, Presidential Advisory Committee on Gulf War Veterans' Illnesses, July 7, 1996, Chicago, IL.

8. Kenneth Bacon, DoD News Briefing, October 22, 1996.

9. Extensive details on this effort are available on the Internet source GulfLINK (http://www.gulflink.osd.mil/).

10. E-mail to author from Mike Fumento, 29 Aug 1997; press release from Rep. Sanders' home page (http://www.house.gov/bernie/Pressrel/8-19-97.htm).

11. The text discussing the Gulf War Syndrome borrows liberally from the GAO report, *Operation Desert Storm: Questions Remain on Possible Exposure to Reproductive Toxicants* (Washington, DC: GAO/PEMD-94-30, 1994).

12. Dr. Joyce Lashof, *Presidential Advisory Committee on Gulf War Veterans' Illnesses: Final Report* (Washington, DC: GPO, December 1996).

13. Major General Blanck, "Talking Paper on Persian Gulf Veterans' Health Concerns," US Army Walter Reed Army Medical Clinic. This paper also notes that of 700,000 Persian Gulf veterans, 1,765 died after the war and before October 1993, as compared with 1,729 of 750,000 non-deployed veterans. As of March 1995, 2,941 Persian Gulf veterans have died, which is less than what would be expected in the matched general population. The collected medical data shows Persian Gulf veterans to be very similar to the overall population, which could not be said for Vietnam veterans suffering from Agent Orange.

14. Robert W. Haley, et alt. "Is There a Gulf War Syndrome?," "Self-reported Exposure to Neurotoxic Chemical Combinations in the Gulf War," and "Evaluation of Neurological Function in Gulf War Veterans," *Journal of the American Medical Association*, January 15, 1997.

CHAPTER 10: CONCLUSION

1. Martin van Creveld, "The Gulf Crisis and the Rules of War," reprinted in Calvin L. Christman, ed., *America at War* (Annapolis, MD: Naval Institute Press, 1995), p. 584, first printed in *MHQ: The Quarterly Journal of Military History*, September 1991.

2. Theresa Hitchens, "Exercise finds U.S. falls short in bio war," *Army Times*, September 11, 1995, p. 30. The war game, called Global 95, was held at the Naval War College, Newport, Rhode Island.

3. Major General Louis J. Del Russo and Colonel Richard D. Read, "Chemical Deterrence—Is a treaty enough?" *Army Chemical Review*, July 1992, pp. 2–4.

4. Radical groups in the United States seem to be the exception, looking at small amounts of biological warfare agents such as ricin and various viruses and substances claimed to be anthrax or botulinum toxins. This may be due to the lack of formal education in chemical manufacturing or lack of willingness to invest in chemical laboratories.

5. Joseph D. Douglass and Neil C. Livingstone, *America the Vulnerable: The Threat of Chemical/Biological Warfare* (Lexington, MA: Lexington Books, 1987), pp. 183–86; and Browder Report, p. 32.

6. Associated Press, "Man sentenced under anti-terrorism laws," *Anniston Star*, pg 6A, May 19, 1995. The two men had discussed cultivating castor beans in order to make ricin, which might have been used to kill government officials. FBI chemists testified that the 0.7 grams of ricin they possessed could have killed 126 people. The Patriots Council, a tax protest group, had also discussed blowing up a federal building, obtaining assault weapons and killing a sheriff's deputy.

7. Karl Vick, "Plea Bargain Rejected In Bubonic Plague Case," *Washington Post*, April 3, 1996. Larry Wayne Harris stood trial for wire and mail fraud charges, since the prosecution could not prove he meant to cause harm with the samples. He claimed that ordering the plague samples was part of research for a book.

8. Thomas Easton, "Nerve agent overwhelms commuters," and "Tokyo Police say injured include possible suspect," *Baltimore Sun*, pp. 1A and 4A, March 21, 1995. As a side note, a great many of the 5,000 injured Japanese had not been on the subways during the accident but imagined nerve agent poisoning symptoms (blurry vision, shortness of breath, etc.). They reported to the hospitals just to be sure, clogging the system even more than the emergency's actual victims had.

9. Mark Matthews and Tom Bowman, "Apparent plan to gas Disneyland during Easter foiled," *Baltimore Sun*, pp. 1A, 9A, April 22, 1995.

10. Major General Barry McCaffrey, Commanding General, 24th IN DIV, letter to Brigadier General Bob Orton, Commanding General, USACMLS, 2 March 1992.

APPENDIX B

1. Tables reprinted from declassified files on GulfLINK, 1 October 1997. Editorial comments are noted in brackets, and minor changes were made to the original abbreviations for clarity.

2. Most of the fog oil was being reserved for VII Corps's mechanized smoke generator companies.

3. The 89th Chemical Company (mechanized smoke generator) commander was two hours late for a maneuver rehearsal and was relieved of command. He had gotten lost in the desert en route to the rehearsal site.

Selected Bibliography

BOOKS

Allen, Thomas B. *War Games.* New York: Berkley Books, 1989.

Association of the United States Army. *Personal Perspectives on the Gulf War.* Arlington, VA: Institute of Land Warfare, 1993.

Atkinson, Rick. *Crusade: The Untold Story of the Persian Gulf War.* New York: Houghton, 1993.

de la Billiere, General Sir Peter. *Storm Command: A Personal Account of the Gulf War.* London: Motivate Publishing, 1992.

Douglass, Joseph D., and Neil C. Livingstone. *America the Vulnerable: The Threat of Chemical/Biological Warfare.* Lexington, MA: Lexington Books, 1987.

Gordon, Michael, and General Bernard Trainor (Ret.). *The Generals' War.* Boston: Little, Brown, 1995.

Pelletiere, Stephen C., and Douglas Jackson. *Lessons Learned: The Iran-Iraq War.* Carlisle Barracks, PA: Strategic Studies Institute, 1991.

Powell, Colin L., with Joseph E. Persico. *My American Journey.* New York: Random House, 1995.

Scales, Brigadier General Robert. *Certain Victory: The US Army in the Gulf War.* Washington, DC: Brassey's, 1994.

Schwarzkopf, General (Ret.) Norman. *It Doesn't Take a Hero.* New York: Bantam Books, 1992.

Spiers, Edward. *Chemical and Biological Weapons: A Study of Proliferation.* New York: St. Martin's Press, 1994.

U.S. News and World Report. *Triumph without Victory: The Unreported History of the Persian Gulf War.* New York: Times Books, 1992.

GOVERNMENT REPORTS

D'Andries, Lieutenant Colonel Michael, Major Jeffrey Bothen and Thomas Huczek. "The NBCRS Project Office and Operation Desert Storm." Aberdeen Proving Ground, MD: CRDEC Historical Records, 1992.

Department of Defense. *Conduct of the Persian Gulf War: Final Report to Congress.* Washington, DC: GPO, April 1992.

General Accounting Office. *Chemical Warfare: DoD's Reporting of Its Chemical and Biological Research.* Washington, DC: GAO, August 1991.

_____. *Chemical Warfare: Soldiers Inadequately Equipped and Trained to Conduct Chemical Operations.* Washington, DC: GAO, May 1991.

_____. *ODS: Questions Remain on Possible Exposure to Reproductive Toxicants.* Washington, DC: GAO, August 1994.

_____. *Operation Desert Storm: DOD Met Needs for Chemical Suits and Masks, But Longer Term Actions Needed.* Washington, DC: GAO, April 1992.

HQ TRADOC. Desert Storm Conference Report. Fort Monroe, VA: March 1992.

House of Representatives Committee on Armed Services. Countering the Chemical and Biological Weapons Threat in the Post-Soviet World. Washington, DC: GPO, February 1993.

Lashof, Dr. Joyce, et al. *Presidential Advisory Committee on Gulf War Veterans' Illnesses: Final Report.* Washington, DC: GPO, December 1996.

Manley, Captain Thomas F. *Marine Corps NBC Defense in Southwest Asia.* Quantico, VA: Marine Corps Research Center, July 1991.

Office of the Under Secretary of Defense for Acquisition and Technology. *Report of the Defense Science Board Task Force on Persian Gulf War Health Effects.* Washington, DC: June 1994.

Senate Committee on Armed Services. *Dept of Defense Response to the Persian Gulf Illness.* Washington, DC: GPO, SH 103-867, September 29, 1994.

Senate Committee on Veterans' Affairs. *Is Military Research Hazardous to Veterans' Health? Lessons Spanning Half a Century.* Washington, DC: GPO, December 1994.

Spector, Daniel E. *US Army Chemical School Annual Command History*, 1990 and 1991. Fort McClellan, AL: US Army Chemical Center and School.

US Army Focal Point for CW/NBC Defense RDA. "Report to the House Armed Services Committee: US Army Program to Improve Chemical Warfare Protection and Training." Aberdeen Proving Ground, MD: US Army CBDA, 31 March 1992.

_____. "Report to the Senate Appropriations Committee: US Joint Nuclear, Biological and Chemical Defense Equipment." Aberdeen Proving Ground, MD:US Army CBDA, 30 July 1992.

US Army Medical Research of Infectious and Chemical Diseases, Annual Historical Report for 1990.

JOURNAL ARTICLES

Adams, Major Jeffery. "Chemical Corps in the Attack—allied troops react to Desert Shield and Desert Storm." *Army Chemical Review*, January 1992.

Barbeau, Colonel Raymond; and Captain Pratya Siriwat. "Lessons from the Gulf—NBC Warning and Reporting." *Army Chemical Review*, July 1991.

Buchanan, Major Robert. "Preparing Coalition Forces for the Chemical Threat." *Army Chemical Review*, January 1992.

Del Russo, Major General Louis J., and Colonel Richard D. Read. "Chemical Deterrence—Is a treaty enough?" *Army Chemical Review*, July 1992.

Feinstein, Lee. "Iraqi Nuclear, Chemical and Biological Facilities Attacked." *Arms Control Today*, March 1991, pp. 19–20.

Fumento, Michael. "What Gulf War Syndrome?" *The American Spectator*, May 1995, pp. 28–30.

Haley, Robert W., et al. "Is There a Gulf War Syndrome?", "Self-reported Exposure to Neurotoxic Chemical Combinations in the Gulf War," and "Evaluation of Neurological Function in Gulf War Veterans." *Journal of the American Medical Association*, January 15, 1997.

"Lineage and Honors." *Army Chemical Journal,* Spring, 1986.

Porter, Kimberly, and Herbert LePore. *Legacy in the Sand: The United States Army Armament, Munitions, and Chemical Command in Operations Desert Shield and Desert Storm.* Rock Island, IL: HQ AMCCOM, 1992.

Roos, John. "Allies Filled Some Big Voids in US Chem Defense Preparedness." *Armed Forces Journal*, October 1991.

Simmons, Captain Gerald. "Desert Storm NBC Operations—NBC training, planning for the 2d ACR." *Army Chemical Review*, January 1992.

van Creveld, Dr. Martin. "The Gulf Crisis and the Rules of War." Reprinted in Calvin L. Christman, ed. *America at War.* Annapolis, MD: Naval Institute Press, 1995. First printed in *MHQ: The Quarterly Journal of Military History*, September 1991.

NEWSPAPER ARTICLES

"Army puts rush on cream to block mustard gas." *The Army Times*, February 4, 1991.

Associated Press. "Man sentenced under anti-terrorism laws." *Anniston Star*, p. 6A, May 19, 1995.

"Biological weapons program in Iraq larger than believed." *Baltimore Sun*, February 28, 1995.

Booth, William. "Gas Masks, Antidote Cause Three Deaths and Illness in Israel." *Washington Post*, January 19, 1995.

Easton, Thomas. "Nerve agent overwhelms commuters" and "Tokyo Police say injured include possible suspect." *Baltimore* Sun, pp. 1A and 4A, March 21, 1995.

Gertz, Bill, and Paul Bedard. "General: Damage in Iraq severe." *Washington Times*, p. A1, January 21, 1991.

Hitchens, Theresa. "Exercise finds U.S. falls short in bio war." *Army Times*, September 11, 1995.

Honey, Peter, and Karen Hosler. "U.S. insists that Iraqi baby formula plant made biological weapons." *Baltimore Sun*, January 24, 1991.

Kamen, Al. "Accounts Differ on Role of Bombed Iraqi Factory." *Washington Post*, February 8, 1991.

Matthews, Mark, and Tom Bowman. "Apparent plan to gas Disneyland during Easter foiled." *Baltimore Sun*, pp. 1A, 9A, April 22, 1995.

Oliveri, Frank. "Pentagon Planners Work to Penetrate Problem Targets." *Defense News*, October 9-15, 1995.

Perry, James E. "Allied Forces Are Preparing For Prospect of Chemical and Biological Warfare." *Wall Street Journal*, January 31, 1991.

Reuters. "Anti-chemical missile sought." *Early Bird Wire News Highlights*, January 24, 1991.

Rocks, David. "US accepts Czech report of chemical traces in gulf." *Baltimore Sun*, p. 3A, June 1991.

Vick, Karl. "Plea Bargain Rejected In Bubonic Plague Case." *Washington Post*, April 3, 1996.

Index

Abrams, General Creighton, 1, 170, 185
Abu-Ghurayb, 27, 94
Air Force, 9, 19–21, 23, 36, 38, 43–46,
    50, 52–53, 65, 72, 74, 85–86, 103,
    111, 130–32, 135–37, 140, 142, 148.
    See also CENTAF
ANBACIS, 64–65, 85–86, 91, 101, 107,
    132, 136, 149
An Nasiriyah, 27, 69, 100, 117–18,
    154–5, 158
Anthrax, 27, 40, 52, 70, 72, 95, 100, 105,
    114, 117, 123, 129, 152, 179
ARCENT, 54, 58, 72–73, 77, 81–83, 86,
    89, 97, 100–1, 107, 117, 122, 138,
    155; G-3 (Ops), 72, 82; NBC Cell,
    23–24, 54, 64, 90, 99, 102, 112, 139,
    see also Lieutenant Colonel Vicki
    Merryman; rear area concerns, 47,
    59, 67, 89, 112, 119, 135–36
Armament, Munitions and Chemical
    Command (AMCCOM), 6, 9, 38–39,
    53–54, 71, 78, 81, 110
Armed Forces Medical Intelligence
    Center (AFMIC), 40, 163
Army Materiel Command, 30, 39, 65–66,
    78
Army Surgeon General. *See* Office of the
    Surgeon General
Army units: 1st AR DIV, 33, 61, 84, 116,
    118; 1st CAV DIV, 22, 25–26, 47,
    49, 66, 81–82, 84, 87, 89, 112–13,
    119, 122, 143; 1st IN DIV, 61, 63,
    81–82, 89, 102–4, 109, 111, 113,
    116–19, 121–22, 143; 2nd ACR,
    59–61, 63, 66–67, 80, 89, 113,
    116–19, 157; 3rd ACR, 25–26, 33,
    47, 49, 60, 63, 81, 88, 102, 104,
    116–18, 122; 3rd AR DIV, 34,
    61–62, 66, 84, 89, 102–3, 111, 113,
    116, 118–21, 143; 24th IN DIV, 22,
    25–26, 32–33, 47–48, 52, 62, 77, 81,
    84, 88, 104, 116–17, 119–20, 127,
    155, 162; 82d ABN DIV, 7, 21, 25,
    36, 47, 82, 84, 103, 119, 155–56,
    159, 162; 101st ABN DIV, 20, 22,
    25, 33, 47–48, 58, 84, 87–88; VII
    Corps, 25–26, 33, 53, 57, 59–63, 72,
    78, 80–81, 84–85, 87, 89–90, 104–5,
    110–12, 116–21, 143, 157; VII
    Corps NBC Cell, *see* Colonel Robert
    Thornton; XVIII ABN Corps, 22,
    24–26, 30, 34, 39, 46–47, 49, 51, 54,
    57–64, 67–68, 78, 80–82, 84, 87–89,
    104, 112, 116–17, 133, 155, 157;
    XVIII ABN Corps NBC Cell, *see*
    Colonel Raymond Barbeau
Arnold, Brigadier General Steve. *See*
    ARCENT: G-3
Aum Shinrikyo, 176–78, 180

Baker, James, 67, 92

Barbeau, Colonel Raymond, 24, 33, 50, 53, 58–59, 69. *See also* Army units: XVIII ABN Corps

Biological Detection Teams, 73, 75, 83–84, 101–2, 105, 112, 114, 121, 140, 170

Biological detectors, 5, 34–35, 51–52, 71–73, 83, 105, 114, 131, 133, 138–42, 149; false alarms, 73, 77, 105, 114, 173

Biological weapons: Iraqi delivery systems, *see* Iraq; storage sites, *see* Bunkers; US retaliation options, *see* Chemical weapons

Blanck, Major General Ronald, 160

Botulinum toxin, 27, 72, 75, 95, 114, 123, 129, 175–76

Bunkers, chem and bio weapons, 27, 69–70, 83, 93–94, 101, 120–22, 153

Bush, President George, 21, 25, 30, 48, 57, 67, 92, 100, 107, 170

Canada: CAM loans, 51, 77–78; military forces, 45, 53

CANE studies, 4, 20, 172

CENTAF, 29, 69, 79, 83, 93–95, 100–1, 109; Instant Thunder, 56

CENTCOM: CINC, *see* General Norman Schwarzkopf; Internal Look, 20–21; J-3 (Ops), 64, 86; Jedi Knights, 56–57; NBC Cell, 23, 58–59, 64, *see also* Lieutenant Colonel Kenneth Silvernail

Central Intelligence Agency, 26–29, 76, 157–59, 161

Chemical Agent Nerve Antidote, 55, 75. *See also* Diazepam

Chemical and Biological Defense Command, 173–74, 178–79

Chemical Defense Training Facility, 4, 6, 26, 131, 134, 181–82

Chemical detectors: false alarms, 38, 54, 85, 96–97, 100–1, 112, 115, 119, 132, 146, 149, 153, 167, 173; ICAD, 77, 115; M1 CAM, 5, 19, 24, 35, 49–51, 53, 61, 85, 96, 99–100, 115, 119, 131–32, 139, 157; M8A1 auto detector, 5, 9–11, 13, 16, 23–24, 38, 52–54, 77, 97, 101, 112, 115, 135, 145–46, 153, 155–56; M256A1 detector kit, 5, 13, 24, 50, 74, 84, 96, 99–101, 115, 117, 119, 145, 153, 155–56; XM21 RSCAAL, 5, 23, 35, 49–51, 73, 84–85, 102, 112, 121, 132, 149; XM93 NBC Recon System, *see* "Fox" NBC Recon System

Chemical RD&E Center (CRDEC), 6, 8–9, 30, 35, 45, 49–52, 64, 71, 73, 78–79, 84, 107, 121, 173

Chemical School, 2, 6, 30, 32–35, 50–51, 63, 78, 80, 82, 113, 138, 174, 181–83; Mobile Training Teams, 35–36, 51, 78

Chemical units: 1st Chem Det (JA), 24; 2d Chem Battalion, 25, 33, 47, 49, 57–58, 62, 66, 79, 82, 84, 89, 113, 118–19, 121; 9th Chem Co (Motorized), 73, 102, *see also* Biological Detection Teams; 11th Chem Co (Decon), 25, 59, 80, 116; 12th Chem Co (Hvy Div), 63, 111, 121–22; 21st Chem Co (Smoke/Decon), 21, 25, 47; 22nd Chem Co (Hvy Div), 34; 25th Chem Co (Hvy Div), 34; 44th Chem Co (Hvy Div), 7, 25, 88–89, 112; 46th Chem Co (Mech Smoke), 80; 51st Chem Co (Decon), 25, 59; 59th Chem Co (Smoke/Decon), 25, 49, 57–58, 79–80, 82, 84, 90; 63rd Chem Co (Smoke/ Decon), 25, 47; 63rd Chem Det (JA), 23; 68th Chem Co (Hvy Div), 25, 47, 82, 89; 69th Chem Co (Hvy Div), 33; 82d Chem Det (JA), 24; 84th Chem Co (Mech Smoke), 80; 87th Chem Co (ACR), 60, 63, 66; 89th Chem Co (ACR), 25, 47, 60, 63, 102; 91st Chem Co (Hvy Div), 25, 32, 47; 101st Chem Co (Decon), 25, 47, 58, 88; 172d Chem Co (Mech Smoke), 80, 113; 181st Chem Co (Decon), 25, 47, 49, 116; 318th Chem Co (Decon), 26, 58, 66; 323rd Chem Co (Decon), 66, 84, 118; 327th Chem Co (Decon), 26,

47, 49, 58, 88; 340th Chem Co
(Decon), 66, 84, 104; 371st Chem
Co (Decon), 26; 413th Chem Co
(Decon), 59, 66, 84; 415th Chem
Brigade, 25; 433rd Chem Det (JB),
26; 457th Chem Battalion, 66, 84,
89, 104; 490th Chem Battalion,
25–26, 49, 58–59, 65–66, 81, 84,
89–90, 111, 118; 761st Chem Co
(Smoke/Decon), 25, 47, 49, 58, 84,
88; 907th Chem Det (JB), 26;
USAREUR NBC recon platoons, 26,
30, 33–34, 47–49, 60, 62–63, 66–67,
81–82, 84, 88
Chemical weapons: Iraqi delivery
systems, see Iraq; storage sites, see
Bunkers; UNSCOM findings, see
United Nations; US chemical
weapons, 19, 48; US retaliation
options, 21, 47–48, 52
Chemical Weapons Convention, 171,
180, 184
Cheney, Richard, 55, 57, 75, 91, 109,
130, 169
Collective protection, 6, 19, 45–46, 53,
92, 98, 132, 145, 149; M20 SCPE,
45–46, 61; M28 TEMPER, 46; M51
shelter, 45–46; vehicle CPE, 5, 65
Czech anti–chemical company, 66,
80–81, 100–1, 153–54

D'Andries, Lieutenant Colonel Michael,
8–9, 31, 59, 115. See also "Fox"
NBC Recon System, Product
Manager for NBC Defense
Decontaminants: DS–2, 10, 44, 53, 85,
144, 163; HTH, 39, 5, 81
Decontamination kits, 23–24, 36, 38, 85,
118, 127, 133, 139
Decontamination systems: German
Kärcher systems, 85; M12A1
PDDA, 85, 132; M13 DAP, 5; M17
LDS "SANATOR," 5, 24–25, 30,
53, 57, 59, 85, 132
Defense Intelligence Agency, 26–29, 85,
95, 157
Defense Logistics Agency, 37, 39, 55,
107, 131

Defense Nuclear Agency, 34–35, 51–52,
64–65, 69–71, 101, 107, 154, 162.
See also ANBACIS, Biological
detectors
Del Rosso, Major General Louis, 30, 75
Deputy Chief of Staff, Logistics
(DCSLOG), 9, 30, 36, 43–45, 54,
102, 107, 139
Deputy Chief of Staff, Operations and
Plans (DCSOPS), 9, 23, 25–26, 30,
35–36, 38, 48, 50, 59, 63–64, 66, 73,
75, 77, 80, 102, 107, 141
Diazepam, 55, 164
Dugway Proving Grounds, 1, 6, 17,
31–33, 49, 67–68, 71, 83, 107, 158,
161–62, 174, 181–83

Edgewood, 1, 6, 9, 28, 45, 49, 73, 141.
See also Chemical RD&E Center,
Product Manager for NBC Defense
Egyptian forces, 23, 51, 82, 101, 115, 117
Evans, Colonel Ron, 31, 59. See also
Product Manager for NBC Defense
Explosive Ordnance Disposal, 112, 121,
156, 161. See also Technical Escort
Unit

Food & Drug Administration, 40–41,
55–56, 60, 75–76, 87, 141–42, 164
Foreign Materiel Intelligence Battalion,
73, 121, 140, 155. See also Joint
Captured Materiel Exploitation
Center
Fort McClellan, 2, 6, 17, 25–26, 31–32,
49, 63, 66–67, 102, 127, 131,
133–35, 174, 181–82. See also
Chemical Defense Training Facility,
Chemical School
"Fox" NBC Recon System: fielding, 5, 8,
26, 30–34, 43, 48–49, 58–60, 62–63,
65–66, 81–82, 84, 88–91, 102–3,
111–12, 119–20, 132–33, 135, 149;
General Dynamics Land Systems, 8,
31–32, 49, 58, 63, 103; maintenance
facility, 49, 66, 72, 74, 111;
operations, 32, 67, 98–100, 105,
108, 115–16, 118–22, 138, 140, 153,
155; Thyssen-Henschel, 32–34,

48–49, 59, 65, 84, 102; training, 30–31, 33, 62–63, 65–67, 81, 102, 122. *See also* Product Manager for NBC Defense

France, 62, 82, 88, 100–1, 116, 127, 129, 153–54

Franks, Lieutenant General Frederick, 15, 26, 60–62, 87, 99, 107, 116, 119. *See also* Army units: VII Corps

Fuzy, Colonel Gene, 51, 141

General Dynamics. *See* "Fox" NBC Recon System

Germany: military forces, 30–33, 44, 48; Sonthofen, *see* "Fox" NBC Recon System: training; Thyssen–Henshel, *see* "Fox" NBC Recon System; US forces in, *see* Army units: VII Corps, US Army Europe

Habbiniyah, 27, 93, 124

Haley, Dr. Robert, 165–66

Hussein, Saddam, 28–29, 56, 75–76, 91–92, 94–96, 98, 107, 129–30, 137, 144, 163

Investigational New Drugs, 41, 55, 75, 141

Iraq: CBW capability, 20, 22, 26–29, 47, 49, 67, 76–77, 79, 85, 89, 92–95, 99–100, 107–9, 112, 116, 120, 128–30, 132, 137; declared CB storage sites, 122–24, 136; EPWs, 115, 118, 155; initiating Scud launches, 68; Khafji offensive, 103–4, nuclear capability, *see* nuclear weapons

Johnson, Major General James, 156. *See also* Army units: 82d ABN DIV

Joint Captured Materiel Exploitation Center, 73, 140. *See also* Foreign Materiel Intelligence Battalion

Joint Chiefs of Staff, 6, 23, 43, 48, 55, 112, 115

Joint Service Coordinating Committee-Chemical Defense Equipment, 43–44, 132

Kelso, Admiral Frank, 22

Khamisiyah, 153, 155–62, 165, 183

Kilgore, Lieutenant Colonel Michael, 113. *See also* Chemical units: 2d Chem Battalion

King Fhad International Airport. *See* Saudi Arabia

King Khalid Military City. *See* Saudi Arabia

Luck, Lieutenant General Gary, 82, 116. *See also* Army units: XVIII ABN Corps

MARCENT, 89, 102, 112, 116

Marine Corps, 20–23, 36, 43–47, 51–53, 57, 77, 79, 103, 110, 112, 114–15, 117, 119–20, 132; minefield breach, 115, 125, 153; NBC recon vehicles, 59, 62–63, 67, 102, 111, 121; purchase of protective suits, 44, 50, 85, 130

Maritime Prepositioning Squadron, 22–23

Mashburn, Colonel Harold, 36, 44. *See also* Joint Service Coordinating Committee-Chemical Defense Equipment

Mask Maintenance Facility, 78–79, 84, 98

McCaffrey, Major General Barry, 22, 43, 52, 81, 88, 98, 127, 134, 182. *See also* Army units: 24th IN DIV

Medical Management of Chemical Casualties Course, 53

Medical Research and Development Command, 6, 55, 85

Medical Research Institute for Chemical Defense, 53, 76, 121

Medical Research Insititute for Infectious Diseases, 40, 51, 71

Medical units, 22, 44, 49–51, 60, 75, 80, 102, 105; forward medical labs, 48–49, 69–71, 81, 114, 138

Merryman, Lieutenant Colonel Vicki, 54, 64, 72, 110

MOPP levels, 10–13, 16, 24, 39, 54, 58, 68, 71, 97–99, 109, 114–16, 118–19, 135, 155–56

Mustard agent, 26–27, 49, 55, 76, 89, 93, 95, 100–1, 115, 118–19, 120–21, 123–25, 129, 147, 152–54, 157–58, 170; dusty mustard, 49–50

Muthanna, 27, 85, 93, 95, 123, 125, 154–55, 157

Natick RD&E Center (NRDEC), 6, 39, 49–50, 98, 107, 175. *See also* Protective suits

NAVCENT, 51, 71, 83

Navy, 9, 20–23, 36, 43–46, 50–53, 64, 67, 71–72, 85, 91–93, 103, 130, 135, 142; Navy Medical Research Unit, 51; Navy forward labs, *see* Medical units: forward medical labs

Nerve Agent Antidote Kit, Mark 1, 14–15, 23–24, 39–40, 43–44, 55, 62, 96

Newing, Major Ted, 30, 33, 59, 72, 102. *See also* Deputy Chief of Staff, Operations and Plans

nuclear weapons: coalition, 19, 21, 29, 70, 76, 91, 127, 130, 137, 171–72; Iraqi, 26, 69, 92–94, 122, 129; proliferation, 136, 139, 172, 184

Nydam, Brigadier General David, 51, 110. *See also* Chemical RD&E Center

ODCSLOG. *See* Deputy Chief of Staff, Logistics

ODCSOPS. *See* Deputy Chief of Staff, Operations and Plans

Office of the Surgeon General, 40–41, 55

Orton, Brigadier General Robert, 30–31, 35–36, 77. *See also* Chemical School

Pagonis, Major General Gus, 58, 65

Patriot missile system, 28–29, 96–97, 112

Peay, Major General Binford, 87. *See also* Army units: 101st ABN DIV

Pine Bluff Arsenal, 6, 45, 61, 78–79, 111, 174. *See also* Mask Maintenance Facility

Polley, Major Walt, 30–31, 33, 63, 113

Powell, General Colin, 34, 51, 55, 57, 61, 75, 93, 95, 109, 117, 127, 141. *See also* Joint Chiefs of Staff

Presidential Advisory Committee on Gulf War Illnesses, 145, 154–55, 157–59, 162, 164–5

Product Manager for NBC Defense, 8, 31, 48–49, 59, 66, 102, 111, 115. *See also* "Fox" NBC Recon System

Protective mask fit validation system, 79

Protective masks: for aviators, 45; MCU-2/P, 67; M17-series, 5, 10, 24, 38–39, 78–79, 84, 110, 118, 145; M24/25, 38–39, 78; M40-series, 5, 8, 38, 79, 110, 130; M43, 8–9, 45

Protective suits: BDO, 5, 24, 38–39, 44, 49–50, 53, 98, 107, 130–31; CPOG, 19, 38, 50, 62, 97–98, 107; Mark IV, 50, 115; Saratoga, 44, 85, 130

Pyridostigmine bromide (PB) tablets, 10, 12, 55–56, 76, 87, 97, 114, 152, 164–166

Read, Colonel Richard, 9–10, 47, 72, 87, 107–8. *See also* Deputy Chief of Staff, Operations and Plans

Reimer, Lieutenant General Dennis, 72, 102, 107. *See also* Deputy Chief of Staff, Operations and Plans

Rhame, Major General Thomas, 113, 117, 122. *See also* Army units: 1st IN DIV

Riot control agents, 7, 100

Rotsker, Dr. Bernard, 161

Salman Pak, 27, 57, 92–94, 122–23

Samarra, 27, 57, 92–93, 95, 123. *See also* Muthanna

Sarin, 4, 26–27, 46, 48, 77, 96, 100–1, 118, 123–25, 127, 129, 134, 145–46, 154, 157, 161–62, 176–78

Saudi Arabia: Dhahran, 20, 23–24, 29,
    31, 34, 46–47, 49, 59, 65–66, 72–73,
    78, 83–84, 87, 96, 98–99, 102–3,
    105, 111, 114, 121, 126, 139;
    Jubayl, 20, 47, 51, 73, 100, 102,
    105; King Fahd International
    Airport, 65, 79, 142; King Khalid
    Military City, 23, 52, 66, 73, 80, 83,
    87–88, 101–2, 104–5, 111, 118–19,
    121, 126, 154; Ministry of Defense
    and Aviation, 23, 36; National
    Guard, 35; Riyadh, 22, 29, 35,
    46–47, 57, 67, 87, 96, 100, 102
Schwarzkopf, General H. Norman, 17,
    20–22, 29, 34, 40, 56, 61–64, 82–83,
    91, 93, 116, 119, 151. *See also*
    CENTCOM
Scud, 11–12, 16, 21, 26–29, 34, 46,
    67–69, 76, 83, 85, 88–89, 92,
    95–102, 104, 107, 109–12, 118, 123,
    127, 135–37, 153, 166, 173
Silvernail, Lieutenant Colonel Kenneth,
    23, 50, 64, 132. *See also*
    CENTCOM: NBC Cell
Smoke operations, 4, 80, 131, 142–44;
    covering breach operations, 113,
    116–17; deception operations, 82,
    104, 112–13; obscuring KFIA,
    79–80; smoke pots at Tuwiatha, 94
Sonthofen. *See* "Fox" NBC Recon
    System: training
Sullivan, Lieutenant General Gordon, 51,
    102

Tear gas. *See* Riot control agents
Technical Escort Unit, 73–74, 121, 125,
    140, 178–79
Thornton, Colonel Robert, 15, 80. *See
    also* Army units: VII Corps
Thyssen-Henschel. *See* Germany
Tuwaitha, 27, 92, 94, 142

United Kingdom, 11, 41, 44–45, 48, 62,
    28, 70, 76, 86–88, 91–92, 99–101,
    121, 151, 164; British 1st AR DIV,
    89, 103, 117–19; CAM loan, 51, 78,
    84; NBC Recon System crews, 33,
    66, 82, 84

United Nations, 68, 91, 95; UNSCOM,
    94, 121–23, 125, 137, 153, 157, 159,
    162
US Army Europe (USAREUR), 19, 26,
    30–31, 62, 102

Vaccines: anthrax, 40–1, 75, 86–87, 141,
    164, 171; botulinum toxin, 40–41,
    55–56, 76, 87, 143, 164; US policy,
    34, 40–41, 55–56, 60, 70, 75–76,
    86–87, 141–42, 148, 152, 164–65
Van Prooyen, Colonel Jan, 31
Vuono, General Carl, 40, 56, 61, 83

Waller, Lieutenant General Calvin, 83,
    101
Watson, Major General Gerald, 34, 51,
    63–64, 77, 86, 185. *See also* Defense
    Nuclear Agency
Willhoite, Lieutenant Colonel Howard,
    30, 32–33, 59, 102. *See also* Deputy
    Chief of Staff, Operations and Plans
Wolfowitz, Paul, 107–8

Yeosock, Lieutenant General John, 54,
    107. *See also* ARCENT

About the Author

ALBERT J. MAURONI has thirteen years professional experience in the area of chemical-biological warfare, including seven with the U.S. Army Chemical Corps. He currently works as a management consultant specializing in Department of Defense chemical-biological defense programs and is a member of the Association of the U.S. Army and National Defense Industrial Association. He is the author of several articles on chemical-biological warfare.